Leaving Pep Band Friends

Leaving Pep Band Friends

Kim I. Maxey

Omberulica Publications

Leaving Pep Band Friends Copyright © 2024 by Kim I. Maxey

All rights reserved. No part of this publication may be reproduced, stored or transmitted in any form or by any means, electronic, mechanical, photocopying, recording, scanning, or otherwise, including information storage and retrieval systems, without written permission from the publisher. It is illegal to copy this book, post it to a website, or distribute it by any other means without permission. Reviewers may quote brief passages in a review.

Disclaimer: This work depicts actual events in the life of the author as truthfully as recollection permits. While all persons within are actual individuals, names and identifying characteristics have been changed to respect their privacy.

Neither the publisher nor the author is engaged in rendering professional advice or services to the reader. The ideas, suggestions, and procedures provided in this book are not intended as a substitute for seeking professional guidance.

The author has no responsibility for the persistence or accuracy of URLs for external or third-party Internet Websites referred to in this publication and does not guarantee that any content on such Websites is, or will remain, accurate or appropriate.

NO AI TRAINING: The author reserves all rights to license uses of this work for generative AI training and development of machine learning language models.

Printed in the United States of America
ISBN: Hardcover 979-8-9911024-0-7, Paperback 979-8-9911024-1-4

Library of Congress Control Number: 2024916329

First Edition

Published by Omberulica Publications
Osseo, Minnesota

For my brother who saved my life.

For my daughter who joyfully expands my life.

TABLE OF CONTENTS

PART 1   LIFE BEFORE

Chapter   1 The Fall Dance..3

Chapter   2 The Pep Band...8

Chapter   3 Gymnastics Class..14

Chapter   4 The Forestview Glen House.....................................18

Chapter   5 A Threat..21

Chapter   6 A Good Move..26

Chapter   7 Contests and Concerts...31

Chapter   8 The Carhop Who Escaped Lightning....................36

Chapter   9 Biking and Hiking...41

Chapter 10 Swimming and Skateboarding..............................47

Chapter 11 Ninth Grade Classes...54

Chapter 12 The Student Council Election................................58

Chapter 13 The Inattentive Band...64

Chapter 14 The Last Chair Flutist...71

Chapter 15 A Girls' Basketball Game..78

Chapter 16 The Concession Stand..82

Chapter 17 The Garage Band Invitation..................................86

Chapter 18 The Optimist Club Award.......................................92

Chapter 19 Something in Common..98

Chapter 20 The Job Offer..101

Chapter 21 An Invitation and Advice..105

Chapter 22 The Winter Dance..110

Chapter 23 Going Steady..115

Chapter 24 All-State Band Tryouts...121

Chapter 25 Exhaustion..126

Chapter 26 The Talk Across the Hedge....................................130

Chapter 27 The Sadie Hawkins Dance......................................136

Chapter 28 The Shadow of "The Move"...................................142

Chapter 29 The State Math Contest..148

Chapter 30 Award Assemblies..153

Chapter 31 The Going-Away Party..157

PART 2   LIFE AFTER

Chapter 32 The Big City..169

Chapter 33 The Quiet Neighborhood..173

Chapter 34 The Big High School..177

Chapter 35 Incredible Thirst..183

Chapter 36 Her Refusal...189

Chapter 37 The Weekend Trip...194

Chapter 38 Intense Heartache..197

Chapter 39 Another New Job...200

Chapter 40 Dèjà Vu with a Twist...203

Chapter 41 The Conflict Over Two Houses.............................207

Chapter 42 Friendly Voices..212

Chapter 43 The Gym Teacher..216

Chapter 44 Two Homesick Sisters..220

Chapter 45 Another New House..224

Chapter 46 Another New School...227

Chapter 47 A Crushing Wave of Despair..............................230

Chapter 48 Hope..235

SUPPORT FOR TEENS WHO HAVE BEEN MOVED

Messages of Support...243

Author's Thoughts on Being Moved as a Teen......................279

APPENDICES

Appendix A Suicide and Crisis Lifelines...............................289

Appendix B Warning Signs of Suicidal Intention.................291

Appendix C Depression...293

OTHER

Poems..298

Book Recommendations Especially for Teens......................301

Acknowledgments..303

About the Author...305

Encouragement..306

Leaving Pep Band Friends
is a true story of the author's experience.

*Identifying information was changed,
and many dialogues were created.*

PART 1

LIFE BEFORE

CHAPTER 1

The Fall Dance

Balloons drifted across the polished wood junior high school gym floor. A group of kids by the stage had piles of black and white ones, while two boys by the bleachers were taping fake spider webs to the walls. Nicky sat cross-legged on the floor, and she pulled out a flat balloon from the bag of orange balloons. She stretched it out three times, put the open rolled edges to her mouth and blew.

She sat with Paizlee and Zoey who talked about which eighth-grade boys they liked. Nicky strained to hear them over the other students' voices.

"Do you think the new boys will come to the dance tonight?" asked Paizlee.

"Let's hope so. I want to dance with Dalton," said Zoey.

"I think he likes you, so he'll probably ask you," said Paizlee.

"Who do you want to dance with, Paizlee?" asked Zoey.

"Gage, but Sutton and Travis better ask me. They're in trouble if they don't!" said Paizlee. She tossed her head and flipped her long bangs away from her eyes.

Suddenly, Nicky's balloon popped, and she felt the rubber smack her face. She held the small mouthpiece between her teeth, but the rest was scattered around her on the floor. Paizlee and Zoey looked at her and started laughing.

"Blow up balloons often, Nicky? You're supposed to stop before they burst!" teased Zoey.

Nicky rubbed her cheek and shrugged. She had been paying attention to her friends, not the balloon. After she picked up the pieces and put them in her pocket, she got a new flat balloon, blew it up and tied it.

The girls continued to chat, then to pause and add balloons to their pile. When they finished, they tied black and white ribbons on some of the balloons.

A boy climbed a stepladder and yelled, "Tape! Tape! Where's the tape?"

Someone ran up with a roll of masking tape and handed it to him. The students attached the balloons around the four doorways as they transformed the gym for the fall dance that would start at 7 p.m. They began to leave, and the school gradually quieted.

As Paizlee, Zoey, and Nicky went through the front door, Nicky's friends turned right on Devon Street, but Nicky turned left.

"See you tonight, Nicky!" yelled Paizlee as she waved.

"Don't worry, someone will dance with you, too!" yelled Zoey.

Nicky smiled and waved at them. She walked fast as she reached the corner and turned right toward Eagleton's Main Street. Her mother worked downtown, and she would drive Nicky home. Her brother, Ryan, who was in sixth grade, usually walked home from school with friends, so he was home by then.

Nicky kicked at a pile of leaves and looked to her right. Even in the fading light, she could see the top of Peaceful Bear Mountain, which her family climbed whenever relatives were in town. She enjoyed hiking to the top.

Nicky turned the corner onto Main Street and went to the law office where her mother had worked for five years. She was the bookkeeper for three attorneys. When Nicky opened the glass office door, a bell rang. Mrs. Weaver, the receptionist, gave her a big smile.

"Hi, Nicky! Your mother was getting worried."

In the back room, Nicky's mother stood at her desk. She smiled and greeted her daughter, who dashed over to hug her. Her mother grabbed her coat and scarf, and they went out the back door. Nicky was almost as tall as her mother, but she felt awkward compared to her graceful mother. In the near darkness, they crossed the parking lot to the old car.

Her mother drove south, and Nicky gazed at the dark shadow of the Ponderosa Hills. Eagleton was in a valley before the last ridge of mountains. Their house was in a town addition called Forestview Glen with a group of other houses.

"How was the decorating committee?" her mother asked.

"It was fun."

"Have you decided if you're going to the dance?"

"I'm going. Can you give me a ride?"

Her mother agreed.

As Nicky walked through the school's front door later, fluorescent lights blazed, and music blared from the gym. She saw Paizlee and Zoey by the water fountain and went over to them. They walked into the dark gym and saw a crowd of people. Kids went in and out of the four doors constantly while the teacher and parent chaperones talked in small groups and monitored them.

The three girls motioned to each other as they saw their friends Kinsey, McKenna, and Lily sitting on the second step of the bleachers. They climbed to the step behind them. The bleachers faced the stage with its long black curtains. The school was old, and the bleachers didn't fold into the wall like newer school bleachers did.

The friends had to shout at each other over the loud music. Nicky sat on the far side, and she tried to read their lips.

"Which boys are here so far?" Paizlee asked Lily.

"I saw Sutton by the stage a while ago," said Lily.

"Did you see the new boys in the hall? We haven't seen them yet," said Kinsey.

Zoey shook her head no.

"Dalton just came in. He's by the refreshment stand," said McKenna.

Zoey tucked her shoulder-length hair behind her ear as she turned her head to look at the refreshment stand, then she nudged Paizlee. Paizlee saw him, and she nodded as she looked at Zoey.

"Are Gage and Trevor here yet?" asked Paizlee.

"No, not yet. Wait! There's Gage!" McKenna nodded her head toward the far door on the right.

Gage stood in the doorway and surveyed the room until Trevor joined him. They walked across the gym to the refreshment stand in the far-left corner to join Dalton. The two new boys greeted each other while Trevor looked around and pushed up his glasses.

Paizlee, Zoey, and Lily left the bleachers to talk to other friends and comment on their outfits. Nicky watched her friends as they mingled in groups, and soon they were dancing. After Paizlee danced with one boy, another one wanted to dance with her. While Trevor sat on the stage with several friends, the new boys had partners for most songs.

McKenna and Kinsey went to get drinks, and soon McKenna was dancing to a fast song with Sutton. Kinsey rejoined Nicky on the bleachers. The two of them were taller than many of the boys in their grade, and they were also shy. Nicky admired how Zoey, Paizlee, and Lily talked and laughed easily, and she wished she knew how to flirt so she could dance, too. But Nicky's tongue seemed to swell up whenever she wanted to speak to anyone, so listening was her default mode.

Nicky saw Paizlee motion to her to go into the hall. The air was cool as they went to Paizlee's locker. Paizlee put on some lip balm and spoke in a low tone while she watched the gym doors.

"Zoey just danced with Dalton three times in a row. He obviously likes her. Did you see who Gage was dancing with?"

"I saw him with Lily at least two times," replied Nicky.

"Me, too. But why would he dance with her and not with me?"

Paizlee quickly shut the door as Gage and Trevor entered the hall and headed to their locker to put on their coats. The two girls watched as they walked the other way down the hall and left the dance.

"Why do they have to leave now?" sighed Paizlee. Then she turned to walk toward the gym door as Nicky followed.

"There are still a few more dances. Let's find someone for you to dance with."

Paizlee approached Travis and Sutton and somehow managed to talk Travis into dancing with Nicky. The two only glanced at each other as they danced, then Travis turned and left her as soon as the dance was over.

But Kirk saw Nicky was alone, and he said, "Hey, your next dance is with me." Nicky didn't like him, but she didn't say no. She went to find Paizlee when the song was over. Only a few minutes later, the lights came on.

On the way home, Nicky's mother asked, "Did you enjoy the dance?"

"I guess."

"Did you dance much?"

"Only twice."

"What about Paizlee? Did she dance?"

"Almost every dance."

"Why didn't you dance more?"

Nicky crossed her arms and wondered if her mother was disappointed in her.

"I just didn't."

"I suspect you waited for the boys to reach out and ask you. You may need to reach out first. I've noticed that you talk easily to the boys in the neighborhood."

"It's different at school. I'm afraid I'll say something dumb. Besides, Ryan's friends are younger than me."

"I see. Maybe you'll get to know more boys before the next dance."

Nicky shrugged and felt doubtful. She was glad she had gone to the dance, and she knew Paizlee would want to discuss it with her at school on Monday. But, as usual, she was the observer. She wondered if she could be more than that.

CHAPTER 2

The Pep Band

After her first-hour social studies class, Nicky bounced up the stairs and through the hall on the way to the band room. Nicky loved playing in the band three days a week. She had more fun in band than any other class, even gymnastics.

"Nicky, wait up!"

Nicky turned, smiled, and stopped until Paizlee caught up with her. As she opened the band room door, the sounds of clarinets, horns, snare drums, and a tuba flowed out into the hall as the band kids warmed up their instruments. The friends retrieved their cases from the racks on the other side of the room, found their chairs in the semicircle, and assembled their flutes.

Nicky sat in the third chair in the inner row of chairs, and she shared a folder of sheet music with Paizlee. Bella sat on Nicky's left in second chair, and Lauren, a ninth grader and the best flutist, was in the chair at the right hand of the director.

Most of Nicky's good friends were in band and she enjoyed making music with them. The eighth and ninth graders were a cheerful group, and many in each instrument section became close.

Nicky loved playing music. She was nine when she began piano lessons with Mrs. Schmidt. Two years later, Nicky saw her first flute. The instrument salesman opened the case, and Nicky looked at the three shiny silver pieces nestled in black velvet. The pieces reflected the light and threw it back in a colorful rainbow, which entranced her.

After the salesman put the pieces of the flute together, he lifted it to his lips and the flute made a long horizontal line away from him to his right. Then he blew a bright string of notes. That was it. Nicky became a flutist at that moment.

"Are you playing in the pep band tonight?" Paizlee asked. Pep band was the group of band kids who showed up and played at games.

"Yes, if my dad gives me a ride," said Nicky.

"My dad usually does, but we're having people over, so Kinsey's mom is driving me instead."

Nicky flashed back to the day she met Paizlee in Ridgeland City when they were only seven. Paizlee came over while Nicky played hopscotch in the driveway and asked if she could play. Paizlee was visiting her grandmother, but she lived in Eagleton. Nicky didn't know where that was. She had only been in the area for six months.

A few months later, Nicky's father got a job in Eagleton and her family moved after school was out. That summer, Nicky had a dance class at Eagleton Senior High School gym, and Paizlee recognized her, then introduced her to Zoey. The girls performed "Three Blind Mice" at the recital.

Nicky and Paizlee met again in fourth grade when they had the same teacher all day. They were in different classrooms in fifth grade, but the next summer, they both began playing flute in school band. Bella joined them, and the three had the same sixth-grade classes together, which deepened their friendship.

Mr. Darnell, the band director, stepped up to his music stand and tapped his baton against the metal stand several times.

He raised his voice. "Quiet! Everyone, quiet, please! We have a hard song to learn today."

About half the kids kept chatting to each other while the other half continued to tune their instruments. Bella leaned back and whispered to Nicky.

"When are they going to grow up?"

Nicky grinned as they shared the joke. The others quieted, and everyone turned their attention to Mr. Darnell, who lifted his arms as he began to direct. Preston, the tall ninth grader who was the section leader, played the snare drum for several bars until the clarinets came in with their first notes. The flutists raised their instruments and, with the rest of the musicians, played when it was their turn.

When band practice was finished, Paizlee looked over her shoulder as she gazed toward the windows to check on the drummers. Preston spoke to Dalton and Gage as they worked. She nodded toward them as they tidied up the percussion area.

"Do you think they'll be at the game tonight?" she asked Nicky.

"Probably."

"Gage is so cool. I wish he'd talk to me."

"You'll just have to encourage him."

"What if he doesn't like me?"

"Of course he likes you! You're cute and friendly. He's smart, so he can see that."

Paizlee looked at the clock and gasped, "I'm going to be late!"

They rushed to store their cases on the far shelf. Preston dashed by them and out the back door to run down the fire escape stairs. His next class was in the senior high school building across the street. He said hi to the girls, but he didn't stop. Nicky thought he was nice.

Paizlee left the band room before Nicky and Bella could get through the crowd. The students had six classes every day, and each class had a different group of kids. Nicky and Bella both had Advanced Math for third hour. Nicky took her seat in front of Gage, who was tossing an eraser with Trevor, who sat in front of her in the next row.

Trevor caught the eraser and looked at Nicky over his glasses.

"I see someone is wearing her pink socks again."

Nicky gave Trevor a frown and looked at her book. She wondered if something was wrong with pink socks. She felt judged, yet defiant. She could wear whatever socks she wanted!

Nicky met Trevor in seventh grade when their teacher picked them to judge holiday decorations. When Nicky arrived, the classroom windows were mirrors that reflected the fluorescent lights against the dark night. The teacher gave them each a sheet of paper, and then she led them to the seventh-grade classrooms. The decorations were green, white, and red with plenty of glitter. Nicky and Trevor selected the classrooms they thought should get first-place, second-place, and third-place prizes. They handed their sheets to the teacher and left. They hadn't said a word to each other.

Trevor was also in her social studies class. On the first day of school, as Trevor fiddled with a pen before class, it broke. Nicky could see the black ink all over his hands. He tried to clean them with spit, but after he wiped his hands on his jeans, he had ink all over them as well. She wanted to get him a towel.

The math teacher entered the room and began the lesson. When the bell rang at the end of the class, it was time for lunch. The kids went to their lockers to store their books. While Nicky was getting her bag, she saw Dalton a few feet away. He was talking with his locker mate.

"Did you see our game last night? I scored a touchdown! It was such a rush."

"Yeah, that was a crazy play. Didn't know Gage had such a good arm. But he sure moves the ball."

Dalton looked down at his friend and grinned. "Yep, we're on a roll!"

Nicky closed her locker and went into the gym to join Alyssa on the bleachers. Alyssa flipped her long hair back as she greeted Nicky. They had known each other since fourth grade. Last summer, they swam at Peaceful Bear Lake several times.

Bella and Paizlee put their lunch bags on the step and bought milk from the lunch lady. When they returned, Paizlee opened her bag and took out an orange. She smiled at Nicky as she handed her the fruit. Nicky peeled it for her friend and handed it back. Nicky peeled Paizlee's oranges because Paizlee didn't like to do it.

"Thank you! Alyssa, are you going to play at the game tonight?" Paizlee asked.

"Yes. I'll have to walk."

"Maybe Kinsey's mom can give you a ride. Hey, Kinsey! Can Alyssa ride with us?" Kinsey sat behind them with McKenna.

"Sure, but we can't fit anyone else. My sister will be in the car, too. She's point guard on the team."

At dinner that evening, Nicky asked her father, "Do you still have to teach tonight?" He taught a night class, but sometimes he had to cancel it.

"Do you need a ride to the game?"

Nicky nodded.

"We have to leave by 6:30."

"Can I go, too?" Ryan asked.

"Remember, you have to finish your art project tonight," said her mother. Ryan scowled and resumed eating.

The girls met in the band room after their parents dropped them off. They got their instruments and walked across the street to the senior high school gym where the girls' B-squad team played their games to join the pep band.

Paizlee climbed to the step behind the snare drums as Bella and Nicky followed. Mr. Darnell handed out the music. Nicky set the stapled half sheets on her lap while Paizlee turned so she could see it.

"We'll start with 'Let's Go Band' and move on to 'The Hey Song,'" instructed Mr. Darnell.

The brass and drums sounded loud as the pep band played the short emphatic notes: ba, ba, ba, ba-da, ba, ba, ba, ba-da. The cheerleaders shouted out, "Go, team, go!" The gym was filled with music, yelling, people running up and down the bleachers, and bouncing balls. Nicky and her friends laughed and cheered between songs.

As Nicky waited for her father to pick her up, she compared how happy she felt to how miserable she had been in seventh grade. That had been a tough year. When she did something wrong, even if no one criticized her, tears filled her eyes. She also became emotional when someone made comments about how she dressed or walked or how tall she was. She would duck her head, let her long hair drape around her face, and run into the bathroom to dry her tears. She knew when kids were just poking fun at her and their words weren't a big deal, yet she couldn't control her crying. Nicky felt as if she didn't fit in with kids who commented on other people and weren't as sensitive as she was.

A week before eighth grade began, she had asked her father, "Do I have to go back to school? I'm a good student. Couldn't I just get books from the library and learn on my own?"

Her father had given her a puzzled look as he said, "Why don't you like school?"

"Kids tease me."

"I think you can handle them. I'm sure you could learn on your own for some subjects, but a lot of things can't be learned in books. What about band or gymnastics? You'd miss those classes."

"I guess so," said Nicky. She sighed.

"I'm sure life will be better this year. You'll be in eighth grade."

Nicky understood she had no choice, and she dragged herself to school. She got familiar with the school routine and became more confident. She befriended kids in each class, felt more relaxed around them, and had few tears.

As Nicky's father drove her home, he asked if she enjoyed the game.

"Yeah. I wish we lived in town."

"Why?"

"Because I could see my friends more often after school."

"You can wish all you want, but we live out here. Weren't you the one who didn't want to go back to school?"

Nicky looked out the car window and considered her father's question as she watched the car's headlights cut through the dark.

"Yes, but I've changed my mind. I really like school this year."

CHAPTER 3

Gymnastics Class

While Nicky and Ryan ate breakfast on Monday morning, their mother looked at the calendar and shook her head.

"It's a busy week. Ryan has his school winter concert Tuesday, and Nicky, you have two concerts, right?"

"No, the band and choir play one concert on Wednesday," said Nicky as she brought her dish to the sink.

"Then the winter dance is Thursday. Are you going?"

"Yeah."

"I feel like a taxi driver taking you to dances, basketball games, and other activities. It will be helpful when you have your driver's license."

"I can't wait. Where's my leotard?"

"I washed it. It's on your bed."

After lunch, Nicky talked to Elena in the locker room as they changed into their leotards for gymnastics class. She pulled her long hair back with a black hair band, and they walked into the gym.

"The beam isn't out," Nicky complained to Elena. "I wanted to practice leaps today." She yearned to do more advanced skills on the beam, which meant she needed to practice. She wished she was only five feet tall, like Bella, because she would feel safer if her spotters could reach her hands.

"I need volunteers to get the big blue mats off the stage," said Mrs. Fleming. Alyssa and two other girls hopped onto the stage and slid the mats over to the edge, where other girls brought them to the floor. Nicky and Bella helped roll them out.

"I'm glad we're doing floor exercise. I don't like beam," said Bella.

"Floor is better than bars," said Nicky. "It seems like I never get time on the bars." She was usually the last in line because the teacher needed to move the parallel bars out for her. Often the class was over before she got her turn on that station.

"Girls, leave one of those mats rolled up so we can practice flying forward rolls. Please line up in two rows. Samantha will demonstrate the skill."

Samantha ran a few steps, jumped up, put her hands out, stretched forward over the rolled-up mat, then curled into a forward roll, and stood with her arms straight above her head.

When she had her turn, Nicky popped up high and flew over the mat. She felt her muscular legs propel her forward and wanted to repeat the skill over and over. She ran to the back of the line to wait for her next chance.

A while later, they practiced forward leaps from one side of the gym to the other. Nicky jumped high as her legs straightened wide above the mat. She leapt four times to get to the far wall where Bella waited. Then she collapsed against it before Alyssa joined them.

Alyssa whispered, "Remember your gymnastics party in October, Nicky? We should do that again."

"It was fun," agreed Bella.

Nicky had invited Bella, Zoey, Paizlee, and Alyssa to her house. Since she didn't have any foam mats, they spread out a mattress and blankets on the linoleum basement floor while they practiced handstands and danced to pop music.

"Let's ask Paizlee if we can do it at her house. She has carpeting in her basement," whispered Nicky.

At the end of the class, Mrs. Fleming called them to form a half circle around her.

"In February, we're having a gymnastics meet here in our own gym. It's the first time junior high girls have had a meet in our district. If you want to compete, please talk to me about it. You'll need to develop a routine or choose a vault skill. Then we'll have a day to try out for the meet. I want to see every one of you at least try!"

As the girls went back to the locker room to change, they talked about the meet and whether they would try out. Nicky wanted to compete, but she wasn't comfortable thinking about an audience. She would ask her mother to help figure that out.

Nicky hurriedly changed and went to her locker for her English and science books. Mario walked into the science classroom with her. Mario was always in a good mood, and he made jokes and comments to the teacher.

"Guess what? My family is moving to California. I can't wait!"

"Why?" asked Nicky. She frowned because she didn't want him to leave.

"My dad got a new job. I get to learn to surf! Our house will be only an hour from the beach. Man, that is going to be fantastic!"

"Surfing sounds fun. When are you moving?"

"After the winter break."

Nicky took a seat at her table while Mario sat next to Dalton on the other side of the room. The teacher started the class.

"Everyone, your homework over break is to figure out what to present as your science exhibit at the science fair in March. If you need ideas, please talk to me this week."

Nicky wrote a note to herself: *Ask Dad for help with science exhibit.* Then she wrote: *Mario is moving to California after break,* then tore out the paper and folded it into a triangle. She would pass the note to Alyssa in the hall because she liked Mario and would want to know. She would be disappointed, like Nicky was.

When Nicky walked into the dance on Thursday night, she wondered if she would see Mario, but he wasn't there. After an hour, Paizlee called to Nicky, and they went to the bathroom, where a few girls were combing their hair. Paizlee started combing her thick hair and waited until the other girls left. Nicky had forgotten her comb, so she used her fingers to straighten out a few places.

Paizlee said, "I think Gage likes me! He asked me to dance four times. Did you see Zoey and Dalton? Every time a dance ends, she grabs his arm and says, 'One more?'"

She looked at Nicky in the mirror. "Why aren't you dancing?"

"I don't think anyone likes me," said Nicky.

"Well, they do, but you have to make it easier for them. When we go back, stand by me for a while and maybe Kirk will ask you. He likes you, and he likes to dance."

"No, please not him."

"Well, find someone! You need to have some fun tonight!"

They left the bathroom and returned to the gym, where Sutton asked Paizlee to dance as soon as he saw her. Nicky stood a few minutes by the door, felt embarrassed, and went back to the bleachers.

The final dance was announced. Nicky put her chin on her hand and bent over while she watched the kids couple up on the dance floor. She saw Gage walk past. Then he tapped her on her right shoulder. She straightened up quickly.

"Nicky, wanna dance?" Gage asked.

"Yes." Nicky accepted without hesitation. She tried not to show her excitement.

Nicky and Gage danced several feet apart, and they didn't talk. She noticed they were about the same height. He said "Thank you" at the end, and so did she. The lights came up, and the kids headed to their lockers. Nicky found Paizlee, and they walked out the door to find their parents.

"I can't believe Gage asked you to dance the last dance! I know at least five girls who are jealous," said Paizlee.

"Really? I'm sure it didn't mean anything," said Nicky.

Nicky felt she shouldn't like Gage the same way Paizlee did. She didn't want to compete with her friend for a boy. But after the girls parted, she replayed the dance with Gage over and over in her head.

CHAPTER 4

The Forestview Glen House

Nicky was reading a mystery novel in her room the day after the holiday when her mother knocked on her door.

"Nicky, would you take Ginger for a walk? She's barking and a walk would calm her down," said her mother.

"I guess so," said Nicky.

Nicky went downstairs, and put the leash on Ginger, an unknown breed who looked like an Irish setter with a copper-colored coat. They went out the basement door as Ginger barked and leaped.

The house was built on a hillside on a full acre. Beyond Ginger's pen, the land sloped to the base of a stream bank, which filled up in rainy springs to become a waterway through the land. Their neighbor on that side lived beyond the bank and up the hill on the main road.

The acre had a variety of places to play, and friends came over to roll down the bank or climb the trees. The group played outdoor ball games, rode bikes, pitched tents and much more. Ryan built a tree house one summer and built a fort with a sign *Boys Only!* the next.

A big ponderosa pine tree stood on the bank of the dry stream, and it had two rope swings. The kids liked to grab hold of one of them and swing out over the creek bed. It hurt Nicky's wrist, but it was fun.

Nicky walked past Carly's house across the street. Her father was a history teacher who took his six kids on explorations around the Ponderosa Hills. They sometimes invited Nicky and Ryan to join them.

Nicky turned left and started walking uphill toward the main road and looked beyond the barbed wire fence which ran along it. She pondered going under the fence and walking across the field into the trees, but she hadn't cleared it with her mother, so she reluctantly turned onto the main road.

Nicky wanted to have a house nestled in the ponderosa pine trees. When she walked alone in the woods, she occasionally saw a deer hiding and looking at her. She would stand still, to not scare it away, but it would disappear in a minute.

She remembered her hike in the forest a few months ago with Fiona and Abbie. They had found branches on the ground to use for walking sticks, picked wildflowers, and enjoyed the fresh air. They had hiked along until they reached a crumbled brick foundation for an old house before they turned back. They saw Peaceful Bear Mountain across the valley.

On her next walk alone, Nicky had found the foundation and started down the dirt lane beyond it. Then she saw a motorcycle at the bottom, and she stopped as her heart started pounding. A man was lying on the grass to the right of the motorcycle with his hands behind his head. She backed up the hill very slowly and quietly until she was far enough away to run home. She wondered what would have happened if he had seen her. Would he have kidnapped her?

As Nicky walked Ginger, she wondered when snow would cover the pasture. In deep winter, it was several feet deep. She usually didn't hike in winter, except when her mother wanted to. On a sunny Saturday, her mother would look out the window and want to get out.

"Kids, get your boots on! It's time for a walk in the Hills."

They would put on their coats, pull on tall snow boots, take Ginger out of her pen, walk up the hill, and climb through the barbed wire fence. In the crisp, clean air, they would find sturdy sticks to help them get over snow drifts. Their eyes got worn out by the glare of the snow as they talked and laughed. By the time they got home, their cheeks would be nearly frozen as they clapped the snow off their mittens and wiped their boots on the mat.

The family might hike more this winter because her mother had quit the bookkeeping job the previous month to prepare to go to college in the fall. In her new position, she helped students study for a high school diploma test, which helped her brush up on her own study skills.

Nicky pulled Ginger around the corner, and they descended past Fiona's house. Four years earlier, Fiona and Nicky had lived next to Eagle Creek. After the creek flooded and destroyed their house, Fiona's father bought the house in Forestview Glen. Nicky's father bought the house behind Fiona's a few months later.

Nicky saw Kelly, a girl in eighth grade who lived close by, walking toward her. They greeted each other, and Kelly petted Ginger.

"Where are you going?" asked Nicky.

"I have to get something I loaned to Fiona because I'm moving."

Nicky's throat tightened. Someone else was moving away?

"When?"

"Next week. I'm going to a new school in January. I don't want to go though."

"I hope it's not too bad."

"I might never see you again. Have a nice life!" Kelly waved goodbye as she walked on.

"You, too."

Nicky liked Kelly, even though they weren't close friends. Nicky thought about the classes they'd had together, and she frowned as she finished the walk. She tugged Ginger's leash as she brought the reluctant dog into her pen. After she settled on the couch upstairs, she looked east through the living room's wide picture window.

Beyond the highway and the school, Nicky could see the hill on the far side of town. Paizlee lived on Pleasant Drive on the left slope, Bella lived behind Paizlee's hill, and Kinsey, Gage, and Trevor lived on Wicker Drive on the right slope. Nicky's brow furrowed as she wondered if one of those friends would move away next.

CHAPTER 5

A Threat

In early January, Nicky babysat the Sumpter children who lived a few blocks away. Mr. Sumpter was a lawyer where her mother had worked, and Mrs. Sumpter was her seventh-grade English teacher. They had a one-year-old girl and a three-year-old boy, and Nicky enjoyed watching them.

The girls' basketball season finished, and the boys' season was in full swing. Nicky went to many of their games, and she laughed and cheered with her friends when the pep band wasn't playing. She watched the dance line perform their new routine, and she wanted to dance with them.

Paizlee called Nicky one night. "Guess what? Gage asked me to a movie! Isn't that great? I can't wait!"

"That's so cool, Paizlee. When did he ask you?"

"After lunch. I was telling him about this movie I heard was good. I said he really needed to go see it, and he said, 'We should see it together.' I said, 'OK! When?' And he said, 'Saturday night?' Then I said, 'I'll meet you in the lobby at 7 o'clock sharp.'"

Paizlee talked about her upcoming date for the rest of the week. She had to figure out her outfit, and she was afraid the movie wouldn't be as good as she heard it was. She called Nicky on Sunday.

"After Mom dropped me off, I saw Gage inside. We bought some popcorn and talked before the movie. I thought the movie was good, but he thought it was just OK. He said it was too much of a romance, and not enough action."

"Do you think you'll see him again?" asked Nicky.

"I hope so! I told him I enjoyed seeing the movie with him and he said, 'It was fun. We should do it again.' But when I told Mom that I might go to another movie with him, she said maybe I should wait until my 14th birthday. But if he asks me, I'll figure out some way to get there."

"I can tell you will," said Nicky.

The next week, when Gage said "Hi" to Nicky in the hall after the pep assembly, she said "Hi" back. He hadn't talked to her since the winter dance, even though Paizlee thought the last dance meant something. When he greeted her the next day, Nicky was happy, but she didn't tell Paizlee.

One cloudy day, Nicky's father drove the family to Ridgeland City. They were a little past the railroad tracks by the Crossings Drive-In when he said, "Kids, we're moving to Texas this summer. There are many technical jobs there, and it would be a good place to live."

Nicky's eyes filled with tears as she considered the possibility of leaving Eagleton. For the rest of the drive, she sat quietly.

Nicky's father grew up on farms, and he hated winter. He was happy when he was stationed on an Air Force base in warm California. After he left the Air Force, he worked for a large company as a field computer technician. The family moved around multiple times while he worked there, but Nicky was too young to remember.

He left that job to follow a dream of owning a horse ranch, but that plan didn't work out. He sold insurance for a while in Ridgeland City before he got the job in Eagleton as a high school electronics teacher. Then the school added a post-high school program, and he taught classes for it. However, he wanted to work with modern technology, not just teach.

After her father's announcement, Nicky's parents talked for hours about how and where exactly to move. They requested information from various Texas cities, and her father researched jobs.

Nicky frowned as she listened to their updates during supper, and she ate less than normal. She started throwing half her lunch away because she wasn't hungry. When she was alone with her mother on the way to a basketball game, she asked the question which had been repeating itself in her head.

"Are we really going to move this time? Dad has said that before, but then we didn't."

"Yes, I think he means it this time."

"But why now? I've got so many friends this year. I don't want to leave Eagleton. Why can't we stay?"

"Maybe you should tell your father how you feel."

But Nicky didn't want her father to be unhappy. She didn't tell her friends because she wanted to ignore the horrendous fear of leaving them. She was having too much fun now. Ryan had many friends, too, and he didn't want to move, either.

Nicky put together a floor exercise routine of tumbling skills and dance moves for the gymnastics meet tryout. Her friends in the class were not interested in competing, but they supported her. After she performed her routine, Mrs. Fleming chose her to compete.

Nicky's stomach was queasy the week before the gymnastics meet in mid-February. The meet took place in the junior high gym. Three judges sat behind some tables on the side wall of the gym to score the routines. Because they didn't have uniforms, Nicky wore the new light blue leotard she had gotten as a birthday present. She felt excited as she did warm-ups on the bright blue mat. The audience, which was mostly students, included Dalton, Gage, and Trevor, and she became more nervous.

During her routine, she did her best skill combination, which was a well-executed cartwheel-round-off with a backward roll handstand. However, she couldn't remember some of the moves she had practiced, and some were out of order. Nicky called Paizlee that night.

"We lost! At least Millie and Eva got scores in the 7s, because I didn't help our team with my lousy 5.8 out of 10," said Nicky.

"At least you tried. What did Mrs. Fleming say about it?"

"She said I did a good job for my first meet. She thinks I'll get better."

"You'll try out again, won't you? You love gymnastics."

"There aren't any other meets this year. Mrs. Fleming said maybe there will be more next year. But I bet she never chooses me again!"

Nicky switched subjects. "When are you talking to Gage?"

"He said he would call this weekend."

"You're so lucky a boy calls you."

"I've never liked anyone like this before. I hope he keeps calling," said Paizlee.

Nicky decided then that she couldn't have a crush on Gage. She would find someone else to like.

On Friday, Nicky's father arrived home with a smile. He pulled her mother into a big hug, and then he explained his excitement.

"The vocational school director offered me a promotion!"

"Does that mean we're staying in Eagleton?" asked Nicky.

"Yes, it does!"

Nicky breathed a sigh of relief. Her father continued.

"I think we should move into town this spring. Mowing and shoveling out the driveway here takes too much time. Plus, your mother and I are tired of driving you to all your activities. It will be worse next year when Ryan is in seventh grade."

"Forestview Glen is such a pretty place, though," said her mother.

"Can we keep Ginger?" asked Ryan.

"Could we live close to Paizlee?" asked Nicky.

"We'll keep Ginger. I don't know what houses are for sale near Paizlee, but we'll stay away from the creeks because we don't want to be in another flood," said her father.

Nicky's family looked at several houses near the schools, and then the agent took them to Sally's old house on Dominick Street. Sally was a teenager who watched Nicky and her brother when she was eight while her mother worked part time. Nicky had liked playing various board games with her and taking walks by Eagle Creek.

When Ryan's friend threw a rock that hit his eye, Sally called her mother, who rushed home and assessed his eye was injured badly enough to go to the bigger hospital in Ridgeland City. Nicky's father was in college summer school at the other end of the state, so he couldn't help. Her mother dropped Sally and Nicky at Sally's house, about a mile away, for the evening.

Sally had four sisters who shared two rooms upstairs. Their big, old house seemed strange and scary that night because Nicky was away from her home, and she didn't know how Ryan was. When her mother picked her up the next day, she was tired as they drove to a former neighbor's house where Nicky stayed until Ryan got out of the hospital a few days later. He had to get glasses after his eye healed.

Nicky's family walked through the old house, which didn't seem scary in the daylight. Their steps echoed as they walked on the wood floors of the empty house. The real estate agent said no one had lived in it for a while, and Nicky wondered what had happened to Sally and her family. Where did they live now?

After her father decided Sally's house was the best choice, her parents bought it and talked with the agent about selling the Forestview Glen house.

Nicky felt cheerful about the upcoming move. Paizlee walked to school along Devon Street, which ran along the side of their new house, as did at least five or six other kids in her grade. Nicky wanted to be more independent and not have to ask her parents for rides to school. She daydreamed about all the exciting things she would do with her friends. She wanted to live in Eagleton until she got married or went to college, whichever came first.

But she worried her father might change his mind and move them away from Eagleton when he got restless again.

CHAPTER 6

A Good Move

The Forestview Glen house sold by the end of the second week on the market. In early March, Nicky's family started improving the new house. When they had moved into the Forestview Glen house, Nicky was nine, and Ryan was seven, so they couldn't help much. This time, their parents put them to work packing up the old house and fixing up the new house.

One day, as Nicky walked to the house in town after school to work on it, Trevor was a half a block in front of her. As he threw a paper airplane into the snowbanks, he had a quizzical expression when he looked back at her. She hid a smile when he looked back again and watched her go into her new house without knocking. Her new closeness to school would surprise others in her grade soon.

In the new house, they put in a new refrigerator, new kitchen cabinets, and counters. They painted the kitchen and living room walls. Upstairs, they put new carpet in Nicky's room, and she painted the upstairs bathroom cabinets. While they worked, they played music, and Nicky sang to songs she liked. She learned what the top songs were, but Ryan told her to stop singing when he couldn't take it anymore.

Nicky and Paizlee started walking together as often as they could. Kinsey and McKenna walked home the same way, and they often formed a group until McKenna and Nicky reached their houses. The other two had to walk another eight to ten half blocks farther.

Nicky and most of the band kids had choir on Tuesdays and Thursdays. The choir director walked into class one day with a box of choir music that she spread on the front table.

"We have a contest in May. Please form groups of three or four, then raise your hand. Chelsea and Hannah will record the names for each group. Then pick a song," said the director.

The buzz in the room increased as the kids began dividing themselves into groups. Paizlee, Bella, Zoey, and Nicky formed a quartet, and they looked at songs until they agreed on one. Nicky chose a piece from a musical as a solo, as did each of her friends.

The March dance featured a live local band. Paizlee looked forward to it because she wanted to dance to some slow songs with Gage. She and Gage had gone to a few more movies together, and she told Nicky about their phone calls.

Nicky was talking to boys in her classes, and she danced more that night. She also intentionally kept away from the bleachers unless she was tired. She felt disappointed that neither Gage nor Trevor asked her. But when Preston asked her to dance once, she decided she liked him, and she thought about him later.

Zoey danced many times with Dalton. Paizlee danced several dances with Gage, but then she avoided him. Paizlee was almost in tears as she told Nicky she had called her father to pick her up early. She wouldn't tell Nicky the reason. Nicky was enjoying herself, so she stayed until the dance was over.

Paizlee called Nicky the next day.

"What a terrible dance!" said Paizlee.

"What happened?" asked Nicky.

"Lily told me that Gage is dating Chelsea. They might even be going steady. I thought he liked me." Paizlee's voice was high, and she was very upset.

"That's awful. Maybe Lily is wrong," said Nicky.

"No, Lily goes to their church, and she sees him talking to Chelsea all the time." She sighed. "I bet he likes the way she sings. She's such a good singer. I wish she wasn't in our second-hour choir," said Paizlee.

"Maybe you'll find someone else to like," said Nicky.

"Oh, please. That's not going to happen here. I've known the boys around here far too long," said Paizlee.

"You never know. Maybe someone will surprise you," said Nicky.

"I wish. No, another new boy will have to move here. That's all I can hope for," said Paizlee.

On a beautiful spring day after the dance, Nicky's family moved. Her father arranged for friends to help with their pickup trucks instead of renting a moving van. They finished by noon and her mother treated everyone to chili for lunch. For the rest of the day, they unpacked and arranged things.

A big snowstorm swept into the area the next morning. The schools closed at noon, and Nicky walked home with McKenna, who asked Nicky to go to her house to hang out. They walked the two blocks to McKenna's house near the funeral home and ran upstairs to her room and played board games.

When Nicky walked home, the snow was already eight inches deep and Central Avenue was quiet, without cars. The tree branches were starting to droop with the heavy snow. She loved how spring snowstorms coated the world in a fresh, white blanket. She thought of the song "Marshmallow World," and she wanted to run down the street and toss snowballs at someone. She tilted her head back, opened her mouth, and caught snowflakes on her tongue.

The next morning, they awoke to 18 inches of snow. The school board canceled the district schools, and the kids enjoyed the snow day. The snow covered her father's car, which made him grouchy, and it was stuck in front of the house. Ryan helped shovel while he played with Ginger. He climbed onto the porch roof and jumped down into the snowdrifts.

The snow melted away within a week. One warm Saturday in April, Nicky carried her purple bike off the porch at the back of the house. She rode up and down the sidewalk while she gazed at the surrounding hillsides with dark pine trees lining the slopes. Then she looked at the house, their new home.

The two-story white house with a large, open front porch stood on the northeast corner of the intersection. It had two spruce trees, four huge ash trees, and a knee-high hedge which surrounded the yard. The yard was small compared to the yard at their old house. Ginger had little space to run around, and they would have to take more walks with her. The house didn't have a garage or driveway, which disappointed Ryan because he wanted to practice basketball.

Her mother hung bright, cheerful yellow curtains in the tall living room windows. Nicky liked the three stained-glass windows the best. They were splotches of color against the chipped white paint. The one high on the south side of the house was round, like a porthole. It had a blue circle in the center, yellow glass in the middle, and eight black spokes that reached to the green edges. The other windows were both on the west side of the house. They were rectangular, with an upper and lower row of green diamonds in a yellow background. The one over the stairway was a full window with only one pink flower in the middle, but the second one sat above the window in the front room, and it had two pink flowers.

When she was inside and the sun shone, the windows seemed to come alive. Sometimes, Nicky sat down on the stairs and let her eyes go unfocused. She felt the yellow, pink, and green colors surround her as if she was part of a kaleidoscope.

The entryway was full of warm mahogany wood, and the front door had a large round window with beveled sides. A wood bench against the stairs opened to store their shoes. Nicky learned the stairs had two steps that squeaked, and she avoided them. The piano sat in the den, which had a fireplace with green marbled tiles around it.

The location was the best part of the move to town. The house was close to many places Nicky wanted to go. Devon Street, which often had cars on it, ran four half blocks west to the school, and eight half blocks east to Nola Drive along the hill. The only stoplight in town was a block away on the corner of Central Avenue.

Main Street was only a few blocks north, with its drug stores, banks, theater, clothing stores, jewelry store, restaurants, and bowling alley. The library was about five blocks west. She could walk northeast to the city park and the football field. Nicky looked at the ridge above Eagle Creek, where the high school boys spelled the name of the town in white rocks.

Nicky lived closer to many band kids now, and she felt they were "her group." Walking home with them and spending time together outside of school helped her to know them better. They smiled when they talked because they cared about and supported each other. She missed her old neighbors, but she saw them at school sometimes. They weren't far away, so they could visit each other when they wanted.

Nicky closed her eyes and turned her face to the sun. Then she looked at the hedge and the buds on the crab apple trees. Soon white blossoms and purple lilacs would light up the street. She relaxed and thought about how content she was. She felt confident everything would keep blooming for her. This was her place.

CHAPTER 7

Contests and Concerts

Nicky's father had a doctor's appointment in a big city, and the family drove together to the Ridgeland City airport in April. Her father had Hodgkin's disease, a type of cancer, two years earlier. Nicky's parents explained the serious disease to their kids, and their worry that he might die. They were all relieved when the treatments worked, and her father recovered. Every year, he needed a follow-up visit with his cancer specialist to check whether the cancer had returned. After watching her father's plane take off, the rest of them shopped for summer clothes.

Her father returned with good news that the cancer was still in remission. He helped Nicky build her science fair exhibit, which they had discussed in January. He taught her how to create an electrical circuit to turn on and dim a light, and she put it together with an explanation. She carried the exhibit to school on the day of the fair and set it up in the gym. During the afternoon, the students visited other exhibits.

Mrs. Schmidt's students performed their spring piano recital at the beginning of May. Nicky played a piano piece, a flute solo, and another song on her flute, while Mrs. Schmidt accompanied her on the piano. Nicky was becoming more comfortable performing in front of people. She worried beforehand, but when she finished, she felt lighthearted and happy.

Nicky's father's college graduation ceremony was on the second Sunday of May, and his mother wanted to attend, so she arrived on the bus on Monday. After school on Tuesday, Nicky's mother drove Nicky, Ryan, and her grandmother to some tourist spots in the Ponderosa Hills. The next afternoon, the four went to Peaceful Bear Mountain and climbed it for about an hour, but they didn't reach the top.

As Nicky and her grandmother sat on the porch on Friday, her grandmother set her glass of iced tea on the little metal table.

"How do you like school, honey?"

"It's good."

"When I went to school, kids had a ceremony when they graduated from eighth grade. Ninth grade was the start of high school. I only went to a few months of high school before my father made me stop to get the harvest in. He needed me to work on the farm, so I never got back to school. You're pretty lucky to have all of these musical events. I never got to play an instrument."

Her grandmother leaned back in her chair and folded her arms as she looked out at the street.

"Do you have friends in town?" she asked.

"Uh-huh. We hang out a lot," said Nicky.

"Good friends are a blessing. But don't let anyone talk you into doing bad things. I'm grateful for some of the friends I made in school. It was lonely on the farm. Do you miss Forestview Glen?"

"Sometimes. But I can walk to school in five minutes here."

"Your mother says you're a good student, and you like math, like your dad. If he had stayed in college when he was 20, he would have become a math teacher, but he joined the Air Force after your grandpa and I divorced. He's been restless ever since, just like his father. I'm surprised your folks have been here for seven years."

"I hope we stay here," said Nicky.

Her grandmother clasped her hands and looked at Nicky.

"Honey, your father had cancer. He's recovered, and now he's got his degree. He can get a better job, and it may not be in Eagleton."

Nicky gnawed on her lower lip. "But I don't want to move again."

Her grandmother nodded. "Of course. Living brings change, though, and as you grow up, nothing stays the same. It isn't easy to learn to adapt to new things, but you've got to do it."

Her grandmother stopped speaking as looked at the street with a sad expression. Nicky gnawed more on her lip. She didn't want anything to change now that her life was going so smoothly.

"I better go rest some, then help your mother with dinner." Her grandmother stood and went into the house.

After a few minutes alone, Nicky wondered what Paizlee was doing, so she went inside to call her.

The next day, Nicky's family and grandmother drove to the other end of the state for her father's college graduation. They stopped at some tourist attractions along the way and stayed overnight in a motel. They dressed up in the morning and went to the university arena to watch her father happily receive his diploma. Her grandmother soon left on the bus.

The next week, the band kids competed at the regional band contest. Nicky got the highest rating on her flute solo. The percussion quintet, which included Preston, Dalton, and Gage, got the highest rating. Paizlee, Bella, Lauren, and Nicky had the second highest rating on their flute quartet.

After band class the following Monday, Mr. Darnell took aside the groups which won awards at the contest.

"Please meet outside by the fire escape during your lunch hour and get into your contest groups. The county newspaper is sending a photographer to take your pictures."

When the flute quartet gathered several hours later, Bella said, "I hope the photographer isn't an amateur!"

"There he is. Is he the same guy from last year?" asked Paizlee a few minutes later as a man with a camera around his neck arrived.

"I don't recognize him. Let's hope he has some experience!" said Bella. She laughed.

"I know him. He's a friend of my uncle. Let's tell him we want to stand on the fire escape for our picture," said Lauren. She walked over to the photographer and told him their plan. The four of them stood on different steps of the fire escape with their flutes for their photo.

Other groups formed and had their pictures taken. Mr. Darnell wanted one of the eighth-grade soloists who got the highest ratings. Gage, Grace, Grant, and Nicky gathered under the fire escape stairs.

"Let's not smile for our photo," said Gage. "It'll show we're serious musicians."

"Sure. No problem," said Grant.

"I want to smile," said Grace.

"I always smile when someone says 'Cheese!'" said Nicky.

"You don't have to smile. Just think of something serious and you'll think serious thoughts," said Gage.

When the photographer said, "Smile everyone," Nicky tried to keep her mouth straight, but she felt a smile creep in.

Later in the week, Nicky grabbed the newspaper from the mail and eagerly looked through it for the photos. The one of the flute quartet was good, and the percussionists had great smiles. But the one of her with the other soloists was awful. Grace was smiling, while Grant and Gage had stern looks. Nicky's eyebrows were raised, and her mouth looked like she had eaten a lemon. She didn't want to go to school the next day because she was embarrassed by the photo.

The next event was the spring band concert. After the regular band played their songs, the stage band performed popular and jazzy songs. Stage band had percussion, sax, cornets, basses, trombones, and a piano. Nicky wanted to be in it, but they didn't want flutes.

After the band played, Mr. Darnell addressed the audience.

"Our 'Outstanding Ninth-Grade Musician' award goes to a young man who is a hard-working, talented, responsible, and a strong leader in his section. The award goes to Preston!"

As Preston shook Mr. Darnell's hand and the audience clapped, Nicky nudged Bella and raised her eyebrows. She still liked Preston and thought it was great he got the award. But Bella shook her head slightly. As they walked to the band room, Bella whispered to her.

"You really shouldn't like him. He spends a lot of time at church."

"So?"

"He wants to be a priest."

Bella shrugged as if she couldn't understand why, and she opened the band room door. Nicky wasn't a Catholic, but she knew once someone became a priest, he couldn't date or marry. Preston wasn't a priest yet, so why couldn't she like him now?

At the choir concert the next week, Paizlee, Bella, Zoey, and Nicky sang their contest song. Chelsea performed a beautiful solo. Other choral groups and singers impressed the audience.

A few days later, those competing in the choir contest got out of school for the day. Nicky, Paizlee, Bella, and Zoey got the highest rating for their song, but Nicky's solo got a lower rating. She was disappointed because she had rehearsed the song intensely at home and thought she would do better.

During the last week of school, the junior high students attended a school awards assembly. Nicky received a certificate of merit for her science fair exhibit, and she got one for participating in the gymnastics meet. Her friends also received various awards. They cheered and clapped loudly as soon as they heard a name they knew.

The day before the last day of school, they exchanged their school yearbooks. Nicky thought a few minutes before she wrote something specific to each friend. Later, she smiled as she reread the notes in the front and back covers of her yearbook.

Zoey apologized for teasing her so much about liking Preston. Her science teacher called her "Miss Quiet." Trevor mentioned her pink socks. Gage called her a "very nice person." Dalton wrote she was sweet and nice, and he hoped to get to know her better.

On the last day of school, Nicky walked home with Paizlee, Zoey, McKenna, and Kinsey. Eighth grade was over, and her outlook was far happier than it had been at the end of seventh grade. She wondered what she and her friends would do in the summer.

CHAPTER 8

The Carhop Who Escaped Lightning

The carhops sat on the bar stools in front of the counter. Nicky sat to the left of Cora. They sat on the top metal bars of the short backs of the stools, not on the black seats, and their feet were on the footrests. Nicky watched the left front of the drive-in, which was her side that day.

The Crossings Drive-In sat on the west side of Central Avenue, north of the highway, between Eagleton Inn and Devon Creek, which was usually dry. The small building was white with red trim, and the front canopy roof was red with yellow trim. Six parking spots lined each side of the center sidewalk under the canopy while three parking spaces were at each side of the small building. Eight tables were inside the building, and a picnic table sat on the north side of the parking lot.

In February just before the move to town, Nicky had talked to Fiona, her neighbor in Forestview Glen, who worked as a carhop at the Crossings Drive-In. She made more money in tips for a shift than Nicky did babysitting for an evening. The hourly wage seemed like a lot of money to Nicky. After the call, Nicky helped her mother pack boxes in the basement.

"Mom, can I work as a carhop at the drive-in this summer?"

"I don't think that's a good idea. You're only 14. Maybe you could try to get a different job."

"But when Fiona worked there last summer, she was only 14."

"Do you know what a carhop has to do?"

"They take orders from customers and bring them food while they sit in their cars."

"Yes. Working with customers isn't easy. Some people can be rude and even mean. You must stay at work through your whole shift, even if you're unhappy. You must be very careful with money. Have you thought about any of that?"

"Not really. But you and Dad always say that I'm capable of doing whatever I want to do. I need money this year. I want some new clothes and a skateboard. I can't babysit the Sumpters because we won't be living in Forestview Glen anymore. How am I supposed to buy things? Can't I try?"

"Let me think about it," said her mother.

Nicky talked to her mother several times after that until her mother said she could apply. She warned Nicky that the owner might not offer her the job, so she should be prepared for that.

Nicky called Fiona.

"Hi, Fiona. How did you get the job at the drive-in last summer?"

"I just went there one day and asked for an application."

"Are you still working there?"

"Yes. I'm quitting in May, though. I'm getting a different job this summer."

"I guess I won't see you if I get a job there. I was hoping we could work together. Do you still like it?"

"It's hard sometimes, but it beats babysitting! It's fun to work with other kids our age."

The next time Nicky went with her mother to the store near the drive-in, she went inside the building and asked the boy behind the counter for an application. He went to the back and returned with one.

Nicky went back a week later and handed it to the woman at the cash register. It was May before the owner, Mr. Sherwood, called her to come in for an interview. They talked for about ten minutes.

"Can you start work on the Saturday after school is out?" he asked.

"Yes."

"You'll only work daylight hours at first. When you show up, one of my daughters will train you. They've been working here since they were about your age, and you can ask them questions."

On her first day of work, she watched the two cooks make burgers, hot dogs, chicken, fries, fried rolls, and other drive-in food. Nicky stood at the back of the kitchen and tried to stay out of the way because only three people could move around comfortably. After several hours, Mrs. Sherwood taught her how to take orders, use the cash register, and count change. She followed Cora as she took food to customers.

The first month was frustrating. She had to talk to people, smile, and never get annoyed. Most customers were nice, but sometimes people were unhappy with their orders, so she had to apologize and take food back to the kitchen to get them another item. A few customers made things up, like when high schoolers came in together in a group. Nicky had to pretend they were right. Sometimes, customers kept arriving, and she didn't even get to sit on the stool.

She got upset when she didn't have the correct money total at the end of her shift. They had to "true up" the total of the orders with the money that should be in the cash register. When they were short, they had to pay back the till out of their tips. Because she was good at math, it always surprised her when her order total wasn't right.

She was exhausted at the end of every four-hour shift, even on slow days. Many days, Nicky cried as she rode home. She wanted to quit, but she knew she better stick it out. She liked having the money to spend.

Secretly, she wanted to be a mugger, not a carhop. The mugger stood behind the counter to fill the drink and ice cream orders while Nicky's feet hurt at the end of the shift from walking back and forth to the cars. But because Preston worked as a mugger, she wouldn't get to work with him if she was also a mugger. The drive-in only needed one mugger on a shift.

As Nicky sat with Cora, the inside eating area was empty. The parking spaces were, too, until a car pulled into a left parking space. The driver and his passenger looked at the menu written on the board that hung below the roof canopy. A few minutes later, Nicky hopped off the bar stool and pulled out her order pad. She used her back to push open the left swinging side door and walked to the car.

The coin changer jangled on her waist as it slid up and down on the polyester pantsuit. The uniforms were navy blue, with some red and white trim on the short sleeves. Buying the uniform took up almost all of her first paycheck.

As Nicky reached the car, the driver rolled down his window, and she leaned over. "Can I take your order?"

"We want two burgers, two orders of fries, and two chocolate milkshakes. No, make one strawberry," said the boy. He and his friend looked about 17.

She used abbreviations to jot down what they wanted.

"Do you want any ketchup?"

"Yeah, bring four packets."

"I'll bring your order out in about five minutes."

As Nicky walked rapidly back into the building, she noticed the darkness in the west. Heavy clouds covered the sky from the ponderosa pine-covered foothills to the highway, the county fairgrounds, the swimming pool, and the railroad tracks behind the drive-in. Nicky saw two lightning bolts, and she wondered how long the storm would last.

The area often had brief afternoon showers in June. A big June storm could bring danger sometimes. When Devon and Eagle Creeks ran over their banks five years earlier, they caused extensive damage to the area, including the rental house where her family lived then.

Nicky handed the order to Shannon, the drink mugger, who looked at it, hung it up for the cooks, and made the shakes. Nicky went to the cash register, put in the items, and took the receipt. Then she put one of the pre-wrapped fork, knife, and spoon sets on a red tray with the receipt.

After about five minutes, Shannon put the food on the tray, which Nicky took it to the car. After she placed it on the driver's window, she gave him change, the she returned to the building.

A loud clap of thunder startled the five kids and rattled the windows. With the thunder, they saw a bright flash of lightning strike the top of the canopy directly above the car Nicky had just served. The bolt streaked down to the left, jumped to the car's antenna, and then along the roof and trunk to the ground. It only lasted a few seconds as the carhops jumped to their feet. The air smelled as if something had burned.

"Did you see that?" Cora shouted.

"I wonder if they got shocked," said Shannon.

Nicky was too stunned to speak.

They watched the driver take the tray off his window and throw it to the ground. He started the car and put it in reverse. The driver wheeled back and out of the space, then turned left on Central Avenue without stopping to look for other cars. His tires left black marks on the concrete. He wasn't taking any chances of being under the canopy for the rest of the storm.

Nicky guessed no one was hurt because the driver could drive. They must have been terrified to see the electricity run along the car while they sat in it. She felt as if she had escaped being hit by the lightning bolt, because it could have struck her when she took the food out to the car.

As Nicky rode her bike home on the wet streets after the thunderstorm passed, she remembered how the driver panicked and left so quickly. She laughed nervously because the situation seemed like a scene from a movie, one which was scary, yet funny.

CHAPTER 9

Biking and Hiking

During June, Nicky rode her purple bike to Alyssa's house every week. The two girls rode to the pharmacy, bought music or candy, and looked at comic books. Nicky's mother drove them, Ryan, and his friend, to Peaceful Bear Lake for picnics. They sat on the small sandy beach on beach blankets and swam in the cool water.

When they were at Alyssa's house, they played video or other games with Alyssa's sister, Hailey. The sisters played duets on the piano while Nicky listened. Alyssa and Nicky sat on the street curb one afternoon as they ate popsicles.

"You're so lucky you have a sister," said Nicky. "It would be fun to play duets."

"It's not fun when we argue, which we do a lot. When are you going to get a new bike? That one is pretty small for you," said Alyssa.

"I know. I've had it since I was eight. The seat is as high as it can go. It's embarrassing to show up for a shift and park it between the bigger bikes. I need to ask my dad if I can get a new one."

"Hope he says yes," said Alyssa.

A few days later, Nicky and her father were in the kitchen.

"Dad, can I get a new bike? My purple one is too small," Nicky said.

"Your bike seems to work fine," said her father.

"But I got it in third grade! I feel like a little kid riding it. I want a 10-speed like my friends have."

"You used to love that bike," said her mother. She came into the kitchen with a bag of groceries, and she unloaded them.

"Used to. That's the problem," said Nicky.

"Bikes are expensive," said her father.

"I can pay for some of it because I work now," said Nicky.

"How about you pay for half? We'll go look for one this weekend," said her father.

"Thanks, Dad!" Nicky was relieved she didn't need to plead with him for long.

Nicky and her father drove to Ridgeland City to a discount store. She found the 10-speed bikes, the kind where the rider leaned over the handlebars, and she chose a bright green one.

"Dad, here's the bike I want," said Nicky.

"That kind? It'll hurt your back. Look at this one," he said as he walked over to a white bike that had a cushioned black seat. The rider didn't need to lean over the handlebars.

"Dad! I can't ride that one. My friends will laugh at me!"

"I think it's better. You'll thank me after a hard day of work."

"It's white! Can't I get a colored bike, a 10-speed?"

"This one has 10 speeds."

She begged some more, but she couldn't convince him to buy a different one, so the upright white bike with a soft seat was what Nicky got. She thought the new one looked too mature for her and felt almost as embarrassed when she rode it as she had with her old one.

When her library books were due, Nicky rode her new bike to the library and lingered among the shelves as she decided which book to explore next. The library had only three rooms, and Nicky was exploring the room of adult fiction books that summer.

July was hotter than usual, and the family used fans to stay cool in the house. The junior and senior high school bands marched in the July 4th Crazy Days parade down Main Street in the dry heat. Only about half of the band members showed up. Paizlee and Nicky marched behind the drummers while Gage played the bass drum.

After the parade was over, Nicky and Alyssa walked home together after Paizlee's mother picked her up.

"Do you want to go to the fireworks tonight?" asked Alyssa.

"Where?"

"They have a huge display at the dam. My whole family is going, well, except my brother. But you could come, too."

"Sure! That sounds fun. Let's ask my mother."

Nicky's mother was fine with the idea. Later, Alyssa's mother picked up Nicky, and she squeezed into the crowded car. They drove until they reached the dam, then spread a blanket on the ground and watched the show. The red, white, and yellow explosions were almost as good as the ones Nicky saw on television.

At the end of Nicky's next work shift, she hopped onto her new bike. She sped along wide Dominick Street, going slightly downhill, shifting gears as needed. She couldn't wait to get out of the uniform. As Nicky crossed Devon Street, she saw Paizlee waiting on the front porch of the old white house. Paizlee was staying overnight with her.

They went inside and scampered up the stairs. Nicky's bedroom was large, with two west windows next to each other. Stuffed animals sat on the bed, and figurines were arranged neatly on a cabinet. The pictures on the wall showed forest scenes and horses. Paizlee put her bag on the floor, and Nicky changed in her closet.

"I was short again today," she said. "I had all of 58 cents left over for tips. What did you do?"

Paizlee told Nicky about her day with her family. Then Paizlee and Nicky biked up the hill and over to Wicker Drive. They saw Gage and Trevor on the corner, so they stopped and talked for a short time with them. Later that night, the girls played some board games.

"I'm so glad Gage and Trevor were outside tonight. Doesn't Gage look taller?" said Paizlee.

"Not really."

"Well, I think he is. I wish he would call me. I want to go to the movies with him again, or get an ice cream, or something."

"I wonder why he hasn't called."

"Lily said today that she saw him walking with Chelsea. Get this, Trevor is dating Hannah." Hannah was Chelsea's good friend.

"Hannah's nice."

"Yeah, they both are. But I still wish Gage liked me more," said Paizlee.

After breakfast, Paizlee and Nicky rode their bikes to the drive-in, where Nicky went in the back door to get her check. She hadn't worked many hours because of a family visit with her mother's parents, who lived a five-hour drive away. The owner had paid Nicky the higher wage, so she must be trained in and performing better.

When the girls went around to the front of the building, Dalton and two other boys stood by the counter with milkshakes. They wore navy caps and dirty white and blue striped baseball team uniforms. Dalton stopped talking to Preston, the mugger that day, to look at Paizlee and Nicky.

"Hi Dalton. How was your game?" asked Paizlee.

"We won by two points," said Dalton.

"Congrats! It's so hot today. Did your dad drive you?"

"No, we biked. We gotta go now because it's a long ride home," said Dalton. He and his friends went out the side door.

The girls bought ice cream cones and went out to the picnic table.

"I just heard from Zoey that Dalton asked her to go steady with him," said Paizlee.

"I saw them at the movies last week. She was flirting with him before the show," said Nicky. "He was smiling a lot."

"I'm glad one of us is dating," sighed Paizlee.

When they finished, they rode back to Nicky's house, where Paizlee picked up her bag and went home.

The next day, Nicky's mother drove Nicky to Bella's house, which she shared with her parents, older sister, and younger brothers.

"Your hair is so cute!" said Nicky.

"I'm getting used to it. My head feels so light, it's weird. But it's better to have short hair with the heat. We don't even have an air conditioner." She rolled her eyes with annoyance.

"Neither do we. I wish we had one," said Nicky.

"My new piano teacher has A/C in her house."

"I didn't know you had a new teacher. Where does she live?"

"In Ridgeland City. After the recital with Mrs. Schmidt, Mom and I decided it was time for a change." Bella played with a pencil on the table. "Let's go for a walk."

"It's going to be a different band without the ninth graders," said Nicky as they passed some old brick houses.

"We'll be the ninth graders! It'll be great being the oldest class in the building. Unfortunately, we're stuck with the same boys. High school boys are better than junior high ones," said Bella.

She grimaced. "The boys in our grade don't even care about true culture. My family went to a touring Broadway play in Ridgeland City last week. The costumes were amazing. I bet we don't know a single boy who would appreciate it."

Nicky wondered if she could appreciate a famous play. Her parents didn't watch plays, but her mother liked some public television shows.

On the way home, Nicky's mother shared an idea.

"Let's go swimming in Crystal Lake after we take Ryan and his friends to Boy Scout camp on Sunday."

"I love Crystal Lake. Could I invite some friends?" asked Nicky.

"I suppose so. I'd like to ride on the pedal boats this time. We always talk about it, but we haven't yet. Then we could stop for dinner at Goldmine Gap."

"How long is Ryan at camp?"

"The whole week. We'll pick him up next Sunday evening."

The temperature was headed toward 90 degrees when the kids piled into her mother's car. When the group got to the camp, the boys grabbed their duffel bags and ran up to the main cabin.

Then her mother drove around curvy roads in the national forest to Crystal Lake. The sky was deep blue without a wisp of clouds. Huge gray boulders surrounded two sides of the lake, which had a small beach. The girls swam in the freezing water until it was a relief to return to the beach and lie in the warm sun. They climbed up the rocks and sat on the biggest boulder.

They put on their tops and shorts to hike around the lake. Few people hiked because of the heat. After they reached the top of a small hill, they hurried down to a cool, shady place to rest in the trees. Her mother looked up at Green Vista Peak and started planning a hike to the top. Nicky, Ryan, and her mother had climbed the three-mile trail the previous year. Nicky felt happy sitting there with her mother and her friends.

The Crystal Lake pedal boats stand wasn't open that evening, so they packed up. They drove to Goldmine Gap, which had many tourist shops, and walked around, then bought some sandwiches for dinner.

"Do you like saltwater taffy? I love it. I'm going to buy some for us," said Nicky. They found a shop, and they took a long time choosing the flavors they wanted.

"Look, they have pistachio," said Bella.

"I like Neapolitan," said Paizlee.

"We need some chocolate, peppermint, vanilla, peach, banana. I like them all, except licorice," said Nicky. She bought the taffy and requested three bags. They divided out the pieces they wanted.

"How about some fudge?" asked Paizlee. "Do you like the kind with nuts?"

"I don't like any nuts in mine," said Nicky.

"Well, I do, so we outvote you," laughed Bella.

The girls pooled their money and bought some fudge with walnuts. They giggled together as they sat in the back of the car. They were worn out and sleepy the rest of the way back to Eagleton.

CHAPTER 10

Swimming and Skateboarding

While Nicky rode her new skateboard, which she bought with her own money, in front of the house, her parents sat on the porch and talked about what classes her mother wanted to attend at the regional community college in the fall.

Her father waved and shouted at a man walking by.

"Hi Ron. How's the TV set working for you?"

"Good. Now the other set is acting up, but we're headed out of town for our summer vacation this weekend, so we won't need it."

"You just let me know if you need me to fix it next week. Where are you going?"

The two men chatted for a while as Nicky listened. Her mother went into the house.

Nicky's family had more conversations that summer because people walked past the house in town more than the house in Forestview Glen. Her father was full of energy and talked to people easily. He knew many people in town because of teaching and working odd jobs. He wired the senior high school gym for video and audio for talent shows and other events, and fixed electronic equipment.

People knew her mother from the years she had worked at the law office. Whenever Nicky was with her parents as they shopped downtown, they chatted with the people behind the counters. They weren't rich, and they didn't give parties, yet people knew her family and seemed to respect them. Nicky felt she was known and trusted in town because of her parents.

Nicky wished she could be friendly with people without feeling intimidated or fearing she would say something stupid. But she was too self-conscious to start a conversation with someone she didn't know. Her jaw locked, and she was silent.

Yet, she was changing. She talked more easily this summer with her friends than she had before. As a carhop, she handled rushes when cars came one right after another. When the other carhop was late or had to leave early, Nicky kept her head up and took each order as it came. She stayed calm through the chaos. She was learning how to handle demanding situations.

The mugger, cooks, and carhops would sigh with relief when they could take a break. They talked about music, school, and their plans for the future. Nicky usually listened, but at times she contributed something she had heard.

When Ryan's camp was over, Nicky and her parents visited Crystal Lake before they picked him up. The cold wind made swimming unappealing. Her father sat in a chair on the beach with a jacket on as he smoked a cigar.

Nicky and her mother rented a pedal boat, which they steered right to the middle of the lake. With tired legs, the mother and daughter laughed as they worried they wouldn't get back to the shore. Once they parked the pedal boat, they rested on the grass. They recovered and walked around the northwest side of the lake.

They drove to the Boy Scout camp, where Ryan's troop showed them around the tents and activity stations. After a Sloppy Joe dinner, and the sunset, the darkness descended. The boys led the families to a campfire. The leaders got their directions mixed up, so it seemed like they were going in circles, which irritated her father, until they finally found it. Each troop performed a skit and told jokes. As Nicky looked at the star-filled sky and the moon, she thought about bounce-walking on the distant orb. Then Ryan grabbed his stuff, and the family drove home in the dark.

At the end of July, Paizlee, Zoey, and Nicky biked down the hill and through the gap to Bella's house. They developed a bunch of code words to use when they were around other people, especially when talking about the boys they liked. They wanted to get together every week until school started, but Paizlee was leaving for a two-week church camp, and Nicky had signed up for a gymnastics clinic.

The gymnastics clinic started Monday in the senior high school gym. The equipment was set up, and the blue mats spread out. The coaches from a big city showed them new skills, and the group practiced over and over. Nicky fell off the beam multiple times. She was stiff on Monday night, and she struggled through the week.

Zoey and Bella planned a swimming and slumber party at Bella's house for Friday. When Zoey and Nicky arrived, they put their bags in Bella's room, left their shorts on the bed, and walked to the pool with just their beach towels around their swimsuits. Nicky shivered and had goose bumps before she got into the water.

"I like your towel," said Zoey. The towel had a red and orange butterfly on it.

"Thanks. It's cold tonight," said Nicky.

"We still have to swim because we're having a swimming party," said Zoey. Nicky got the message: Zoey would be the leader that night.

"Bella, toss that beach ball to me! We can play a game in the water," said Zoey.

"Over here!" yelled Nicky.

They played with the beach ball for a while until Zoey admitted she was freezing. They walked back to Bella's and had some spaghetti.

"What should we do now? Bella, do you have any board games?" asked Zoey.

"We have Yahtzee, Monopoly, and Sorry. But I'm sorry, we can't play Sorry because my brothers hid some of the pieces." Bella grinned.

"Let's play Monopoly," said Zoey.

"I like Monopoly," said Nicky.

Bella got out the game, and Zoey won. They played music and sang along. They made up lyrics and laughed when the words didn't make sense. Bella's sister told them to turn down the volume. They snuggled into their sleeping bags and kept talking.

Zoey told them about some strange things which happened after a relative died. A door repeatedly swung open by itself, and drafts circulated throughout the house. Zoey and Bella talked about how they believed good people's spirits went to heaven after they died. Nicky's family didn't attend a church, and she had never thought about death. After Zoey told some ghost stories, her friends said goodnight and were quiet. Nicky didn't fall asleep right away because she was thinking about the ghost stories.

At home, she asked her mother what happens after a person dies. Nicky's mother said people around the world had different answers to that question. She got a big book off their shelf titled *The World's Great Religions*. Nicky looked through it and saw pictures of Christians, Jews, Hindus, Muslims, Buddhists, and people of other religions. They all believed differently about what happened after death.

During the last weeks before school started, Nicky worked many shifts at the drive-in. When she made mistakes, she was able to control herself and not get upset. Her confidence and bravery grew when she handled situations well. At the same time, she wasn't sure she wanted to work at the drive-in anymore because she wanted to be involved in other activities when school started.

After Paizlee got back from church camp, she went to Nicky's house as the sun set. The air was cool after a sweltering day, and they rode their skateboards up and down quiet Dominick Street while they talked.

"Nicky, look!" said Paizlee. "Isn't that Gage and Trevor?"

Nicky looked up Devon Street and saw two boys on their bikes about a block away. "Maybe."

They waited until they were sure and then called out to the boys, who stopped right by them.

"Cool skateboard, Paizlee. Can I try it?" said Gage. He laid his bike on the ground.

"OK, but don't wreck it. I know you won't. I just had to say it. Where are you guys going?" asked Paizlee.

"We're just riding around," said Gage.

"Hey, Nicky, can I ride your skateboard?" asked Trevor.

"Sure."

"This is definitely a girl's skateboard. Mine is bigger than this."

The boys sped back and forth as the girls watched, then Trevor stopped, picked up Nicky's board, and played with the wheels. They talked about movies, games, music, and vacations. Nicky felt relaxed because they couldn't see each other very well in the dark. The streetlight threw some light through the tree branches, but the shadows made the street seem smaller.

"Nicky, when is your next shift at the drive-in?" asked Gage.

"Tomorrow afternoon."

"Maybe we'll see you there."

After they left, Nicky and Paizlee kept talking until Paizlee's father picked her up and took her home.

Gage and Trevor rode their bikes to the drive-in the next day to get ice cream cones during Nicky's shift. They sat at one of the tables and looked at menus. She took their order for twist ice cream cones.

"How old is your brother? Is he going to be in our school next year?" asked Trevor.

"He'll be in seventh grade," said Nicky. "Do you have brothers or sisters?"

"They're all graduated now so I'm the only one living at home."

"My sister is graduating in May. My brother just got into West Point. I'm going to the Naval Academy," said Gage.

"You'll never make it," said Trevor. "Your brother is way smarter than you."

"Yeah, but I will." Gage glared at Trevor.

Nicky gave them their cones.

"Isn't that uniform a little big for you?" asked Gage.

"Are you going to grow into it before school?" asked Trevor. The boys laughed as they ate their cones.

When she came back inside from taking another order, they were debating how much to tip her.

"I think she only deserves two pennies," said Gage.

"Naw, she did OK. Let's give her three," said Trevor.

Pennies? Really? Why even leave a tip? They sauntered out and hopped on their bikes. Nicky put the pennies in her pocket.

Several days later, they were back at the drive-in, and they were goofing around even more as Trevor took his watch on and off. They whispered and laughed every time she looked at them. Then they left without taking the watch. When Nicky saw it, she ran outside to yell at them, but they didn't hear her. Nicky called Trevor and left him a message saying if he was looking for his watch, it was at the drive-in.

The two boys called her a few times, told jokes, teased her, and laughed. During one call, Trevor was at Gage's house, and he tied his shoe on his head. He was dancing around while Gage tried to describe him, but Gage was laughing so hard he couldn't talk. Nicky laughed as he described Trevor's antics.

A few days before school started, Nicky visited Paizlee, and they ate snacks while they talked at her patio table.

"It's official," said Paizlee. "Gage and Chelsea are going steady. Lily told me."

"How does she know?" asked Nicky.

"She saw Gage kissing Chelsea at the movies last Saturday. Trevor had his arm around Hannah. Other people saw them, too."

"I saw all of them at the county fair while you were at church camp. They were on the swing ride together, and I saw them buy cotton candy and play some toss games. They looked like they were having fun."

"It's so unfair." Paizlee took a sip of soda pop. "Why doesn't Gage want to date girls in our grade?"

Nicky shrugged and didn't reply. She didn't think dating between grades was a problem.

"I would never want to date a younger boy. They're immature and they do gross things." Paizlee shuddered.

"But so do boys in our class."

"But Gage is definitely more talented than most of them. He's smart, he's good at sports, and he's good at music. Maybe he has higher goals, so he wanted an older girl."

"Maybe he likes her for other reasons, like she's nice. Can you believe he's only been here a year?" asked Nicky.

"He's not a new boy anymore. I wonder if any boys will move here this year." Paizlee looked across the lawn with a dreamy smile.

They won't be Gage, though, Nicky thought as she put her chin on her hand. The summer was over, and she wondered if she would have any classes with him. Gage and Trevor's attention that month had been exciting, and she didn't want it to end.

CHAPTER 11

Ninth Grade Classes

On the first day of ninth grade, Paizlee, Bella, Zoey, and Nicky walked to school together and talked excitedly. They wanted to know who their teachers would be and who would be in their classes.

The students checked an alphabetical list posted in the hall with students' names and their homeroom numbers. Nicky's homeroom was English, and her locker was located in the busy first floor hallway near an exit. The students received their schedules, and the girls compared them as they walked home.

The next day, a full day of classes, Nicky left English and went to band. The flute section had five new eighth-grade members. Bella was first chair, and Nicky shared a folder with her as second chair.

A new gymnastics coach greeted the girls in third hour. She was shorter than Mrs. Fleming, and she had more gymnastics experience. Elena was in the class again, but Bella wasn't.

Nicky's fourth-hour class after lunch was Honors Algebra with the same people who had been in Advanced Math. The students had to walk through the senior high school gym to get to the classroom, but they were told not to walk across the gym floor. Instead, they walked up the gym stairs, held the railing along the edge of the upper bleachers, then rushed down the stairs on the other side.

Nicky's fifth hour science class was down the long high school hall, where the older students had most of their classes. She saw them laughing in groups and sitting on the benches which lined the glass walls that surrounded the two outside areas. Elena was in science with Nicky, and they walked back to the junior high building together. It was a long walk, and they had to hurry.

Her sixth and last hour class was social studies with the same teacher she had in eighth grade. Elena was in that class, too.

Lily and Nicky switched lockers on Monday so Lily could share one with her good friend. Nicky's new locker was upstairs next to the band room door in a hall that only band kids walked through. She would have to carry more books and notebooks with her at one time because she couldn't return after any of her afternoon classes. But she liked the out of the way hall better.

As she walked to her new locker the next morning, she saw Gage standing at the locker next to hers. Her eyes widened with surprise.

"Hi, Nicky. Looks like we're neighbors. What's up with your hair this morning? It's messed up. Didn't you comb it?" said Gage.

"Yes, but it's windy. Didn't yours get tangled?" said Nicky. She was embarrassed that he noticed, and she got out her comb.

"No, my hair never tangles," said Gage as he grinned at her.

The next day, he said, "You're wearing your pink socks again. Don't you have other colors?"

"Yeah, but I like these."

"You should wear other colors, too. Do you think kids will start listening to Mr. Darnell this year?"

"They paid more attention after the winter break last year."

"Not much." Gage shook his head with disgust.

As the days passed, sometimes he complimented her outfits, but usually he tried to get a rise out of her. Nicky felt like she was a turtle, and he was poking a stick at her to see what she would do. She didn't respond to his poking right away as she tried to figure out if he was serious or cynical. She was puzzled as she looked at him, and she said, "Yes," or "Really?" or "Maybe." She didn't want to say something dumb, especially not to Gage.

Grant, who shared the locker with Gage, was friendlier. Grant had broad shoulders, and he was a wrestler. He played baritone horn in band, and he couldn't wait to get his driver's license because he lived out of town. He always said "Hi, Nicky! How are you?" or "Wasn't that math assignment tough?" or "See you later at the game!"

Nicky babysat that Saturday night for a woman she barely knew. The two kids were cute and behaved well, but Nicky saw many wine bottles in the kitchen garbage. At 1 a.m., Nicky called her mother.

"What should I do, Mom? She isn't back yet."

"You should try to get some sleep. She'll probably be back soon. But if something happens, let me know right away."

Nicky pulled a blanket over her and laid down on the couch. She slept a little. Dawn arrived before the mother returned and went into her bedroom. An hour later, Nicky called her mother for a ride home because the woman was still sleeping. Nicky could smell the alcohol and assumed the woman had gotten drunk, which made her uncomfortable. She decided she wouldn't babysit there again. She felt bad for the children.

On Monday, Nicky saw Gage at his locker.

"Hi, Nicky. How was your weekend?"

"I babysat, but it was awful. How was yours?"

"I did some stuff. Hey, I've been kidding around a lot with you. I decided that I'll be nicer to you from now on. I just wanted you to know." Gage shut his locker and went into the band room.

Nicky was relieved because he confused and upset her when he tried to be clever. She wanted his attention, but not his zinger remarks.

As she took attendance in junior high band a few days later, Gage's name was crossed off. Mr. Darnell said Gage had transferred into the senior high band. She was disappointed, but also envious.

Nicky was tired of the lack of discipline in the band room. The musicians talked and talked even when Mr. Darnell asked for quiet multiple times. It seemed worse than the start of school last fall, and the more responsible students got impatient. Many eighth graders didn't play well yet. Nicky guessed that was how the ninth graders last year felt about her class as eighth graders. Even though she still had many friends in junior high band, she began to wonder if she could get into the senior high band. But she didn't want to hurt Mr. Darnell's feelings.

Even though Nicky didn't feel well Thursday, she went to school so she could go to the ninth-grade football game with Paizlee that afternoon. With Gage as the quarterback, the team won 16-0.

On Friday night, Bella, Paizlee, and Nicky sat in the outdoor stands by the high school pep band at the football game. Gage and Preston played the snare drums. When Paizlee left to talk to Lily. Mr. Gillette, the senior high band director, sat down next to Bella and Nicky. He had directed them in sixth-grade band, and they saw him often in the band room.

"Do either of you know anything about All-State Band? It's a band you have to qualify to get into. Only the best players throughout the state get into it. It meets in the summer, but students try out for it in January."

"I bet they're good," said Bella.

"Do you have to be first chair to try out?" asked Nicky.

"No, you don't, although usually, the best player in our band is first chair. The two of you are so close in ability that you could both try and see what happens. At least start thinking about it. Even if you don't get in this year, you'll know the process and have a better chance next year. I know that one of you will make it before you graduate."

Someone called his name, and he went back to the other side of the band.

"Should we try out, Bella?"

"Definitely! I bet that band sounds a lot better than ours does!"

Nicky nodded as they laughed together.

CHAPTER 12

The Student Council Election

Before Mrs. Colsen started her lesson in Nicky's English class on Monday morning, she stood in front of her desk and asked for the students' attention.

"As you all know, we have a Student Council election coming up."

The Student Council worked on the pep assemblies, the junior high float in the Homecoming parade, and they helped with other events like dances with the Pep Club. During the first week of school, each homeroom class had voted for one student to be their representative. That person would attend meetings during lunch several times a month. Nicky had not been on Student Council before.

Everyone in the school got to vote for the new Student Council president. The ninth grader who got the most votes would win, and the person who had the second most votes would be vice president.

Two years ago, Nicky didn't know any of the candidates, so she voted for the best speaker. Last year, she knew some of the candidates, so she voted for the one she thought had the best speech and could be the best leader. This year, she knew her classmates well and felt confident she would choose the best leader, even if they didn't have the best speech. She knew who was active and smart, so she would select the candidate who was qualified.

Her teacher continued. "Most elections have two or more candidates. But, so far, only Lance has told the Student Council supervisor he wants to run for president. Do you think having only one choice is a real election?"

Some of the class shook their heads no.

"Even if you feel intimidated about stepping up, you each have the potential to be a leader. Let's talk about what a leader is. Give me some qualities a leader shows."

Mrs. Colsen went to the chalkboard, wrote the word "Leader," and underlined it. The students offered their thoughts. When they finished, their list included: "Has good ideas." "Talks a lot." "Listens to others." "Honest." "Works hard." "Smart." "Wants to tell others what to do." "Wants to help others." "Makes decisions." "Responsible." Mrs. Colsen put down her chalk.

"That is a great list. Even if you feel you aren't so good in some of the qualities on our list, you may simply need an opportunity to volunteer for a leadership role. You might find out that you like being a leader. It can be fun.

"If anyone in here has been on Student Council before, please consider throwing your name into the hat. Even if you haven't, you could still enter the election and win it. Please talk to me after class is over."

Nicky wrote the words in her notebook. She had most of the qualities, except "talks a lot" and "wants to tell others what to do." She had never thought she wanted to be a leader, but the school needed a real choice. Someone should run against Lance to make him sweat a little. She realized she could be that someone, even if there was no way she would win.

But what if Nicky did win? She thought about how she wanted to help with activities this year and be more involved in the school. Since she lived in town, she could walk to school whenever she had to, even before or after classes.

At the end of English class, she went up to Mrs. Colsen.

"I'd like to be in the election."

"Wonderful. You need to talk to Mr. Weaver. Do you know where his classroom is?"

"Yes," said Nicky.

Before she went to lunch, she found Mr. Weaver upstairs, sitting at his desk. He taught the English Literature elective, which she had last year, and he was the law office receptionist's son.

"Mr. Weaver, I'd like to run for Student Council president. Mrs. Colsen said I didn't need to be on Student Council. Can I run?"

"Of course, Nicky! Why do you want to run? What's inspired you?"

"I want to get more involved in school and help out."

"Being involved is a good reason."

"What do I have to do?"

"You need to work on a speech. Do you remember the speeches from last year? Tell the kids how you could help, and why they should vote for you. Include some changes you'd like to see happen. You also need to advertise. Make lots of signs! I'll add your name to the ballots."

"OK. Thanks, Mr. Weaver."

As she left his room and went past the library to go to lunch, she felt a rush of energy. Why couldn't she be Student Council president? She was responsible and smart. It would be something new to run in an election. She told her friends during lunch.

"I'm going to run for Student Council president! I just talked to Mr. Weaver. I need to write a speech and make some signs. Will you help me?"

"You're going to run for president? I don't believe it!" said Zoey. "You're too quiet. I bet you can't even speak in front of people. I predict you'll fall down from embarrassment while giving your speech."

Zoey had a point because Nicky didn't like speaking in public. She remembered the speech teacher catching up with her one day in the hall.

"Nicky, I haven't seen you in eighth-grade speech class yet. Please join us as your second semester elective."

Nicky had nodded, but she didn't want to take the class. At the time, she couldn't imagine she would ever volunteer to speak in front of people. Instead, she took drafting where she didn't have to speak. Now she wished she had taken the speech class after all. At least the election speech only lasted a few minutes. The rest of the preparation would be fun.

Bella, Alyssa, and Paizlee offered to help her make some signs and try to get people to vote for her. They gathered colored construction paper and crayons, then wrote, "Vote Nicky for Student Council president!" They taped the signs up along the halls.

Even Ryan helped her. He promoted her to his classmates before class. "Vote Nicky for Student Council president. She's my sister."

Mia also decided to run. Mia was in Nicky's math class, she was in band, and she had been on Student Council before, like Lance. Her experience gave her an advantage over Nicky. Nicky heard Lance had some doubts. He thought it would be easy to win when he had no competition. But with two smart girls against him, he wasn't so sure. His friends persuaded him to stay in the race.

As election day approached, Nicky began wondering why she had volunteered. Both of her opponents knew a lot about the Student Council, but what did she know? Nothing. But she wasn't a quitter. She said she would run, so she had to follow through.

When election day arrived, the whole student body gathered in the senior high school gym to hear the candidates speak. Nicky felt like the entire world was there to judge and criticize her speech. She was incredibly nervous, but she tried not to show it. The three candidates drew straws to determine the order of their speeches. Lance was first, Nicky was second, and Mia was third.

Lance gave a good speech. He stressed his two years on Student Council, and he gave some ideas about what he would like to do for the school. He had a cheering section who loudly supported him.

Nicky's speech wasn't as long. Her hands were shaking behind the podium as she held her paper and looked out at all the faces waiting for her to speak. She leaned closer to the microphone. It was her first time speaking into one, and she was glad it didn't squeak.

"Hi, I'm Nicky. Thank you for considering me for Student Council president. Even though I haven't been on the Council before, I think I could be a good president. I have an outside perspective, but sometimes that's good. To be a leader, you need to think clearly and work hard. Being popular isn't enough.

"I think we need teachers to communicate with us more. I want some posters in the school which will inspire us to be great. I have other ideas, but I'll learn if they make sense if you choose me. So please vote for me to be your next Student Council president."

The audience clapped, and a few kids even cheered as she finished. She had adequately delivered the speech, even though her voice was not as strong as Lance's. She sat down on the bleachers with relief.

Mia's speech was entirely different because she didn't actually have a speech.

"Hi, I'm Mia. Everyone, please stand up."

People looked at each other with confusion, but some of Mia's friends stood up, so many other people stood up. Nicky didn't want to, but she did.

"Now, everyone, sit down." People started giggling or moaning as they sat down.

"I believe this shows my control and power over the students at this school. I would be the best president. Vote for me!"

A lot of kids liked the joke. They laughed and looked at each other. Nicky thought Mia should have prepared an actual speech. Instead, she had shown the power of telling people what to do, even when they didn't understand the purpose, which was disturbing to Nicky. Mia would have a better chance of winning if she had offered some ideas.

That afternoon, the three candidates found out Lance had won the vote. Mr. Weaver wasn't sure yet who had gotten second. Nicky was not surprised or disappointed she had lost to Lance, and she was certain Mia had the second most votes.

Mr. Weaver found her at her locker after the Council meeting the next day. Nicky wasn't at the meeting because she wasn't the representative for her homeroom.

"The Student Council had a vote about who should be vice president. You won!"

He explained that even though she had gotten the second most election votes, some Council members were unhappy she had never been on the Council before. Mr. Weaver decided a vote was the best solution. The majority had voted for Nicky.

"Really? That's great," said Nicky.

She was surprised she had come in second in the election. It felt good to know people had voted for her. She wondered who opposed her becoming vice president. She hoped Mia would still like her since they would be on the Council together. They had known each other for a long time.

Nicky felt a little proud she had tried something she never thought she would do, and she won a role she was comfortable with. She could be part of the Council, but not the main leader. The position was fine with her.

CHAPTER 13

The Inattentive Band

Nicky gave Mr. Sherwood her notice she wanted to quit working at the drive-in. Earning money had been satisfying, and sometimes she had fun working, yet the demanding shifts exhausted her. She had more homework and activities at school, and she was bored with the job. She planned to try some other job next summer.

On Thursday, the junior high pep band went to Sparta to play for the ninth-grade football team and to cheer them on. Paizlee and Nicky sat together on the bus.

"You know how Dalton has been calling me since July to ask what he should do about Zoey? He still seems clueless how to treat a girlfriend," said Paizlee.

"But they've been dating for a while," said Nicky.

"Yeah, but boys need help. Of course, Zoey knows he calls me, so she asks me what he said, or sometimes she tells me to tell Dalton something. Sometimes I tell him, sometimes I don't."

"It's weird. Why don't they talk to each other?"

"They don't understand what the other one wants. I give them ideas about things to do together, too. Anyway, when Dalton called Sunday, I told him to stop talking to me about Zoey."

"What did he say?"

"He asked why, and I told him I'm Zoey's friend and I'm tired of being in the middle of their relationship. He has to talk to his own friends. But he said his friends don't give him the same kind of advice and he wants to keep talking to me."

"You are good at giving suggestions."

"Yes, but if they are going to date, they need to talk together and leave me out. When Zoey called, I told her the same thing."

"To stop talking about Dalton?" asked Nicky.

"Yeah, but she got mad and hung up. Then yesterday, I heard from Lily that Zoey told her she broke up with Dalton."

"What? Why didn't Zoey tell you herself?"

"She was still mad at me. Besides, I already know she's interested in someone else. Dalton is too, so it's just as well."

"Who are they interested in?"

"I'm sworn to secrecy, so I can't tell you."

"Oh. Well, at least you aren't in the middle of them anymore."

The bus arrived at Sparta's football field, and the kids ran off the bus. The night was warm, and the Eagleton fans were excited to cheer their team on to a win. The final score was 26-0, with Gage and the running back enjoying many completed passes. The enthusiastic kids cheered all the way back to their school.

"We're the best! We're the champions!"

The next night, Nicky worked her last shift as a carhop with Preston as the mugger. It was his last shift also, which was ironic because they had only worked together a few times in the summer. She was relieved at the end of the night as she biked home. The next morning, though, she was a little sad. Because Nicky had worked, she had confidence to run in the Student Council election. She was uncertain how to buy things she wanted without the money she earned by working.

In band the next week, Nicky approached Mr. Darnell and said she wanted to challenge Bella for the first-chair flutist position. Nicky yearned to be first chair. She loved playing her flute, and she wanted to take band all the way through college, maybe at the same college where her mother took classes. She might become a professional flutist and play in an orchestra after she finished school.

Mr. Darnell said he couldn't tell any difference between them, so he asked Mr. Gillette to supervise their evaluation. The high school band director chose some music and told them to practice it for a few days. Nicky practiced the piece until she played it well, and she was sure she would win.

Mr. Gillette called Nicky into the office first because she was the challenger. She played the prepared music for him, and she messed up a few times on the piece. However, she did well on the scales and the sight-reading, which was music she had never seen before.

Then Bella went into the office. Nicky could hear her, and she listened carefully. After Bella finished, she opened the office door and joined Nicky in the band room. Mr. Gillette stayed in the office.

"I'm sure you won. I messed up the sight-reading something awful," said Bella.

"But you did great on the prepared music. I did a lousy job on that," said Nicky.

Mr. Gillette took a few minutes before he opened the office door and came into the band room.

"Congratulations, Bella! You won by one point more than Nicky. You two are so close, it's tough to know who is better. As you played, I thought Nicky was better overall, because of scales and sight-reading. But Bella was better at the prepared music, which counts more in the total score. If you both keep practicing, you'll be well-prepared for All-State tryouts in January."

"Thanks, Mr. Gillette," said Nicky and Bella. Nicky was disappointed. But she would keep practicing and try again another time.

As the days passed, Nicky became fed up with the junior high band. Many of the eighth graders wouldn't pay attention and it got worse every day. Mr. Darnell couldn't control them, and most students ignored him. They didn't seem to care how they sounded. Sometimes he would throw down his stick, storm into his office, and shut the door. Nicky wanted to enjoy practicing together and not have to wait for others to quiet down.

Gage and Kinsey had moved into senior high band, which met first hour instead of second hour. Maybe Nicky could get into it, too. Being with older kids might mean she would play more. But she would miss being in junior high band. She would especially miss Paizlee, Bella, and Alyssa.

Nicky would also have to give up choir on Tuesday and Thursday because she would have band every day, not just Monday, Wednesday, and Friday. She would miss being with her friends in the choir, but she wouldn't miss the singing. Her voice wasn't strong, and she wanted to play her flute more than she wanted to sing.

Nicky didn't care about leaving her first-hour English class, either. One boy gave her trouble when he imitated her voice and picked on her. She weighed the pros and cons of transferring to the older band as she went into the principal's office to talk to the secretary.

"Hi, Mrs. Halston."

"Hi, Nicky. Congratulations on becoming Student Council vice president. What do you need today?"

"Thank you. I'd like to get into senior high band."

"You're not alone. Four of your classmates have requested that. What's wrong with junior high band this year?"

"Many of the kids just want to talk and not play, so I'd like to be in the next level where maybe they don't talk as much."

"Mr. Darnell isn't happy about the moves. His best players are leaving." She dug into the filing cabinet and brought out a form.

"You'll need to get Mr. Darnell's signature on this form and then get Mr. Gillette's signature. Then return the form to me. We also need to change your class schedule for your first and second hours. What do you have the first hour?"

"English with Mrs. Colsen."

"Oh, so you need a different English class. That'll be tough. Mrs. Fleming teaches the only second-hour English class, but the class is full." She stood up and opened the principal's door. "Principal Dahlke, we have a request."

Principal Dahlke came out of his office. "Hi, Nicky. What can I help you with?"

"Nicky would like to switch into senior high band. She needs Mrs. Fleming's second-hour English class, but that class doesn't have any more seats in it. What do you suggest?"

"Why do you want to leave the junior high band, Nicky?"

"People don't pay attention." Nicky felt defensive, and she was afraid they wouldn't let her move. But she wanted the switch, and she was prepared to argue.

"Mr. Darnell may implement some discipline if you give him some time."

"But I want to be in the better band, so I can improve before All-State Band tryouts in January. Our band doesn't play enough."

"I see. Let me think about what we need to do about the rest of your schedule. Please talk to Mr. Darnell and Mr. Gillette first and come back with the signed form. If they agree with the change, we'll take the next step."

"Thanks, Mr. Dahlke."

Nicky left the office with the form. The next time she saw Bella, she told her how she could get into senior high band, too. Nicky thought she would like to have Mrs. Fleming as an English teacher, since she liked her in gymnastics class. Nicky didn't want to shift other classes, so she hoped she could get into the second-hour class.

The Student Council met twice that month during lunch. They took their lunches into Mr. Weaver's classroom, and they ate while they discussed the agenda. Nicky was shy in her new role, and she wasn't sure what she was supposed to do. She listened a lot, and occasionally she spoke up. She voted on issues with the other members.

One of the first decisions for the group was the float design for the Homecoming parade. Lance asked people to raise their hand if they had an idea, which he wrote on the board. Some kids wanted to put animals like bears or dogs on the float. Some suggested entertainment shows they liked. Others wanted a school spirit theme with their mascot and a large drawing of the school.

Nicky suggested they recreate the five colorful Olympic rings and make signs about their team having Olympic strength, power, and spirit. After everyone voted on the idea they liked, the Olympic rings idea won. Nicky felt like she had contributed something.

For several weekends, she worked with other Student Council members to finish the float. They had to decide who would ride on it, since it represented the whole school. Many kids were already marching with other groups, like the cheerleaders or the football teams. Nicky couldn't because she was in the marching band. Eventually, they decided on Lance and two other popular council members.

On the way home one day, Nicky and Paizlee saw Trevor pass them in his new vehicle, a landscaper-type motorized cart. It was rust-colored and narrow, with two seats inside and a small open area in the back where two could sit. He already had his provisional driver's license. He sometimes offered them a ride home, and they sat in the back for a bumpy ride.

Paizlee called it "The Thing" because she thought the cart was ugly. Nicky thought it was cool Trevor could drive around town already, even if only in the daytime. She and her friends planned to take Driver's Education class in the spring after they turned 15.

At the end of September, the two sixth-hour social studies teachers arranged a history field trip. On the bus, Nicky found a window seat. Her teacher took attendance, and when she called Gage's name, no one answered. Mr. Neville, his teacher, said Gage was excused. Nicky could feel the disappointment in the air. Many girls hoped he would be there. Nicky heard other people talk about him during the half-hour bus ride.

"Is he sick?"

"He was in school today."

"He should have come on this trip, then."

"He's lucky he got out of it. I wish I could have."

Nicky was anticipating the field trip because she liked history, but it might have been more enjoyable if Gage had been along.

The classes visited a museum which recreated the atmosphere of the 1870s. Nicky read many of the placards while most of the other kids looked quickly at the exhibits and then went outside where they could talk to each other.

The next stop was the cemetery on the hill, which was full of famous people's gravesites. It was the first cemetery she had ever visited. Her ancestors were buried in cemeteries far from Eagleton.

Most students wandered around in small groups, but Nicky stayed by herself so she could read inscriptions with the person's name, birth, and death dates. She wondered what the person buried there looked like, how they lived, and how they died. Sometimes there was an engraving which indicated whether the man was a miner, a farmer, or a banker. Mothers lay buried next to their children with the same date of death. Graves of Chinese laborers who worked in the mine were beside graves of children who died during an epidemic of smallpox. Nicky thought about the fascinating stories of people's lives, past and present.

The park-like cemetery grounds seemed quite beautiful and peaceful on the warm summer-like day. The sunlight filtered down through the trees and gave the cemetery a cheerful atmosphere. The tops of the pine trees swayed in the breeze, but their trunks sheltered the cemetery, and only a slight current of air reached the ground. Nicky could hear the rustling treetops swaying back and forth as if in time to a secret beat of music only they could hear. She felt like she was in a trance.

The past month seemed like a dream. She was busier than she had ever been, yet she was eager to do more with her friends and for the school.

CHAPTER 14

The Last Chair Flutist

Dalton walked behind Nicky as she stood with her locker door open after school on Thursday. She continued to gather her things until she noticed he was beside her.

"Where's Gage? Did he go into the band room?" asked Dalton.

"Yes."

She looked up at him, and he smiled at her. She smiled back.

"I voted for you, and I'm going to ask you to the winter dance."

He turned, opened the band room door, and strode inside.

As the door closed behind him, Nicky's jaw dropped. She was perplexed because she still thought of Dalton as Zoey's boyfriend. They had hardly spoken, although he had been in classes and in band with her. He had phoned her in the summer to ask how long Paizlee would be at church camp. Why had he declared his intention about the dance? Why had he mentioned the winter dance when the fall dance was coming up? She decided he was joking with her.

"Dalton said he's going to ask me to the winter dance," Nicky told Paizlee on the way home. "Do you think he means it?"

"He said that? He didn't mention it to me," said Paizlee.

Gage, Trevor, and Dalton ran past them, got into a huddle, and called out a play. Gage pretended to throw a ball, and Dalton ran back to catch it. He was next to the girls when he said, "Hey Nicky, I'll call you sometime soon." Then he ran back to Gage and Trevor.

After the boys sped ahead, Paizlee exclaimed, "He's serious! He really intends to call you."

"Do you really think so? I don't want to be disappointed if he doesn't. And what about Zoey? Doesn't she still like him?"

"Zoey is already talking to a different boy, but I can't tell you anything else about it."

While she did homework after dinner, Nicky thought about Dalton and what he had said. She daydreamed about what they would talk about when he called. Maybe they would go to a movie together.

When Nicky talked to Mr. Darnell about transferring to the senior high band, he looked at her sadly.

"Are you sure?"

"Yes. I'm going to try out for All-State Band, so I need to get better. I'll be motivated to work harder in senior high school band," she said.

He reluctantly signed her form.

As Mr. Gillette signed the form, he said, "Great! Can't wait to have you as a student."

After she got the band directors' signatures, she talked to Mrs. Halston about the full second-hour English class. Mr. Dahlke said he would ask the class whether someone wanted to switch their schedule. At lunch several days later, he called her aside and said a student wanted a change and Nicky could take her seat. Somehow, it all worked out, and she was going to be in the class she wanted.

But now she realized she had a new problem. She wouldn't have any classes with Dalton because junior high band and choir were the only ones they had together. After worrying about it that night, Nicky decided the next morning she wanted to be in the senior high band, and wanting to see a boy would not deter her.

The junior high and senior high bands marched in the Homecoming parade. The Student Council float looked good. Nicky observed the other floats carefully. If she was on Student Council in senior high, she wanted to have better ideas about what made a great float. The senior high Pep Club had the best one in the parade.

Paizlee and Nicky went to the Homecoming game later, despite the light rain. Nicky's father drove her to the game, and he stayed to watch it. When she was in elementary school, her father took Nicky and Ryan to football and basketball games. Whenever a group of high school boys from his class saw him, they gathered around him to discuss the game. Nicky always felt her father was special because he was a teacher.

That night, as he walked past the stands, a few guys yelled, "Hi, Mr. M! Stay cool!" He smiled, waved, and went to sit by the adults on the other side of the stands.

The pep band wasn't playing because of the rain. The girls saw Dalton sitting with two of his friends, but they didn't see Gage or Trevor. Chelsea was there, but she was not with Gage. Paizlee was burning with curiosity, and she wanted to talk to her. Nicky was reluctant, but Paizlee motioned for Nicky to come with her, and the two climbed up the bleachers to sit next to Chelsea.

"Hi, Chelsea. Isn't the game good?"

"I guess. But it's starting to rain harder. I think I'll leave soon."

Paizlee took a breath and then went ahead. "What I was wondering is, how is Gage? I mean, I usually see you sitting by the band next to him at games, but he isn't here. Is he OK?"

"How should I know? I didn't feel like being with him tonight." Chelsea was curt and went back to looking at the football field.

"Oh, I'm sorry. Well, have fun." Paizlee quickly withdrew and Nicky followed her back to where they had been sitting. Paizlee started whispering and making predictions.

"I bet they're having trouble and Chelsea didn't want to say so. If she doesn't want to be with him tonight, maybe she's thinking of breaking up. Maybe they already broke up. I haven't heard about it yet, though. But I predict even if they're still dating now, they won't be dating any more in a few weeks. I hope Gage is OK. He might be heartbroken."

"She probably wouldn't tell us if she's planning to break up," said Nicky.

"True. I hope she doesn't hurt him too badly."

Nicky looked at her friend and nodded. She knew Paizlee enjoyed thinking Gage might be unattached again soon.

After the halftime show, the girls saw Gage and Trevor walk from the entrance to the football field, stop to talk to some friends, and turned around without sitting in the stands. Both girls were disappointed, but they talked about other people and watched the game. They covered their heads with their jackets as the rain came down harder. Despite the rain, the team won 20-14.

On Monday after Homecoming, Nicky was finally in the senior high band. Kinsey and McKenna waved when they saw her come in. She was assigned to the last chair of the flute section, but she would challenge someone to advance. The kids talked in the senior high school band, too, but less than the junior high band. They played more often and better. She liked Mr. Gillette as a director, and he had a sense of humor.

In English class, Mrs. Fleming assigned Nicky to the first row against the wall, with Gage on her left and Lainie in front of her. Five or six extroverted students were in the class, and they raised their hands to participate in lively discussions.

In mid-October, Nicky and her friends walked to the fall dance in the junior high gym. When they first got to the gym, Kinsey was afraid Gage wouldn't come, since Chelsea couldn't come because she was a sophomore.

As one of her Student Council duties, Nicky worked in the refreshment stand for the first 45 minutes. She dug out cans from the cooler to pour soda pop into plastic cups on the table. When someone bought a cup, she took their money and put it in the coin box. The kids were supposed to drink the pop at the refreshment stand and throw the cup in the garbage next to the table. But some kids walked off with the cups, and later she had to walk around and pick up the empties. While she was working, she overheard only snippets of the conversations around her. Gage and Trevor visited the stand before Nicky's shift was over, and she hoped Kinsey saw them.

Lance was the DJ, and he had many requests for songs. Nicky overheard Mrs. Fleming, who was one of the chaperones, ask Lance to play a song, which he did about ten minutes later. She heard someone else ask for five different songs all at once.

Lance said, "That's enough! I can't remember all of those. Sutton, get some paper and keep a list."

After her shift, Nicky walked around with her friends to their lockers and then sat on the bleachers. It was always strange to be in the school hallways in the evenings, when it was dark outside. As she and Paizlee re-entered the darkened gym, Nicky heard a favorite song, and she was ready to dance.

Trevor asked Nicky to dance several times. Another boy asked Nicky to dance once slow. McKenna and Grant danced right next to them and later she said Nicky looked funny because she was taller than he was. McKenna was taller than Grant, too, but Nicky didn't point it out. Nicky wanted to dance with Grant, but they didn't.

Gage asked Kinsey to dance two times, and Kinsey asked him once. Gage asked Paizlee several times, and she smiled and lowered her chin to look up at him as they talked during the dance. Gage and Nicky danced to a slow song a few dances later, but Nicky didn't flirt as Paizlee had. As soon as that song was over, Dalton asked her to dance to a fast song, but he seemed distracted and talked to a friend nearby instead of to her. She felt a little rejected and wondered why he had done that.

After the dance, she rejoined her friends in the hall. As they talked, Nicky relaxed because she was having a wonderful night, and she smiled frequently.

Later, Gage, Trevor, and Grant sat behind McKenna, Paizlee, and Nicky on the bleachers. The music was loud, and the lights flashed around the dance floor. The boys yelled some corny jokes like, "What did one light bulb say to the other? Watts up?" and "Where do cows go on a date night? To the moovies!"

The boys roared with laughter, but Nicky was sure some of the laughter was fake. The girls mostly just rolled their eyes. Then Gage told one about a librarian. The boys laughed again, but Nicky didn't laugh, and she frowned a little at him.

"Do you want to dance?" Gage asked Nicky at that moment.

"Well, I don't know," Nicky began. She paused because she intended to say, "Only if you stop telling those bad jokes!" But Gage looked at her funny as she said, "don't." She realized quickly he was afraid she would reject him. Maybe no one had ever said no to him before. Instead, Nicky switched and said, "Sure." She didn't want to hurt his feelings, plus she wanted to dance with him again.

During the slow dance, she had her hands around his neck, and his hands were around her back. He stepped in closer than he had before. Nicky enjoyed being close to him. At the end of the song, he thanked her and left the floor.

Nicky danced 11 times at the dance. Because she had a good time at it, she didn't want the night to end, and she could hardly wait for the next one in December.

On Thursday, Nicky and several friends went to the ninth-grade football game. The team won and were undefeated so far. The guys were performing well, and they might win their division that year.

The students got their picture packets. Nicky carefully cut her photos apart that night and thought about who she would trade with. She wrote on the backs of some of them.

To Paizlee, "To my best friend who makes everything more fun! Love, always."

To Bella, "To a wonderful musician, dancer, and great friend. What would I do without you?"

To Alyssa, "To a wonderful friend who loves music and helps make lunch fun."

To Dalton, "To a super boy who is a good drummer and always has a smile."

To Grant, "To a great wrestler and friendly locker neighbor."

To Gage, "To a cool guy who keeps me on my toes."

To Trevor, "To a quiet guy who always has the right answer in math."

The next day, she brought the photos to school and traded them with her main group. When someone else wanted to trade, she wrote a nice phrase on the back. She gave away most of her photos. That night, she sat on her bed and laid out all the photos she had received. She turned them over one by one and reread what her friends wrote to her.

Paizlee wrote, "Thanks for being here to listen to my fantasies, dreams, loves, woes, hurts and feelings. Need I go on? But mostly for being my friend."

Bella wrote, "To my competitor and friend. Nothing more to say because I know we'll always communicate since we're such close friends."

Alyssa wrote, "To my best friend. Have fun this year."

Grant wrote, "To a great friend and a great band member. Next time, look at the arrow and go down the stairs in the right direction."

Nicky giggled, because one time, when she was in a hurry, she went up the down stairs and bumped into him.

Dalton wrote, "To a real nice and sweet girl I know. Have fun in the future."

Gage wrote, "To a person who has total control of herself. You really are nice, and I tease you too much."

Nicky liked what everyone had written to her. Even Gage had written something nice.

CHAPTER 15

A Girls' Basketball Game

Carrying their flute cases, Nicky and Paizlee climbed down the fire escape stairs. They crossed the street and entered the senior high school gym by the back door. They heard the beat of the bass drum as kids swarmed up and down the bleachers. Eagleton's A-squad girls' basketball team was on the floor, running through some drills before the game started. The opposing team entered the gym from the main door and hustled into the visitor's locker room.

Paizlee and Nicky climbed up the bleachers to sit on the right side of the pep band. Paizlee sat beside Nicky and held her music so they could be together. Some of the older flutists greeted them.

Only a few ninth graders were in the senior high pep band. Kinsey was in the brass horn section, and she waved at them. Her sister, Shannon, was on the girls' A-squad basketball team, and she played that night. Kinsey was on the B-squad girls' basketball team.

The percussionists sat in front of the flutists. Nicky didn't know how anyone heard the flutes because the drums were so loud. Gage played a snare drum and Preston played the bass drum. Nicky started warming up with the others and the cacophony increased. She focused until she felt ready, then she set her flute on her lap.

Mr. Gillette lifted his arms and directed the band as they played the first pep song. The music rang through the senior high school gym as the ball players gathered in their groups to listen to their coaches' instructions. The rhythm of music, the thumping of the basketball, the chatter, and the excitement rushed through Nicky. She loved feeling pumped up with the energy. As the game got underway, the referee soon blew his whistle and stopped the game.

Paizlee asked, "What happened?"

Gage turned around and started explaining. "That girl hit the girl who was holding the ball, and the ball went out of bounds. Do you know anything about this game?"

"Not really," said Paizlee. "Would you teach me?"

"OK, so…" Gage told them the basic rules. As the game moved on, Gage explained the action to the girls.

Nicky learned about basketball from her father who watched many games. In seventh-grade gym, the girls had a module on basketball. They had learned all the rules then, but Paizlee probably forgot. Their gym teacher, Ms. Tanner, said the team needed tall girls, and she tried to persuade Nicky to join the basketball team. But Nicky wanted to be in gymnastics, not play basketball. Ms. Tanner kept pressuring her that fall, and Nicky felt like crying several times because she didn't like saying no.

After the halftime break, the band put away their instruments in the band room. Nicky and Paizlee returned to the bleachers, and Kinsey joined them.

"Gage looked like he was ready to leave. He's probably outside right now. Maybe we could talk him into staying," said Kinsey.

"Let's go find him!" said Paizlee.

The cool night air felt good against Nicky's flushed face. Gage and Trevor came out of the band room and flew down the fire escape.

"Hey, Kinsey. When you dribble the ball, you should do a crossover as you approach the basket. Like this," said Trevor. He bounced a pretend ball, crouched down, then switched the ball to the other hand as he approached her.

"I know how to do a crossover," said Kinsey. She frowned at him.

"Can you do it while you cut up to the basket, like this?"

"Yes, we practice those moves all the time."

"You have to work on your passing game. You're just the center, so you have to play defense, but you could grab the ball, move to the basket, and score!" He pretended to sink the fake basketball.

"I know that. Why are you talking to me like I'm stupid?"

Kinsey was getting annoyed with him. He was bouncing and moving around her like she was a pole.

"Hey, guys, you're arguing, so I'll be the ref. Trevor has one minute to tell Kinsey something, and Kinsey has one minute to respond. Trevor's turn, go!" said Gage. He looked at his watch to keep time.

"Her coach probably doesn't tell her enough, so I thought I would give her some tips," said Trevor.

"Time! Kinsey. Respond. Go!" said Gage.

"Ms. Tanner played ball in college and she's a really good coach!"

Trevor and Kinsey went back and forth several times until Trevor started fake dribbling his basketball around her, ran up the fire escape stairs, hopped off and ran around her again.

"Trevor, the hoop is over here!" Paizlee said as she pointed nearby.

Trevor looked at her, and he put his right hand to his mouth and his left hand to his ear as if he was an announcer.

"It's the first living basketball hoop in the world! Can the center make the basket? No, the center is paralyzed, so it's up to the guard."

"You are so obnoxious," said Kinsey.

"Two points! The crowd goes wild!" said Trevor.

Paizlee and Nicky laughed as they watched, even though Kinsey didn't see the humor yet.

"I'm sorry, Kinsey, but Trevor is acting so funny," said Paizlee.

When Kinsey realized Trevor was entertaining them and not really making fun of her, she laughed, too.

Then Gage and Trevor switched gears. They ran up four or five steps of the fire escape and jumped off. They pretended like they were jumping off a diving board at a world competition. Kinsey and Paizlee acted like the judges and gave them scores.

Nicky felt like an outsider, even though she was part of the group. The others joked and teased each other, but she was tongue-tied and quiet, and she couldn't make anyone laugh. Her shell of silence was too strong, and she doubted if they needed her around.

Kinsey turned to Nicky when the boys paused to take a breath.

"Hey Nicky, did Paizlee tell you about her dream?"

As Kinsey asked this, she and Paizlee bumped shoulders and exchanged a look. Paizlee had told Nicky about her "marriage-go-round" dream on the way to the game. Paizlee, Bella, and Nicky were on a merry-go-round with the guys they liked as they waited to be married. Paizlee was with Gage, Bella was with her favorite pop star, and Nicky was with Dalton.

"Remember, Nicky, you were with the guy you like?" asked Paizlee.

"Nicky likes someone? Who?" asked Gage.

"Come on, tell us who he is. We won't tell anyone!" said Trevor.

Nicky just smiled, shook her head, and then glared at Paizlee. How could her friend do that to her? They didn't talk about the boys they liked in front of any boys! Gage and Trevor continued trying to get Nicky to tell them who she liked, while Kinsey and Paizlee laughed at Nicky's discomfort. Nicky felt frustrated, and she wanted to tell the boys to be quiet.

Then two groups of boys came out of the gym, and they yelled at each other. Nicky and her friends sat down on the curb and waited to see what would happen. Two boys walked by and told them it was a fight between the rival team's fans and Eagleton's fans. The girls got off the curb to leave, but they had been having so much fun, they changed their minds. They agreed to run home if anything happened. Nothing came of the threats, though. One group went back into the gym and the other group walked across the street and past the fish pond.

When they decided to leave, Trevor gave Gage a ride home while the girls walked together. Nicky was glad the fight distracted the boys. She didn't want Gage and Trevor to know she liked Dalton.

CHAPTER 16

The Concession Stand

The varsity football team played the conference championship game on a Friday night in late October. The freshmen had won their division, and the high schoolers said their team had to win so the freshmen didn't show them up. Even though cold, light rain fell, the excitement was high in the stands, and the cheerleaders kept up their chants to help the fans stay warm. At every touchdown, the Eagleton supporters cheered.

Nicky arrived at the game with her flute to play in the high school pep band, but Mr. Gillette canceled the performance because of the rain. She walked from the stands on the north side around the outer track to the concession stand on the south side of the field.

The debate class sold the snacks that night, and Paizlee had a shift. She had invited Nicky to come and keep her company after she finished playing in the band. After Paizlee ushered her inside, Nicky went to the far-right corner of the small wooden shack, put down her flute, and watched her friend wait on people. The friends talked when there were no customers.

Then Grant and Josh came up to the counter and started talking with them. Lily came into the shack, and she brought warm excitement with her. She immediately took over the conversation. Lily was not self-conscious, and she laughed as she said whatever was on her mind. She was one of the most outgoing people Nicky had ever met. Lily could make herself a part of any group, and she especially loved groups with boys in them. Nicky sometimes wished she was more like Lily, who always seemed to have fun.

At halftime, the Eagleton seventh-grade football team played for ten minutes. Nicky's brother and Grant's brother were on the team, and Grant and Josh left the concession stand to watch them. Nicky told Paizlee she wanted to see her brother play, so she would come back later. Nicky sloshed through the wet grass until she could see the seventh-grade team clearly. The boys' uniforms and faces were coated with mud.

Before long, Nicky was cold and her jacket hood dripped water on her face, so she turned around and walked back to the concession stand. She wanted to be inside and warm again. As she approached, she saw McKenna, Gage, and Trevor walk up to the counter. She stood in place for a minute before she decided to join the group. As she made her way up to the stand, she saw a senior supervising Paizlee, which made her hesitant because the older girl might object if she went inside when she wasn't in debate class. Her first thought was always to stay out of the way, so she stayed outside by the corner.

"Nicky, why are you outside? Come in and get dry!" said Paizlee.

Nicky went in and stood in the corner again, happier and more comfortable. She appreciated seeing the expressions on the faces of everyone while they talked. She set her flute case on the floor.

"Are you having a good time?" asked Gage.

"Yes, but it's cold."

"For sure, it's freezing tonight. Why is your family so tall?"

"Beats me."

He laughed when she said that, and he smiled frequently as they talked. He had changed from the previous year when he was serious and not talkative. He was more relaxed, and he started conversations more easily.

"Did you get the essay done for English?" asked Nicky.

"Not yet. But it'll be A plus work when it's done." Gage grinned with confidence. Nicky always felt self-doubt about her work.

Trevor told jokes to get some laughs, and he told some dirty ones. Paizlee pretended she didn't understand them. Nicky felt she had to smile because she was afraid people would think she wasn't smart enough to know what they were talking about. But she didn't like those kinds of jokes.

The game ended, and the Eagleton team won the conference championship title. Fans left as soon as they heard the announcement. Paizlee had to babysit, and she went to find the family who would drive her to their house. Nicky joined McKenna and Lily to walk home.

Trevor had his dad's car, and he offered them a ride. He had driven some children to the game, and he needed to drive them home first. The girls joined Gage and Trevor as they walked over the gravel parking lot to the back row of cars. Lily and Gage sat in the front seat next to Trevor, while McKenna and Nicky sat in the back with the two young kids. After Trevor dropped the kids at their house, McKenna and Nicky moved apart.

"Hey, let's go to the cemetery! It's right ahead!" said Gage.

McKenna and Nicky looked at each other and shook their heads.

"No way! It's dark! Cemeteries are spooky in the dark," said McKenna.

"I think it would be fun to drive around and see if there are any ghosts out tonight. Let's go!" said Lily.

Trevor looked in the rearview mirror at Nicky, who hunched her shoulders and grimaced.

"Nah," he said. "It's still raining. Let's think of something else to do."

Gage leaned forward and glared at him. "Fine, but let's drive around. It's not often you have the car at night." He sat back. "I can't wait until I can drive. I'm getting a truck."

McKenna objected. "Dad said he'd ground me if I wasn't home right after the game. He grounded me last week, and now I'm on probation. He said I'm too young to be running around at night."

"Fine. Let's take McKenna home, then let's drive up Central and turn around before the highway," said Gage.

"Maybe we can stop at the drive-in," said Lily.

Nicky worried about Trevor driving on the busier street. She wanted to ride with them so she could hang around with the group, but Central would have more traffic than normal because of the football fans driving home. Trevor looked back and saw her biting her lip.

"I don't like driving in the rain. Besides, I don't want to get into trouble either," said Trevor. Nicky was relieved, and she relaxed as she appreciated Trevor's thoughtfulness.

"Spoilsport," said Gage. Trevor just shrugged.

"Isn't it great we won the championship? Everyone at school will be so pumped up on Monday," said Lily.

Lily turned to Gage and asked him some questions about what he was doing over the weekend. Trevor stopped at Nicky's house and McKenna got out with Nicky. While Lily chatted nonstop, Trevor and Gage waved goodbye to the girls, and Trevor drove off. McKenna said goodbye and left to walk to her house. Nicky stood on her porch and watched Trevor turn right to go back up the hill. She listened until she could hardly hear the car engine. She wished she could stay with them.

CHAPTER 17

The Garage Band Invitation

When Nicky went into the band room on Monday morning, she didn't have her flute. She had left it in the concession stand on Friday. But she looked on the rack, and it was on the top shelf. Someone had found it, and she was grateful. She had never left her flute anywhere before.

She sat down and looked around. Many of the older kids acted the same as the junior high kids. They played with their legs crossed, their backs slumped, and they made sarcastic comments. Almost everyone talked as soon as the song was over. Even though they did that, the band still got through the songs. Nicky felt lonely without her ninth-grade friends in the flute section. She was happy Bella would be in senior high band at semester time.

After lunch, Nicky was at her locker with Alyssa when Dalton, Grant, and Josh came out of the band room.

"Let me have your books," said Dalton.

"Why?"

"Sheesh! I just want them."

"Why?" Nicky asked. She held her books loosely at her side.

Grant threw an eraser to Josh, who then backed up and threw it back to Grant, who moved behind Nicky. As she glanced at them, Dalton grabbed the books from her. He charged down the hall and around the corner. She tried to follow, but Grant and Josh blocked her.

"Alyssa, he has my books!" Nicky and Alyssa dodged around the two boys and rounded the corner.

Zoey saw them from the end of the hall. "What's going on?"

"Dalton took Nicky's books!" said Alyssa. "Did you see him?"

"He went into Mr. Neville's room!" Zoey went in, but Dalton came out and dashed down the stairs. Nicky started down the stairs, but Alyssa and Zoey stopped at the top.

"I have to get to Mr. Neville's class, but I hope you get your books back," said Alyssa.

"I have to check out a book before math," said Zoey.

Downstairs alone, Nicky couldn't find Dalton. She gave up looking and walked to math class without her books. Dalton finally came in with her books just before the bell and gave them to her.

"Here are your books. I just wanted to carry them for you." He shrugged and left. Nicky was confused as she wondered why he wanted to carry them.

The next day after lunch, Dalton and Gage were at Gage's locker when Alyssa and Nicky walked up. Nicky opened her locker and then took out her math and science books.

"Hey, give me your books!" Dalton took hold of the edges.

"Maybe I don't want you to have them," said Nicky.

"Come on, let me have them!" He gave Gage an exasperated look as he tugged on her books. She tugged back, so they went back and forth.

"I think he likes you," said Gage to Nicky.

She ignored him. The comment wasn't helpful, and Dalton's cheeks turned red. Nicky and Dalton tugged her books back and forth.

"I think he likes you," repeated Gage. She again ignored him.

He said it again, louder. "I THINK HE LIKES YOU!"

Nicky turned to Gage fiercely and said with force, but not volume, "Shut up!"

At that moment, Dalton grabbed her books and took off with them.

"He did it again!" Nicky looked at Alyssa in disbelief.

They followed him down the stairs and through the downstairs hall. They found Dalton sitting on the bleachers in the junior high gym.

"Can I have my books now, please? I need them," said Nicky.

He looked at Nicky and grinned as he said, "OK, here they are." He stood up, passed them to her, and left. He didn't apologize.

Alyssa went back upstairs to her class while Nicky looked for notes Dalton might have put in one of the books or notebooks. She didn't find any. She didn't like how he demanded her books instead of asking. She hoped he wouldn't do it again.

A few days later, Grant and Gage sat by her after band as she took apart her flute.

"Want to join our garage band? Gage, Trevor, and I are starting one. I play guitar with Trevor, and Gage is the drummer, of course. We're going to practice at Gage's house," said Grant.

"That sounds fun."

"We need a lead singer and piano player. We want you! Come on, say yes!" said Grant. He smiled widely and nodded as his eyebrows rose.

"Why do you want me?" Nicky asked.

"Because you can help us get famous," said Gage. "Every band needs a tall girl singer. If we practice every weekend, we'll be good."

"So…you want me because I'm tall?" asked Nicky. She looked from Grant to Gage with a confused expression.

"Not just because of that! You're cute, you sing, and you play the piano. You can even play your flute if there's a part," said Grant.

"I don't know," said Nicky. "I don't have the greatest voice."

"But we want you!" said Gage. He emphasized "you."

"I'll think about it," said Nicky.

For the next few weeks, each of the three boys bugged Nicky about joining their new band whenever they saw her.

"Are you going to join our band?" Trevor asked her after math.

"I'm not sure. Have you started rehearsing yet?"

"Yeah, we got together last week."

"What are you going to call this so-called band?"

"I don't know. Hey Gage, what are we going to call it?"

"We still have to discuss that," said Gage.

A few days later, Nicky walked up the stairs after gymnastics. She felt sore, but she liked the exercise when she could move her body and relax her brain. They had been working on jumps on the beam that morning. The gymnasts were preparing a winter program for some of the elementary school kids, and she was practicing a routine for it.

Gage and Grant were at their locker getting lunch sacks when Nicky greeted the boys as she opened her locker to get her own lunch.

"We decided on a name for the band," said Grant.

"What?"

"Nicky's Harem! See, since you'll be the only girl and we're all boys, we thought it would be funny! And people will remember it," said Grant.

Gage nodded and then burst out laughing as he turned to his friend. Nicky squinted her eyes as she looked at them. She didn't believe they meant it. They must be teasing her again. It must be a joke.

People teased Nicky daily. Sometimes she liked the attention, but most times, it was maddening. Zoey, who was a graceful, advanced dancer, commented when she didn't stand up straight, or she slumped down in a chair and said she should be more ladylike. McKenna and Kinsey sometimes made comments about how fast she walked or clothes she wore. Bella and Paizlee sometimes teased Nicky, too, but they were good friends, and she could usually laugh with them.

When boys teased her and she asked why, they said, "Because we like you!" Paizlee told her they teased her because she got so "hyper." Usually, she was a quiet, reserved girl who paid attention in class and listened intently to people. But when she was teased about something she said or did, then she glared, frowned, and tried not to retort. For a while, she could be patient, but when they kept it up, she felt like she was a tortured babysitter. She got annoyed, which made them laugh at her. At least it was one way she could make them laugh.

Nicky definitely didn't want to be in a band called "Nicky's Harem." That was too horrifying for words. But she thought she and

Paizlee could have fun with the new band. Paizlee would have to be the group manager to keep Nicky company.

Nicky was in the band room for practice lessons later that week as Gage, Trevor, and Grant practiced stage band music. Trevor played the guitar in stage band even though he wasn't in regular school band.

As she passed Gage, she told him, "I'll be in your band…if you choose a different name. And you have to let Paizlee be the manager."

Gage grinned as he pounded on the drum set.

"She said yes! We have a lead singer!" He shouted to the other guys, who cheered.

Nicky hid a smile as she went into the practice room.

After she agreed to be in the band, she practiced piano for an hour or more for five days straight. She still didn't think she had a strong or pretty voice, but when no one was home, she sang. She wanted to be good for the new band, whatever they called it.

On a nice autumn day in early November, the two sixth-hour social studies classes had another field trip. As the kids climbed onto the bus, they laughed and talked. Nicky looked at them for a few minutes before she turned her head and looked out the bus window. All she heard was noise. She didn't want to go on the trip today. The field trip in September had been good because she had been in the mood to think alone without her friends nearby.

But Nicky had news to share. After a schedule switch, Trevor was in her English class. She knew he and Gage would disrupt the class and she was apprehensive, yet excited about the possibilities, too.

Before the bus left, she heard Gage ask Mr. Neville if he could do extra credit instead of going on the field trip. Maybe that's what he did in September. Mr. Neville shook his head and Gage slowly climbed the bus steps with his head down. He abruptly took a seat a few rows in front of her where Lily and her friend started talking to him. He folded his arms and ignored them.

The bus of students arrived at the local military fort, where they gathered outside the small museum. They listened to Mr. Weaver's father, the town historian, talk about the early history of the area. Then

Nicky's class went inside the museum to look at the displays while Gage and the rest of Mr. Neville's class waited on the bus.

Nicky read about the early fort and town and looked at the artifacts, but she felt bored. She didn't want to be there, and the military artifacts didn't interest her. When her group came out into the sunshine, the other class was lined up for their turn. Gage looked at her as she walked past.

"Well, was it interesting?" he asked.

"Not especially."

He grunted as if her opinion confirmed his suspicions.

The group's next stop was the military cemetery for another lecture. The cemetery was small and not half as interesting to her as the cemetery on the hillside had been. When she walked over someone's grave, Gage was nearby and pointed it out.

"Nicky, you just stepped on that guy's grave! Now his spirit is mad at you."

She jumped away as he smirked. She didn't know how to behave in a cemetery, so she wondered if it could be true. Gage walked toward the bus, and the class was soon behind him. Nicky was glad to leave.

CHAPTER 18

The Optimist Club Award

Sometimes Nicky aspired to be a math teacher because she liked it. Her father helped her if she asked him a math or science question, which wasn't often. He explained math concepts clearly, and she wanted to be like him. He talked with Nicky and Ryan about science and other technical articles, which he read in the newspaper.

Nicky's father believed women could learn hard science subjects as easily as boys could, and he helped her have confidence in her ability. But he didn't want her to be a teacher because he thought they were underpaid.

One night in late October, her father looked at want ads in the Ridgeland City Journal. He said there were many ads for computer programmers, and he read a few aloud to her. Nicky looked up from the dining room table where she was doing homework.

"What does a computer programmer do?" she asked.

"Mostly, they design ways for the computer to store information or to give them the same answer every time they ask it a question. They use logic to write up those instructions, such as, if this happens, do this, or if that happens, do that. Computer instructions are written in a code specific for that type of machine."

"Maybe I could become a computer programmer."

Her father chuckled before he replied. "No, you don't want to hang out with those nerds."

But Nicky liked using logic when she solved math problems. Because her father worked with computers, she probably could, too. She was puzzled by his discouraging reply.

A few days later, her father flew to Magnus City in another state for a job interview. He was enthusiastic when he returned the following day. He liked the company and the people who interviewed him. He said if they made him a decent job offer, he would accept it.

Nicky's stomach tightened up while he talked at dinner, and she pushed food around her plate but didn't eat it. She hoped he wouldn't get the job offer. The prior winter, when her father wanted to move to Texas, he didn't have any interviews, and they didn't move. But an interview meant a move was more likely. Nicky knew little about Magnus City, but she knew its winters were cold. Since her father didn't like the cold, maybe he would decide against going there.

A week later, Nicky missed the first ninth-grade boys' basketball game in the afternoon because she was sick at home. She wondered how Gage, Dalton, and Trevor had played and if they won. Dalton was one of the tallest players, but Gage was a forward and extremely competitive. After the basketball game, some of her friends called out to her as they walked past her house.

"Hey, Nicky!"

"We missed you!!"

"Get well soon!"

Nicky looked out the living room window and waved at them. She missed the school Open House on Thursday and the Veteran's Day high school band concert on Friday. She watched television, and she tried to read a book, but she felt lonely and wondered what was happening with her friends. After a few days away from school, she felt like a piece of herself was missing because she hadn't been with them.

The snow started as Nicky went to sleep. She awoke in the middle of the night, got out of bed, and looked out her window to the west. The red stoplight reflected in blurry splotches on the wet, black pavement. The snowflakes covered the sidewalks, and the streets would be white soon. The streetlight made a bright circle of yellow as she watched the snow accumulate on the grass. She loved smooth, unmarked snow. The blanket of white made the world new.

Nicky wished she could paint the scene with watercolors. Her mother, who loved painting and art, had encouraged her to start drawing. But Nicky was unsatisfied with her own attempts at art. She only completed paint-by-number kits where she had a plan to follow.

As Nicky crawled back into bed, she thought about moving. They had moved to the house in town only eight months ago. She was having such a great time that fall. She had many wonderful friends, and she didn't want to leave them. But she knew most kids in school wouldn't miss her if she moved away and they would soon forget her. She hadn't thought often about Mario and Kelly, but at that moment, she wondered where they were and whether they were happy.

Maybe her father wouldn't get that job. She tossed and turned as she thought about moving, but eventually, she fell back asleep.

When she returned to school on Monday, Paizlee opened the classroom door while the kids were reading their English assignment. She looked at Nicky before she went over to Mrs. Fleming and whispered something to her. After Mrs. Fleming nodded, Paizlee motioned to Nicky to leave the class with her.

In the hall, Paizlee whispered that Mrs. Colsen, Nicky's old English teacher, wanted to see them. Paizlee said they were getting some kind of award. They went into Mrs. Colsen's empty classroom to learn more.

"Hi, girls. Thanks for stopping by. Both of you are getting a special honor."

Paizlee and Nicky looked at each other. "What is it?"

"The businesspeople in town have a club called the Eagleton Optimist Club. Have you heard of it?"

They both shook their heads no.

"The Optimist Club honors 10 students every year for Student Appreciation Week. Five students are from junior high, and you two are among them. You'll each get the award."

The girls smiled at each other and Mrs. Colsen.

"That's terrific! Why did they choose us?" asked Paizlee.

Mrs. Colsen picked up a note. "'This award emphasizes the positive achievements of young people.' Principal Dahlke recommended you because you both get good grades, and you show good citizenship."

"That was nice of him! When do we get it?" asked Paizlee.

"Tomorrow morning," said Mrs. Colsen.

"Who else is getting it?" asked Nicky.

"Zoey, Steve, and Marla will also get the award." Steve was in eighth grade and Marla was in seventh grade.

"Have you told Zoey yet?" asked Paizlee.

"Yes, so all of you know. Here's a note for your parents with the details. You will have breakfast at Eagleton Inn tomorrow with the Optimist Club and get your award there. Be sure you get there on time! This award is a privilege, and you want to show you deserve it."

In the hall, the girls whispered together.

"Why do you think they really chose us? I mean, other kids get good grades and are good citizens," said Paizlee.

"Maybe because we're involved in so many activities," said Nicky.

"You're Student Council vice president, and on honor roll, but why did they choose me?"

"You're in debate, Pep Club, band, and choir, so you deserve it. I wonder why they didn't ask Bella. And why did they choose Zoey?"

"Yes, I wonder, too. We should dress up for the ceremony. Let's talk to Zoey at lunch and coordinate outfits! See you later!" Paizlee went up the stairs to her class while Nicky returned to English.

The next morning, Nicky was up early to prepare for the award breakfast. Paizlee's mother picked up Zoey and her mother, as well as Nicky and her mother. Their fathers couldn't go. As the group entered the Eagleton Inn restaurant, Nicky saw Mr. Sherwood, her former boss, but she didn't know the other businessmen in the club.

The Optimist Club president stood up at the front of the room and gave an introduction.

"Too often adults think young people are troublemakers, and they don't recognize the many young people who contribute positively to our world. Our Optimist Club has confidence this group will help make the town successful in the future. We encourage your ideas and participation."

Each student was given a plaque and a certificate. The certificate said, "For upholding the dignity of youth, for a sincere devotion to our welfare, and for generous and unselfish contributions to society."

A county newspaper photographer took their pictures, then they ate breakfast. Nicky never ate breakfast away from home, so the meal was special by itself. Their mothers and the girls thanked the Optimist Club members and left. School didn't start for almost an hour.

Nicky rode with Paizlee to her house while Paizlee changed her outfit for school because she didn't want to wear the dress. They talked animatedly about the exciting morning. Nicky felt eager to win similar recognition in the future. She wanted to contribute as much as she could to make her town even more special.

The next day, the ninth graders had an assembly. Dalton stood up from his folding chair and motioned to Paizlee when he saw her enter the gym, and Nicky and Bella followed Paizlee to where he sat. Dalton still called Paizlee every week. When people teased her about liking him, she replied she didn't think of him as a romantic boyfriend, just a friend who was a boy.

The principal stood at the front and asked the kids to pay attention because they were going to learn about the dangers of driving. A state trooper gave them a lecture and said once they realized how awful a car accident could be, they would want to avoid having one. The film showed multiple car accidents, with images of injuries and deaths of drivers and passengers. Students started groaning, and the fake groans were so loud Nicky was unable to hear the movie. She doubted most of the kids would be better drivers after the film because they didn't even pay attention.

Then they saw a film about the National Parks. It had many wonderful nature scenes. They learned the history of Yellowstone National Park. Nicky had visited Yellowstone once with Ryan, her mother, her grandmother, and cousin, Sophia. As they drove through the park, they looked for deer, elk, and other animals. Nicky enjoyed it so much she wanted to return someday.

All three grades gathered in the junior high gym the next day to watch the high school drama club perform a play. The band kids sat in the chairs in front of the stage again. The girls sat behind Gage, Trevor, Grant, and Josh, who made comments between the acts.

"Hear the applause! Feel the excitement in the air! They love our band!" said Gage.

"They can't stop clapping!" said Trevor.

"Let's take a bow! They want more!" said Grant.

The new band still didn't have a decent name, but Nicky thought of it as the "Wicker Drive Band."

Nicky had a piano lesson every week, but she was leaning toward quitting the lessons. She wanted to practice popular songs for the Wicker Drive Band instead of lesson songs. Nicky hoped the boys would ask her to join them soon.

CHAPTER 19

Something in Common

Bella was in a small room in the back of the band room when Nicky joined her to practice their flute lesson. They played a little and talked more. Gage saw them through the window then came inside, and he started talking. Nicky lowered her chin, looked up at him, and responded as if what he said was immensely interesting. Bella looked at her oddly, so she stopped after a few minutes. She had imitated Zoey for some reason. Then Mr. Darnell opened the door and looked at Gage.

"I figured I would find you here. Get your sticks and leave them alone now." Gage rolled his eyes as he shut the door behind him.

The high school class schedule was five minutes different from the junior high schedule, which meant the ninth-grade band members had extra time before their second-hour class. Gage and Nicky usually grabbed their books from their lockers and went back into the band room to sit on the chairs by the door. The other freshmen disappeared to go to their lockers, which were farther away.

One morning, Mr. Darnell went to the blackboard, then turned and looked at them.

"Don't the two of you have somewhere else to be?"

"Not until the bell rings," said Gage. He and Nicky kept talking.

When Nicky had her next flute lesson, Mr. Darnell helped with trill fingering, which sometimes confused her.

"I think Gage likes you. He's always around you," said Mr. Darnell.

She understood he meant it as if Gage wanted to date her. It was funny a teacher would comment like that, but Nicky didn't mind.

She shook her head. "No, he doesn't. He has a girlfriend already."

"He probably won't be with her for long." He smiled as he opened the door and left the practice room.

Nicky dismissed the comment. She didn't think Gage would break up with Chelsea for her.

A few days later, Gage and Nicky walked down to English together, and he said she shouldn't slouch in her chair because it was unattractive. Then he tormented her in class as he nagged her to sit up straight. Trevor overheard and looked at Nicky with a half-smile, as if he was concealing some secret. The boys wrote jokes on a blank piece of her notebook paper and snatched it away before she could see what they wrote.

After lunch, Nicky was at her locker when Gage opened his.

"Hey, Nicky. Sorry we kept teasing you in English. Sometimes, we get on a roll."

"I know. Could you tone it down tomorrow?" she asked.

"Maybe, but I'm not promising."

On the way home, Nicky told Paizlee what Gage had said. Paizlee was quiet for a moment before she commented.

"Kinsey thinks Gage likes you because he teases you so much."

"He's just a friend, you know, like Dalton is to you," said Nicky. She didn't want Paizlee to feel hurt. Yet, in spite of contradicting her friend, she was flattered others thought he liked her.

After they parted, Nicky admitted to herself she thought about Gage frequently, and school was definitely more exciting because he was there. But he said nothing to hint he wanted a date, and he didn't call her on his own. She wouldn't allow herself to believe there was more to the situation. She didn't want to admit she had feelings for him, and how she wished Gage was attracted to her.

During the next algebra class, the teacher left the room after the lesson, and her classmates talked. Nicky tried to focus because she wanted to get the homework done so she could watch a show in the evening. Zoey asked her a question, but Nicky just shrugged her shoulders and looked down at her notebook as she finished a problem.

Zoey called Nicky after dinner.

"Are you mad at me? You seemed mad in algebra."

"No, I'm not mad at you," Nicky said.

"But I kept trying to talk to you. You wouldn't talk to me."

"It wasn't you. It was something else." She didn't want to admit she wanted to finish the homework and not talk to people.

"Was it something Gage did?"

Nicky scrunched her eyes and looked at the phone with confusion. Why did Zoey think she was mad at Gage? Her focus had nothing to do with him.

"No, it wasn't about him, either."

Dalton called Nicky during the show she didn't want to miss, but she talked to him anyway.

"Who are you talking to?" Nicky heard his sister ask.

"You don't know her." His sister asked three more times.

"I'm talking to Nicky. Stop bugging me."

Nicky heard her say, "Nicky? I heard she was in love with Gage."

"Go away, I'm talking!" Dalton said. She had irritated him, and he said it with an edge.

Nicky was shocked because Dalton's sister was a year younger than them. Why would eighth graders be talking about her? Who else was speculating about her feelings for Gage? She didn't appreciate being the subject of gossip.

"My family's moving to California this summer," said Dalton.

"How awful. Why?" She was alarmed. His family had only moved to town the previous year, and he fit right in with the pep band kids.

"We have relatives out there."

"I wish people didn't move away. My father might move us, too."

"Really? That's too bad. Well, I guess that gives us something in common."

CHAPTER 20

The Job Offer

The Saturday before Thanksgiving, Nicky and Ryan were watching television. Nicky heard her father open the door and bring in the mail. He gave a cheer. "I got it!" he exclaimed.

"That's wonderful!" her mother said.

"Kids, please come into the kitchen. We have to talk to you."

They all went into the kitchen, and Nicky sat with her back against the wall with Ryan at her right side. Her mother poured some coffee into a mug, then she and her father sat across from them.

"Remember the job interview I went on? The company offered me the job! I'm taking it. Your mother and I have already talked about how this will go. First, I'll accept the offer. Then, I'll give my notice to my manager, and I'll teach my last day before the winter break. My new job will start the first week of January."

The kids sat in silence. Nicky tried to listen, but her head was reeling and she had an acid taste in her mouth. She swallowed.

"I'll get training for the first few months. I need to attend a school out of state, but luckily, the new company will pay for my room and board. I'll find an apartment out there while you and your mother stay here in Eagleton. We have to prepare the house and find a realtor to sell it. You kids need to cooperate, understand?"

They nodded. Nicky looked down at her hands in her lap.

"Then I'll move to Magnus City and find us a new house. After we sell this house, we'll move into the new house."

"Are we going to live right in the city?" asked Ryan.

"No, there are many schools and areas in the metropolitan region. I want to be near the office, though, because I don't want to drive far during rush hour traffic. It isn't like here. In rush hour, cars are lined up for miles. You'll have to go to new schools, but we know you two are smart, and we know you'll do well wherever you go to school."

"It'll take a little time to adjust, but we hope you'll like the new schools eventually," said her mother. She looked at her husband as she supported his decision.

"It'll be great! I know you need more opportunities and better schools. You need to get prepared to go to college, and the schools here aren't as advanced as Magnus City schools. This isn't simply good for me, it's good for you guys as well," said her father.

"When will we move?" asked Ryan.

"It depends on when I find a house. We might move out there in the spring."

"Before the end of the school year?" Nicky's voice rose with horror.

"Maybe. We'll have to see."

"I'll really miss my friends here." Nicky's voice was soft because she didn't want to challenge him.

"I suppose a better school is a good idea," Ryan said.

He was trying to be agreeable. Nicky guessed he was upset, too. He was well-liked, and he had many friends in Eagleton. He couldn't even remember the other places they had lived.

"You'll start thinking about new places and new things. This is a wonderful thing for all of us," said her father.

Ryan looked at him over his glasses. Nicky put her elbow on the table, dropped her chin into her hand, and frowned.

"Can we go now?" asked Nicky.

"Yes. But be sure and talk with us if you need to," said her mother. "We know this will be a big change."

"I'm going to write the acceptance letter right now!" Her father was happy and excited to go on a new adventure.

Nicky jumped up and ran upstairs to her room. She threw herself on her bed and pounded her pillow. She screamed silently. No! No! NO! This couldn't be happening!

Unlike last winter, her dad had a job to go to. He wasn't stating his intention to move because this time he was going to move them without even caring how he would tear them away from everything they knew. She loved her friends. What was she going to do? She started crying, heaving with sobs. Her life was over!

When she was younger, moving was often exciting. She didn't have any choice but to go along. But she and Ryan were older this time, and her father should at least ask them if they wanted to move. Instead, he only wanted to hear they were on board.

Her grandmother had warned her this would happen. She knew her father was happy, but Nicky doubted the rest of them were. Her mother would have to transfer to a new college. They would all have to adjust to living in a city. Before they lived in small Ridgeland City, they lived in a big city on the west coast, but for less than two years. Living there differed greatly from living at the edge of the Ponderosa Hills.

Nicky needed to spend time with her friends because she didn't have long before she would be taken away. She cared so much about all of them. She wanted to call Paizlee, but she couldn't stop crying.

A snowstorm raged all day on Sunday, with high winds, cold temperatures, and nine inches of snow. School was canceled on Monday because the rural roads weren't plowed yet, so Nicky couldn't go to school to distract herself. Ryan and Nicky kept getting into arguments, and Nicky wanted to get out of the house to see her friends, but she couldn't.

"We're moving! It's not fair," she said when she called Paizlee.

"But you can't move! This is awful," said Paizlee.

"I still can't believe it. I don't want to move," said Nicky.

"Dalton is moving, too. I'll be stuck here alone."

"You've got many friends in Eagleton. I'll be the lonely one."

They discussed the situation more and commiserated.

Nicky called Bella next.

"You are so lucky. I wish I could get out of this one-horse town," said Bella. "But I'll miss you in high school."

After Bella, she told Alyssa.

"Gosh, I had no idea you would ever leave. When?"

"Maybe in the spring. If we leave before the end of school, I think I'll scream," said Nicky.

"We need to spend time together as much as possible."

On Tuesday at school, Nicky told other people. The news traveled fast, and kids told her how sorry they were she was leaving Eagleton. She tried not to cry when they sympathized with her.

At Thanksgiving dinner on Thursday, Nicky's father made a toast.

"We're grateful this year for a new beginning. My job will give us a chance to do new things. Cheers!"

The family bumped glasses. Her father told them he had given his notice to his manager. He described what he knew about his new job, talked about his hopes for finding good schools, and said he was eager to see what the kids would do with their new opportunities. He was certain they would all be happy in Magnus City.

Nicky kept her gaze on her food as she played with it. She was conflicted because she usually looked up to her father. But now she felt he didn't understand what he was doing to them. She believed he only wanted something different for himself. He couldn't predict the future for her. She dreaded the thought of leaving Eagleton.

CHAPTER 21

An Invitation and Advice

Paizlee visited Nicky on Friday, and they talked all afternoon. After she left, Nicky thought about how boring life was when she wasn't with her friends. How would life be bearable in a new place without them?

Paizlee's mother drove them to the high school basketball game that night. Nicky noticed Gage paid a lot of attention to Kinsey, who looked like she was having a great time. Trevor wasn't there, and Nicky wondered why. She felt despondent and spoke little.

Josh's sister, who was in band also, had heard the news about Nicky's family leaving. She leaned over to Nicky. "Do you want to go get drunk? It might help you forget you're moving."

No one had ever asked Nicky to get drunk before. She had never even had a drink. Getting drunk sounded like it would make her feel worse.

She said, "No, I don't want to."

Josh's sister shrugged and turned to talk to her friend.

As Kinsey, Paizlee, Gage, and Nicky walked home, Gage started reenacting a comedy sketch he had seen. Nicky fell back from her friends and watched him until she was laughing. Gage used different voices as he performed all the parts. It was the first time she had laughed in days.

After senior high band was over on Monday, Gage asked if Nicky had seen a different comedy sketch, and he started acting that one out for her. Nicky giggled, which egged him on.

As Mr. Darnell walked by, he commented to Gage. "Now I understand why Nicky keeps telling me you're crazy."

"I never said that!" Nicky protested. But, just to tease Gage a little, she paused. "At least, not in those words."

Gage pretended to pout. "I'm not going to talk to you anymore. Just watch me." He crossed his arms and looked the other way.

"I'm sorry, Gage. I was just kidding."

"I forgive you. But just remember, I might stop talking to you if you aren't nice to me." He grinned at her, and she felt a strange feeling of warmth. Somehow, she knew he would keep talking to her.

"Teenagers!" said Mr. Darnell as he shook his head and left.

Nicky told her mother she didn't want to take piano lessons anymore. After Mrs. Schmidt changed where she taught piano, Nicky felt distracted during the lessons. Besides, Nicky had to think about Student Council, homework, friends, band, and now, the move. She wanted her mother to tell Mrs. Schmidt. But her mother said Nicky had to tell her in person. The piano teacher stopped by their house.

"Mrs. Schmidt, Nicky needs to tell you something," Nicky's mother prompted.

"I want to quit piano lessons," said Nicky.

"I'm sad to hear that. Why do you want to quit?" asked Mrs. Schmidt.

Nicky shrugged. "I have to play my flute at games and there's more homework this year."

"We could change the lesson plan. Maybe instead of me choosing your music, you could choose songs, and I could help you learn them."

"Maybe."

"I could find a time to stop by here after the other lessons, so you wouldn't have to go anywhere. You could also drop to two lessons a month. I hate to see you quit when you're playing so well. There's more to learn."

The teacher was disappointed, and Nicky wavered. Yet, she still wanted to quit.

"I know. But I don't have time to practice. Plus, we're moving."

"Your mother told me. Moving gives you more to think about. I'll miss having you as a student. If you change your mind about lessons, you can call at any time and restart them."

Nicky's mother walked Mrs. Schmidt to the door, and they talked for a few minutes. Nicky felt bad after the piano teacher left. Mrs. Schmidt had taught her a lot about music and discipline. She also felt relieved because she had one less thing to worry about.

Mrs. Fleming changed the English class seating arrangement on Monday. She moved Nicky to the second-row third seat. Gage sat in front of Nicky. Trevor sat on her right in the first row by the wall. The boys still weren't separated, and they continued to goof around after they finished their assignments.

The class had a study hall with a substitute teacher the next day. Trevor and Gage whispered to each other, and then they looked at her and laughed. They laughed so hard Nicky thought they would fall out of their chairs.

On Wednesday during class, Gage and Trevor continued to bug her. They wrote on her paper, tore the page from her notebook, then dropped the paper on the floor and leaned over to grab it. She ignored them, but it didn't help. They wouldn't stop.

When Gage and Nicky were at their lockers, he pointed to his upper left arm, which was nearest to her.

"Hit me. Right here in the arm. Hit me."

"I can't hit you!"

"We were terrible today. If I were you, I would hit me." He nodded to encourage her.

She smiled at him and shook her head no. He didn't know when to stop sometimes. It helped when he apologized.

"Don't say I didn't give you the chance," he said. He opened the band room door and raised his eyebrows before he went in.

The next time Bella and Nicky were at their flute lesson, they talked about stage band. The junior high group needed a new pianist. Lauren had played piano for them before, but she was in high school now. The two girls were each interested in replacing her, but they decided Bella would ask if she could play it because she played better than Nicky. Nicky continued to wish the stage band needed a flutist.

Grant asked Paizlee to go to the winter dance with him. She declined for several reasons, which she explained to Nicky. He was such a nice guy and Nicky could see them together, but he wasn't who Paizlee wanted to be with. Later that week, Nicky saw him sitting with another girl and flirting with her. She noticed more couples holding hands each day.

On Sunday, Dalton called Nicky.

"So, what boy do you like? You know, like like," said Dalton.

"I like a few boys, but I don't want to tell you who," she said.

"Come on, tell me. I really want to know."

"Um, well, I liked Preston last year."

"But what about this year?" asked Dalton.

"Why do you want to know?"

"Dalton! Get off the phone!" Dalton's mother yelled loudly. He said goodbye and hung up.

Dalton called again Tuesday night. He wanted to ask Nicky something, but for 10 minutes, he wouldn't say what it was. She kept prompting him because she wanted to know.

"OK, OK, so here's what I wanted to ask. Are you going to the winter dance? I mean, are you going with someone?"

"Yes, er, no. Yes, I'm planning to go. No, no one has asked me."

"So...would you go with me? We could have a lot of fun!"

Nicky was quiet for a minute as she considered his question. No one had ever asked her to a dance before. She might not have another chance in Eagleton. She liked Dalton and how cheerful he was.

"Sure. I'll go with you."

"Great! I'll call tomorrow and we can talk about it."

Nicky called Paizlee as soon as they hung up.

"Paizlee, Dalton asked me to the dance! I thought he forgot about what he said before. But he said he thought we'd have a fun time."

"Oh. Well, everyone seems to be going with someone. But I thought Dalton had decided not to ask anyone."

"Is it OK? Maybe I should say no."

"It's fine. I only wish someone I want to go with would ask me."

Dalton started calling Nicky every two or three days. She wasn't used to talking to a boy multiple times a week. Sometimes there was a show she wanted to watch, or she had homework to do, and she didn't want to talk to him. But she didn't tell him to stop.

In algebra, the teacher gave lectures on graphing equations, and Nicky couldn't wrap her head around the new topic. She kept scratching out the notes she had written. After school, she and Gage were at their lockers, and she was scowling as she pulled out her math book to take home.

"What's wrong today?"

"I don't get this graphing section."

"Don't worry about it. You can get sick if you worry about things too much. You could get an ulcer."

"An ulcer?"

"Yeah, I did before we moved here. My stomach hurt a lot, and the doctor said I was too worried about things. He said I should lighten up."

"An ulcer sounds terrible. Did it go away?"

"Mostly. Sometimes it bothers me though. Don't get one!" He shook his finger at her.

"I'll try not to, but I'm very worried about moving. And this graphing stuff."

"Just ask Mrs. Matthews to explain it better tomorrow."

"Yeah, I should. But I really don't want to move, Gage."

He closed his locker. "Who knows if it'll happen. Don't worry about it until it does."

CHAPTER 22

The Winter Dance

On the way home from school, Nicky told Paizlee another story of Gage and Trevor's torture of her in English.

"You're always talking about Gage, Nicky. I know you have a crush on him." Paizlee frowned at her, then looked away.

"No, I don't! I like Dalton now." She was afraid Paizlee was mad.

"But you talk more about Gage than you do about Dalton."

"I do like Dalton! Dalton is nice to me, except for when he took my books. But Gage and Trevor are so irritating."

"I don't know. I hear girls say you and Gage should go to the winter dance together instead of you and Dalton."

"Gage is with Chelsea. Anyway, I'm not interested in him for a boyfriend. We're just friends. Besides, you still like him, right?"

"No, I've decided I like someone else better. Gage is just a friend for me now, too."

"Tell me who you like! Do I know him?"

"I don't think so. Hi, Kinsey."

Kinsey had slowed down so they would catch up to her.

"Have you seen the new boy in the drama club? He's a sophomore, and he's handsome. My sister told me all about him. I heard he plays basketball."

Paizlee's eyes lit up, and she spoke rapidly. "I saw him when I was out with my family for dinner on Saturday. What's his name?"

As Nicky left them, Kinsey and Paizlee were still discussing the newest new boy.

While she washed the dishes after supper, she thought about Gage, and how, when he wasn't around, she felt disappointed. She liked Dalton in a different way. She felt guilty, but she didn't have to like only one boy, did she? She was only 14.

On the day before Gage's 15th birthday, Paizlee called.

"We should get Gage a birthday card," said Paizlee.

"I drew one for him. But it's dumb," said Nicky.

"What does it look like?"

"It's a football player in a helmet. The jersey has Gage's number 10 on it."

"You should give it to him! Can I sign it, too?"

"If you want, but it's not that great."

"Homemade cards are special. He'll like it. I'll sign it before school. Then we'll find Gage after lunch."

The next day, Gage and Grant stood by their locker as Nicky and Paizlee walked up and greeted them. Nicky's hand shook as she pulled her books and the card from her locker. She bit her lip and suddenly handed the card to Paizlee, whose eyebrows rose in surprise.

"What's that?" asked Gage.

"Happy Birthday! We have a card for you," said Paizlee. She handed it to him.

"Really?" He looked at the card. "Who drew this?"

"I did," said Nicky. Her cheeks burned, and she felt stupid she had thought the card was good enough for him, so she turned and ran down the hall.

"Where are you going? Thanks for the card. I like it," said Gage to her back.

Paizlee caught up to her and asked, "Why did you run off?"

"I'm a terrible artist. I don't know why I drew the card."

"But he said he liked it."

"He was just being nice."

"He wouldn't say it if he didn't mean it. I wish you weren't shy sometimes," said Paizlee.

"I'm sorry." Nicky dropped her eyes and held her books tightly. She had embarrassed both of them. They split up as they went to their next classes.

On Saturday night, her parents hosted a goodbye party for her father at their house. Nicky helped prepare the food.

"Nicky, as people start to arrive, please take out the chips and pass them around," said her mother.

"Why? I don't want to be at your party."

"Nicky! We rarely have parties, and I need your help."

"It's only adults. They can help you."

Her father overheard the conversation. "That's enough. You're old enough to cooperate when we ask you. I'm very disappointed. You need to do what your mother asks, especially when I'm away."

"But some of your friends smoke. I'm allergic to tobacco smoke, in case you forgot."

Her parents weren't convinced the smoke would harm her. When the first of their friends arrived, she ran up the stairs and stayed there until everyone left. After the party, she did all the cleanup, which took several hours. Her parents were angry, but she didn't care.

On Friday, the day of the winter dance, Nicky strained her right leg muscle during gymnastics class, and she limped a little. Dalton bought a pink carnation and gave it to her after lunch. It looked nice on the new purplish-pink sweater her mom had bought for her. She wore it for the rest of the day, and Dalton smiled when he looked at her. His attention made her feel special.

Later, Nicky and Dalton met at the front door under red, white, and green balloons. They hung their coats in Dalton's locker and sat down together on the bleachers in the dark gym. Then Dalton went over to Gage, Trevor, and Grant, who were choosing the music.

It felt weird to be with Dalton more and sitting with her friends less. Nicky noticed the ninth-grade girls and boys who were couples that night. She and Dalton danced with other people, but they danced together most dances. She felt less independent, which was uncomfortable. It had been fun to dance with many partners at the fall dance and not feel tied to one person. Then again, she was on the floor more often at this dance. Gage asked her to dance once, but Dalton kept looking at her and squinting his eyes, which made her uneasy.

Someone dedicated a love song to Dalton and Nicky, and they danced to it. She was reluctant because she and Dalton weren't in love. They were simply at a dance together.

When Dalton went back over to the DJs, Lily pulled Nicky aside.

"Did you know Dalton was going to ask Noelle to the dance? She was expecting him to."

Noelle was a friendly, pretty girl who Dalton talked about sometimes, so Nicky wondered why he hadn't asked her.

"Oh, I'm sorry. I hope she isn't unhappy."

"Naw, she flirted with Lance, and he asked her instead. I guess Dalton likes you better." Someone called to Lily, and she darted away.

Nicky felt unsettled. Dalton probably would have been happier with Noelle, who was easier to talk to than Nicky. Plus, she didn't limp.

Paizlee wasn't as cheerful as usual, even though she was dancing with many different boys. After each dance, Nicky wanted to talk and laugh with Paizlee, McKenna, and Kinsey, but Dalton always came along and sat with them so they couldn't talk openly.

At the end of the dance, Paizlee's father picked up Paizlee and Nicky. They were both quiet. When Nicky went inside, she decided not to go to another dance with a boy because she missed having fun with Paizlee.

On Wednesday, Nicky's leg muscle still hurt, but she performed her routine in the gymnastics demonstration for the elementary school class. After the program, her pain was intense, and she felt like crying. As she limped down the hall at the end of school, Dalton caught up with her. He had church school, so he didn't ride the school bus home that day. After Paizlee joined them, the three walked slowly together as Nicky limped the four blocks.

Dalton said he had to ask Nicky something important. Paizlee waved goodbye. Dalton and Nicky sat on the front porch, but they went in when they got cold. They drank some soda pop and ate potato chips as Nicky propped her foot on the coffee table.

"We have a good time together, right?" said Dalton.

"I guess so."

"Maybe we should go steady?"

"You…want to go steady with…me?" Her eyes opened wide as she considered the question.

"Yeah, we could see ball games and movies. We could keep each other company."

"We need more soda pop," said Nicky.

As she limped into the kitchen, she wondered what to say. Nicky was flattered, but she wasn't sure about going steady because it meant spending more time with him and less with her friends. She wanted to ask Paizlee for advice. But Dalton was on her couch and waiting for an answer. As she limped back with the cans, she decided to try having a boyfriend, at least for now.

She said, "Sure, let's go steady."

Dalton smiled widely.

"Great! We're going to have fun together! But I've got to go because I'm going to be late to my church class, so I'll call you later."

As Nicky iced her leg muscle, she imagined what the two of them would do. She knew going steady meant they would talk more and maybe hold hands. She felt some doubts about being a girlfriend, though. She was more at ease doing things with her close friends or alone. Yet, the situation was exciting, too. A boy liked her enough to want to spend time with her. Maybe she wasn't as boring as she thought she was.

What would Paizlee and Zoey say when they heard? Would they be mad at her?

CHAPTER 23

Going Steady

The technical school manager gave Nicky's father a going-away party on his last day of work. It was the last time he would see the other teachers before he started his new job.

After the holiday, her family cleaned the house from top to bottom. Her mother took pictures of the rooms for the real estate agent to show to people who were looking for a new house. The house was officially up for sale as the agent set up appointments to show it.

Nicky was sad because she wanted to stay in the house. They had only lived there nine months. How could anyone like it the way she did? She couldn't think about what would happen if it sold before school was out.

Nicky visited Paizlee before the first showing. Paizlee wasn't surprised Dalton had asked Nicky to go steady. But she warned Nicky that he liked other girls, too, and talked about them with her.

Dalton asked her to go to the movies with him the next night, and she agreed. During the whole movie, she felt like giggling. Dalton talked without thinking and sometimes his remarks made little sense, or they were funny in some way. Halfway through the show, he put his arm around Nicky. She wanted him to do it, but she had to suppress more giggles. A boy had his arm around her. How strange.

Tessa, who was in their grade, sat three rows in front of Nicky and Dalton with a friend. Tessa and her friend looked back multiple times to see what Dalton and Nicky were doing. Nicky had known for at least a month that Tessa liked Dalton because of how she looked at him and said things to draw his attention.

While she watched them, Nicky wondered if she was doing the right thing. Maybe she should never have said yes to Dalton. Maybe he would be better off with Tessa, Zoey, or Noelle.

The night before New Year's Eve, Nicky's parents told her she could only talk on the house phone for a half hour at a time starting on January 1st because she tied up the phone line. They said no when she asked if she could have her own phone. But she had a boyfriend now and lots of friends, so she griped about the phone rule.

Her parents went to a New Year's Eve party, and they stayed out late. Nicky and Dalton talked for a long time that night because the time limit started the next day. She was in an unusually talkative mood, and they laughed a lot together. She was smiling and lighthearted when she went to bed.

The next morning, Nicky quietly went down the stairs as she tried not to wake her parents. But she saw her mother in the kitchen, wiping tears and blowing her nose with a tissue.

"Are you all right, Mom?" asked Nicky.

"Oh, Nicky. I didn't hear you. I was thinking about how much I'll miss your father while he's away. When we move, I'll miss people here. But enough of that. Do you want pancakes for breakfast?"

"Sure."

The night before her father left for his new job, he gave Nicky and Ryan a lecture.

"Kids, listen to me. When your mother asks you to do some work, just do it and don't whine. She has to study for her classes, and she doesn't need to worry about you misbehaving.

"Don't fight with each other. Ryan, you need to be the man of the house and shoulder some responsibility. I don't want to hear your mother complain when I call. I'll be visiting occasionally, but it will depend on the work schedule."

They were put on alert: life would be different. His leaving meant a big change in their house. Her mother drove her father to the Ridgeland City airport the next day.

On the first day back to school, Nicky sat down in the tenth chair as usual. But she saw her former foldermate had moved.

"Nicky, you can be ninth chair now. Raya quit band."

"OK. Why?"

"She had too much to do. Enjoy your own music stand!"

When Bella joined the high school band after the new semester, she shared the stand with Nicky. Nicky enjoyed playing with her friend again. Grant, Alyssa, and McKenna joined the older band at the same time and pulled in chairs to fit into their groups.

"Nicky and Bella, here's some extra music for you, and I'd like you to come in for some extra flute lessons before the All-State Band tryouts later this month. Can you manage that?" said Mr. Gillette asked them at the end of the class. They nodded.

They practiced seriously during the extra lessons. They knew it was a long shot to make it into All-State band, but the attempt would give them experience for next year. Oh, that's right. Nicky wouldn't be in Eagleton next year. Sometimes she forgot.

During one practice, Bella told Nicky about a talk with Zoey.

"I told Zoey you're going steady with Dalton. She didn't ask a single question or make a comment. I thought she would be upset."

"I guess that's good, right? I mean, she didn't want to date him anymore."

"Yeah, but normally she would say something like, 'Fine with me.' But she didn't. I think she's hiding her jealousy."

"She would only be jealous if she wanted to get back with him."

"She still really likes him because she still talks about him a lot."

Nicky felt bad as she thought about Zoey's reaction. She asked Paizlee on the way home.

"I can't talk about that. We had a guest speaker today in German. She's in college, but she's from Germany. The teacher said we could only talk in German while she was there. It was fun to talk with her."

"Will you teach me some German? My family lived in Germany for a while and my brother was born there. Dad taught me how to count and say the days of the week."

"Call me tonight and I'll read you the lesson while I study."

After that, Nicky decided she wanted to catch up and be in the same German class as Paizlee, Gage, and Trevor next year. She would get a book and learn over the summer. They could practice talking in the German language together.

Oh, right. Nicky reminded herself again she wouldn't be in Eagleton next year. She just wanted to forget.

One morning, Paizlee told Nicky, "Last night Dalton called. We were talking about the future. You know, someday, when we're married and have families."

"When you're married? To each other?" Nicky asked.

"Not to each other, silly!" Paizlee said emphatically. "After we grow up. I want to have three kids, and he said he isn't sure how many he wants. How many do you want?"

"I don't know."

Nicky assumed she would get married and have a family someday. She didn't want to think beyond having fun with a boy now, though.

"Did you remember the February dance is girls-ask-boys?" asked Paizlee. "Are you going to ask Dalton?"

"Yes, I suppose so." Nicky felt reluctant as she remembered the winter dance.

"Well, he expects you to, so you'd better do it!" said Paizlee.

"But maybe it would be better to hang out with you."

"Don't worry about me. It would really hurt him if you don't ask him."

On the phone that night, Dalton hinted about the dance.

"There's a dance coming up…"

"I know."

"Somebody already asked me to go. I haven't given her an answer. But if you want me to go with you, you'd better ask soon!"

Nicky was confused. They were "going steady," so they should go together. Was he considering the other offer? Who asked? She wondered if it was Zoey or Noelle.

"We'll see…" She teased him a little, but she wasn't sure what she was going to do.

The next week, Dalton walked home with Nicky, then he hung out with her until he went to church. Dalton had gotten three love letters from someone. She could tell he was flattered, and perhaps he wanted her to write some to him, but she wouldn't because someone else might see them. Dalton got three more notes the following week, and he told Nicky about each one.

On Thursday night, Dalton wasn't at the high school basketball game.

"Did you hear who wrote the notes to Dalton?" Kinsey asked.

"No," said Nicky.

"I don't know for sure, but I have my suspicions," said Paizlee.

"I just found out. Tessa wrote notes to the guy McKenna liked to make him think they were from McKenna. To get back at Tessa, McKenna wrote notes to the guy Tessa liked, Dalton, as if they were from Tessa. Isn't that ridiculous?"

"It doesn't seem right. They might hurt his feelings," said Paizlee.

The gossip confirmed Tessa had a crush on Dalton. Nicky knew the girls were joking around with the notes and they weren't thinking about consequences. But she wondered if Dalton would be happy or disappointed about Tessa's crush.

Nicky got into a squirrely mood after that. She didn't want to care how many other girls liked Dalton. He liked her best. She talked to everyone who came by, and she laughed out loud when others made jokes. She ignored her inner voice, which told her to be quiet.

Trevor looked at her funny. Finally, he asked, "Are you drunk?"

"No! Of course not!" she said. She giggled for a few minutes as she thought about how differently she behaved that night. But she wasn't a drinker, and Trevor knew that.

When she went home, she had more doubts about dating. She wanted to belong and do what the other kids were doing, like having a boyfriend. But sometimes, she didn't want a boyfriend. She didn't think she was a good enough girlfriend. Maybe she should give it up.

When Dalton called next, he told her he found out McKenna had written the notes for Tessa. He sounded disappointed. Nicky didn't ask him who he wished had written them. She didn't want to know.

There was a gymnastics meet on Tuesday, but Nicky hadn't tried out for it. Dalton came to her house, and they walked to the junior high gym together. She couldn't relax as she watched the girls at the four stations because he kept talking.

Nicky got a ride to another high school basketball game on Saturday night with Trevor, Gage, Dalton, and Grant. She expected to see Paizlee in the car, but she wasn't. Maybe Paizlee's father wouldn't let her ride with Trevor after dark. But it was only four blocks for Nicky. She sat in the back as the boys played with the radio and tried to find their favorite songs. They were joking around, and she laughed with them. She felt warm and happy watching her friends.

Nicky's father called his family on Saturday mornings. After her mother talked to him, Nicky talked to him. He asked how her classes were going, but she had little to say except, "Fine."

She told him she was preparing for All-State Band tryouts, yet nothing else seemed important enough to share. She didn't tell him about what she did with Dalton and her friends.

After her brother had a similar brief conversation with him, her mother talked cheerfully about her classes and conversations with the realtor. When they hung up, the three of them went back to their normal routines. Nicky felt strange when she talked to her father on the phone, knowing he wasn't in Eagleton. He was in some other place without them, living a separate life.

CHAPTER 24

All-State Band Tryouts

The All-State Band tryouts took place on a cold mid-January day. Fourteen people from Eagleton auditioned at one of the Ridgeland City high schools. Nicky and Bella rode with Alyssa, Hailey, and their mother, who drove. Nicky enjoyed the ride as she looked at the north ridge of the Ponderosa Hills on her left side and the expanse of mountains flowing away like a dark blanket on her right. When they arrived, the girls remembered they had been to the high school for the choir contest last spring. They remembered some of the school's layout, which helped them relax a little.

The high school band musicians from across the state gathered in the auditorium. The written music test was handed out, and the students began completing it. Nicky wasn't sure about four of the questions, but she knew the others. When they finished, the band directors handed them the audition schedule on the way out of the auditorium. Nicky's time was right before Bella's, but they had to wait an hour.

At her time, Nicky nervously walked into the room and sat down in the folding chair. When she played the prepared music, her flute seemed different as she tried to catch her breath. She goofed up on parts she never goofed up on. She played the scales well. Then the judge gave her a difficult sight-reading piece of music, and she made many mistakes. But when Nicky finished, the judge told her she should be proud of her sight-reading.

After Nicky left the room, Bella went in. Nicky stayed outside to wait and to listen. Bella must have been nervous, too, because she didn't do as well as she usually did. Nicky knew Bella was a better player than she was, yet the sight-reading threw her friend. Bella would have next year to try again. Nicky wondered if she would ever get a chance to try out for an All-State Band in the future.

The girls were glad the tryouts were over, and the results would be revealed next month. They had all practiced intensely, and they wanted to celebrate. They ate at a restaurant with Alyssa, Hailey, and their mother.

A new stage band piano arrived and sat against the wall behind the director's podium in the band room. Bella played it for stage band rehearsals held during lunch hour.

"The stage band songs are so easy even a sixth grader could play them," said Bella. They were standing in front of the piano.

"I'm glad for you," said Nicky.

Then Nicky sighed. Her mood was gray since the All-State Band audition. When she got up every morning, she reminded herself her family was leaving Eagleton. Every time she enjoyed an activity, she thought about how she would never get to do it again with her friends.

"You've been sighing a lot lately. What's wrong?"

"I guess I'm just sad."

"Because of moving?"

"Yeah. I can't stop thinking about it."

"I wouldn't be able to stop thinking about it, either. But I'd be researching to find out all about the new place."

"You wouldn't really just want to leave us, would you?"

"I guess not. Mostly, I'd miss you and Paizlee, though."

Nicky grimaced and touched her forehead. "I keep getting headaches."

"Have you told your mother?"

"Not yet. What will I do after I move, Bella? Who will I do things with?"

"You'll make new friends. New kids move here all the time, and they make new friends."

"But I like the friends I have now, like you. I might not be able to make new friends."

Dalton came through the band room door. "Hey, what's wrong? You look like someone just died."

"Nicky doesn't think she'll make new friends after she moves," said Bella.

"I wish I wasn't moving," said Nicky. She shook her head.

"I wish I wasn't, either. But what can we do? Our parents will make us. I mean, we don't have a choice. We're stuck."

"I know," said Nicky. She frowned and wished she had a choice. If she did, she would stay in Eagleton.

That night, Dalton told Nicky the German club was going to a movie.

"We each get to ask one person to go with us. I wanted to ask you to go with me. But the teacher said we could only ask a friend who wasn't of the opposite sex. It's ridiculous!"

"Who will you ask?"

"I think I'll ask Paizlee to ask you to go as her friend, but you'll really sit with me."

"But if Paizlee asked me, I would go and sit with her."

"Couldn't you sit with both of us?"

"But Paizlee should only ask me if she wants me there. Don't you get it?"

"No."

"She would feel left out."

"Well, I'm still going to ask her to do it. I bet she will."

Nicky was very conflicted. It wasn't fair Dalton would put her friend in such a situation. Later, Paizlee told her Dalton had asked her to bring Nicky along as her friend, and she said no. She would have asked Nicky if Dalton hadn't been dating her. Paizlee decided not to go at all. Dalton asked Grant to go to the movie instead.

The freshmen went to a senior high pep assembly in the senior high school gym on Friday. Dalton came over and sat by Nicky. A senior girl Dalton knew went up the bleachers by them, and she gave Dalton an A-OK sign. Nicky felt embarrassed. She was now a girl evaluated in relation to a boy. She was part of a couple, which felt incredibly odd. She wasn't his possession.

The next basketball games were after school, and Nicky and Alyssa went together. The ninth-grade team won their game. Ryan helped his seventh-grade team win. The high school games were on Saturday night, and both teams won in overtime. The wrestlers won their matches, too. The teams seemed to be on fire in their divisions.

After lunch on Monday, Dalton came up to Nicky at her locker and asked her where Grant was. She told him she didn't know, and Dalton left to look for him. As Nicky walked down the hall, she saw Dalton talking with Zoey. Zoey saw Nicky and went into a classroom on the left. Dalton followed Zoey. Nicky wondered what they were talking about as she passed the door.

Later, Bella, Kinsey, and Nicky were in the band room for lessons.

"Do you think Zoey still likes Dalton?" asked Kinsey.

"Of course she does!" laughed Bella. "Before the winter dance, Zoey heard Dalton was going to ask Nicky to go with him to it, and she was upset. She told me she had a way to get Dalton to stop liking Nicky."

"What was it?" asked Kinsey.

"Well..." Bella paused for dramatic effect. "She thought by telling Dalton Nicky had a big crush on him, he would be turned off and stop liking Nicky. But, instead, Dalton liked Nicky more!"

"That explains why he kept trying to find out which boy I liked before he asked me to the dance," said Nicky. "He asked me over and over."

"Of course he did! He wanted to see if Zoey was telling him the truth! But her strategy backfired," said Bella.

"I thought you liked Gage in December, Nicky," said Kinsey.

"I liked Dalton. Anyway, Gage was with Chelsea, and he still is. There's no point in liking him since he will never be available."

"Yes," said Kinsey. She nodded slowly. "Gage is still with Chelsea. I wish he didn't have such a serious girlfriend."

Dalton walked Nicky home from the evening's wrestling match. He put his arm around her while they walked. Then on the porch, he leaned over and kissed her on the mouth. It was her very first kiss.

"Good night, Dalton," she said softly as she went inside.

Maybe nothing was going on with Zoey after all. As Nicky got ready for bed, she thought about the kiss, and she dreamed about it.

CHAPTER 25

Exhaustion

In early February, Nicky and Paizlee went ice skating at an outdoor rink halfway between their houses. Nicky had new ice skates to try out. They skated up and down the rink, then tried to move backward and twirl. Nicky wasn't very good, so she fell before she got far, and she sat on the ice.

"Why do boys yell at refs?" Nicky asked. Since the basketball game the previous night, she had been stuck on that question.

"Who knows? They get angry easily, I guess."

"When Dalton stands up and yells, I want to tell him to sit down. I can't figure out why I care." Nicky got up from the ice.

"You have to care what he does now because he's your boyfriend."

"Wasn't the dance line routine good last night?" asked Nicky. She had watched them with longing.

"Bella and I have been practicing some steps to prepare for the auditions in April. They win state competitions, so we have to be practically perfect to make it on the team." She skated backward.

"I wish I could try out," said Nicky. She was reminded again of what she couldn't do because of the move.

At the next game, Nicky felt dizzy while playing her flute. She didn't feel well as she walked home with Kinsey. When she got inside and took off her coat, she realized she didn't have her flute. How could she leave her flute somewhere again?

"Mom, I left my flute in the stands. What am I going to do tomorrow for the piano recital?" Mrs. Schmidt had asked Bella and Nicky to play a duet on their flutes, and they had agreed. Nicky had to have a flute.

"You need to find it because we aren't buying you another one. I'm not sure what you can do for tomorrow. Could you borrow someone's flute?" said her mother.

The next morning, Nicky called Paizlee and the other flutists she knew, but most weren't at home, or they kept their flutes at school.

"Hi Kira. I left my flute in the bleachers, and Mr. Gillette is out of town this weekend, so I can't get it. Could I borrow your flute?"

"You could, except it's at school. I could ask my sister if she could let us into school. She's a teacher. I'll call you back," said Kira.

Kira called to say she could borrow the key if they picked her up and she went with them. In the band room, Nicky rushed over to the instrument shelves, but she didn't see her instrument, so she borrowed Paizlee's flute. Nicky thanked Kira when they dropped her off.

"Kira, you're a lifesaver. Please thank your sister."

"Sure. See you at school on Monday," said Kira.

Nicky and her mother picked up Paizlee after lunch to go to the recital. When Nicky asked Paizlee if it was OK to play her flute, she said it was. While she listened to the piano pieces, Nicky wanted to take lessons again. She was relaxed as she played the duet with Bella.

After the recital, Nicky, Paizlee, Bella, and the older girls, including Chelsea, chatted as they ate some cookies. They were from three different grades, but they had music in common. Nicky wished she could be at another recital with them.

On Monday, Nicky returned Paizlee's flute to the rack, then she went to Mr. Gillette's office to see if he had found her flute. It was on his desk, and he handed it to her.

"Nicky, isn't this the second time you left your flute at a game? You need to be more careful."

"I'm sorry. I didn't feel well that day. I've been exhausted lately."

"Are you practicing for the music contest?"

Nicky nodded, then criticized herself as she went to sit down. If she left her flute somewhere after she moved, it might be stolen.

A few days later, Bella, Nicky, and two of the sophomores practiced their flute ensemble together. Nicky played the lowest part, and she was out of breath each time she played it. The sophomores left after several run-throughs.

"Bella, I feel like I'll collapse. The low part is hard to play, and I lose my breath," said Nicky.

"You volunteered to play it, so you're stuck with it now," said Bella.

"I've been so tired. By third hour, I feel like I need a nap."

"Maybe you're just mentally tired. Are you still worried about Zoey?"

"Yeah, I saw her talking with Dalton again this morning, and I'm sure she's trying to get him back."

"You're smarter, though, and musical. He must like that."

"Zoey is smart. She's in math with us, and she's a cheerleader now."

As Nicky sat in her next class, she hoped Dalton would end their relationship and go back to Zoey. She didn't think she could break up with him. She was hesitant to confide in Paizlee because Dalton still called her friend often. Nicky didn't want her friend to be in the middle and have to keep Nicky's feelings secret from Dalton.

After four weeks away, Nicky's father came home the first weekend in February. He told them about his job, the people he met, and the places he visited. She was distant with him. If he didn't have the new job in another place, she could stop feeling so anxious about leaving.

Nicky told her father her eyes had been bothering her, and she had headaches. He suggested she needed glasses, so her mother made an appointment in Ridgeland City with an optometrist.

At the next basketball game, Paizlee, Dalton, and Trevor were absent, but Gage was at the game.

"Where's Trevor?" asked Nicky.

"Hannah broke up with him. He's taking it hard," said Gage.

"Oh, that's too bad."

"Don't tell anyone, but he's pretty hurt right now."

"I won't tell." She meant it because she was getting tired of all the gossip.

After the game, she and Gage walked home and discussed the upcoming band contest. She was self-conscious as she wondered if anyone saw them who would think they were doing something wrong. She didn't want people to talk about her anymore.

The next time Dalton called, he told Nicky three secrets. One was Nicky's secret. The second one was Gage's secret. The third secret was one of his own.

"Preston was surprised when I told him you liked him last year," said Dalton.

"I asked you not to tell anyone," Nicky said. She was irritated.

"Well, I don't know why you would care now. It was last year."

"I do care. Please don't tell anyone else."

"Did you know Gage liked you last year?"

Nicky's jaw dropped as she tried to understand why Dalton would tell her about Gage's feelings. If Gage wanted her to know, he would tell her.

"Everyone around here likes each other," he said. "A few weeks ago, I almost had a crush on Paizlee."

"Dalton, you and Paizlee are just friends."

"Yeah, I know. But she's always so nice. I like talking to her."

And you don't like talking to me, thought Nicky. When they hung up, she felt angry. If she told him anything, he would tell multiple other people because he didn't know what discretion was. Nicky tried hard not to repeat secrets other people told her. Nicky often took a breath before she talked, in case she would decide not to speak. She didn't want to hurt anyone with her words, and she criticized herself if she thought she said something dumb. But Dalton talked carelessly sometimes. It was one of the ways they were different.

Dalton scared her, and Nicky wasn't sure what to do. Everything was mixed up in her head, and she was exhausted thinking about the problems. She wished she could talk to Paizlee again, the way she used to before a boy got in the way.

CHAPTER 26

The Talk Across the Hedge

Before her father went back to his training, Nicky's family had a birthday celebration for her. At school, Paizlee gave her a present. Dalton gave her a card and a birthstone necklace. As other people said "Happy Birthday" to her in classes and in the halls, Nicky realized she had many friends and acquaintances.

Before math class, Trevor said, "Now you're 15, you need a philosophy of life."

"Definitely. You need to know what's important to you," said Gage.

"Really? I never thought about it. What's yours?" asked Nicky.

"Mine is to work hard and you'll succeed," said Gage.

"Mine is to be open to new experiences," said Trevor.

Nicky thought for a minute. "I guess mine is to be nice to people and care about them."

They both nodded and said that was a good philosophy for her. They sang "Happy Birthday" to her on the way out of class.

She was so tired she left school after math, and when she got home, her mother took her to the medical clinic. The doctor said her allergies were acting up, and he gave her an allergy shot.

After she was home from the clinic, Dalton called from the band room. He and some other male voices sang "Happy Birthday" to her over the phone. When she started crying after she hung up, it made no sense at all. She had such good guy friends.

Dalton visited Nicky on Thursday afternoon. But Nicky was not in a talkative mood, and he talked more to Ryan than to Nicky. She thought about moving every day and how it would change her whole life. She didn't know how she would make new friends. She would miss the small town, which was so familiar. If the house sold soon, she might be gone before the weather was warm enough to climb Peaceful Bear Mountain again.

On Friday afternoon, Dalton called. He said, "I heard Gage and Chelsea are having problems. I think they're breaking up."

Nicky didn't respond because she didn't want to sound interested.

"I also heard Grant and his girlfriend are breaking up, maybe even before the dance."

"Oh. I thought they really liked each other."

"She's mad at him, I guess. I hope we won't have problems like that."

He apparently hadn't noticed she wasn't smiling lately. She was unhappy being part of a couple, but he couldn't see it. She choked every time she started to express herself.

"We're going to the dance still, right?"

"Um…yeah." She chickened out again. She should tell him she didn't want to go to the dance with him. But she couldn't.

"Are you going to the wrestling match tonight?" said Dalton.

"Yeah, I need to play in the band."

"I'm not sure if I'm going. If I do, I'll call you later."

"OK," said Nicky.

He called later and said after he drove his sister to the movie theater, he would be at the wrestling match. When she got to school, she went up the fire escape to the band room to get her flute from the rack. She didn't want to be with Dalton that night. She wanted to talk to other kids, not be someone's girlfriend, and only talk to him.

When she walked into the band room, only a few pep band kids were in the room, and she didn't see Mr. Gillette. Gage was pacing, and he looked nervous. His arms were around his stomach, and his face looked pale.

"Hi, Gage. What's wrong?"

"I'm directing the band tonight. Mr. Gillette can't be here, so he asked me to do it."

"That's great. Why did he choose you?"

"I told him someday I want to direct the Naval Academy band. This afternoon he said, 'Here's your chance to lead a band and get some practice.'"

Gage didn't look happy to get the chance, however.

Nicky felt concerned about him, so she reassured him. "You'll do fine. You're a good drummer, and you keep us all on the beat."

He nodded, but he didn't say anything as he clenched his jaw.

She went across the room, sat down, and put her flute together. Dalton walked through the fire escape door and sat by her.

"My sister is at the movies."

"OK." She barely looked at him.

"I made it in time, so we can walk over to the gym together."

She bent her head, and she didn't answer.

"What's wrong?"

"Nothing."

"Aren't you going to talk to me?"

She shrugged as she avoided his eyes.

He got up and went back out to the fire escape. He made a comment to Gage as he passed him.

Gage came over to sit by her. "Dalton said you wouldn't talk to him. Are you mad at him?"

"I don't know. I don't know anything. Maybe I just don't want to talk to him tonight, that's all."

"Why?"

She shrugged. "I don't want to talk about it." She remembered Chelsea feeling the same way about Gage.

He looked hurt. She hadn't been friendly to him, either. He was still sitting in the chair as she left the room. She felt guilty, but she didn't want to talk to Dalton or Gage about how she felt.

In the gym, she saw Dalton sitting with a group of friends on the far side of the band. Nicky sat on the other side of the band.

During the match, Gage directed the band to play songs everyone liked the best. Nobody criticized him, they just followed his arms as he kept the beat. After the last song, he looked at Nicky and lifted his eyebrows, as if to say, "Glad that's over."

Nicky went to the band room to put her instrument away. She thought if she was quick, she could leave without seeing Dalton again. She hurried toward the door. But, as she was leaving, Dalton called to her to stop.

"Hey, Nicky! I can give you and Gage a ride in my car. Gage wants to go see Chelsea at the movie."

She felt cornered, so she nodded and followed them to his car parked across the street by the fish pond. Dalton drove to the movie theater first and dropped off Gage. Since Gage was meeting Chelsea, they had obviously made up.

Dalton and Nicky went to her house, listened to a few songs in his car, got out, and stood on the porch. There was still snow on the ground, and it was cold, but she didn't invite him in. She wanted to tell him she didn't want to date him anymore.

"What's wrong with you tonight?" asked Dalton.

"I...well, I just feel...I don't know."

"Come on, you might as well tell me."

"Don't you ever...I mean, you know, just want to be by yourself?"

"Yeah, sometimes. So what?"

"Well, for me, I mean, it's weird but...oh, I'm not sure I can..."

"Can what?"

She was ready to cry from frustration because she couldn't say what she wanted. They saw Gage walk up the block.

"Dang, the movie's over! I have to go pick up my sister," said Dalton.

He ran to his car. As he tried to pull away from the curb, he got stuck in the snow, and the car's rear wheels spun around. Gage stopped and helped him push the car out. After Dalton left, Gage and Nicky stood by the street with the short hedge between them.

Nicky realized she had to talk to someone. She wouldn't call Paizlee for help because the subject was her relationship with Dalton. Gage rarely gossiped, and she believed he would keep her secret. Gage had seemed genuinely concerned about her earlier in the band room, so she decided to ask him.

"Would you help me with something? You can't tell anyone else what we talk about, though."

"Sure."

"I'm so…down. When I see Dalton, I feel worse."

"Do you like Dalton?"

She nodded.

"Are you happy being with him?"

"I was at first."

"What happened?"

"He doesn't, well, understand me, I guess. Whenever I tell him something, I know he'll tell other people. Dalton gossips so much. Everyone here does, except you."

"But you should tell him how you feel."

Nicky looked down at her snow boots. "I don't want to talk to him," she said quietly. She looked at him across the hedge.

"What do you want to do?"

"I want to break up with him, but I don't want to hurt him."

"He should know if you don't want to go steady with him."

"People will think I am an idiot. He's such a great guy."

"Don't worry about what other people think. Just do what you know is the right thing for you."

"I feel so guilty."

"Don't. He'll be OK. Do what you need to do."

His words made sense. She knew he wanted to go home and get warm, but she was glad he didn't leave.

"Did you like directing the band?"

"Yeah, but my stomach hurts. I need to go drink some milk until it feels better."

"Oh. Well, thanks for talking with me."

"Any time." He turned, walked along the hedge, and up the street.

When she got inside, she felt calm. Gage had reminded her she shouldn't let what other people thought rule her life. Her father was always saying things like, "If everyone was jumping off a high bridge, would you do it?" Of course not. She needed to think for herself.

But she wanted to fit in. She didn't want to be different. She just wanted to be one of the gang. Friends were starting to date, so she wanted to date, too. At least, she had thought so.

Yet she knew she wasn't interested in being Dalton's girlfriend anymore. She had to be honest with him.

CHAPTER 27

The Sadie Hawkins Dance

In the car on the way to Bella's house to practice for the band contest, Nicky's mother glanced over at her.

"Your father and I decided not to sell the house now. We'll try again in a few months. I want you kids to finish the school year, and I want to finish my semester to get the college credits."

"Oh, good."

Nicky felt relieved because now she could enjoy the rest of the school year without the fear her father would call and say they were moving in a month. She knew her mother had a lot to take care of without her father at home. Nicky tried not to complain about anything. She tried to be responsible and follow the rules, like her father had warned them to do. But holding in the dread about leaving was hard. Even though she wanted to talk to her mother, she didn't want to burden her.

"I saw you outside with Gage last night. I was worried you were getting cold out there. Is everything OK?"

"He was helping me figure something out."

"Is it anything I can help with, honey?"

"No. I need to break up with Dalton. He kind of took over my life and I want it back."

"I see. Dalton seems nice, and he calls a lot. He might be upset when you break up with him. That's a difficult situation and you should tell him soon, but tactfully. I've also heard you talk about Gage with your girlfriends. Do you like him?"

Nicky stared out the window. Even her mother wanted to know how she felt about Gage. "No, he's only a friend. He's been dating Chelsea for a long time. I guess they're in love or something."

"They're very young to be in love. That must be tough for you if you like him, too."

"I guess. I mean, I don't want to be interested in a boy who already has a girlfriend. Besides, Paizlee really likes him. I would never hurt her."

At Bella's house, Bella and Nicky talked a lot as they practiced. Nicky confided she was going to break up with Dalton, and she asked Bella not to say a word to anyone. Nicky trusted Bella wouldn't, yet it also made her feel more pressure to talk to Dalton as soon as she could. Keeping secrets was too hard in their group.

When Dalton called next, she lost her nerve.

"I saw you and Gage talking after I left. What were you talking about?"

"Just things."

"You must have been talking about something. Tell me what it was."

"We talked about band and stuff."

"Did you talk about me? If you talked about me, I want to know."

"We talked about a lot of things."

"What did he tell you?"

"Nothing!"

"He said something, I can tell. I need to know!"

He was so insistent, and she was getting upset. But his demands made her not want to tell him anything, and she just wanted to get off the phone.

"Dalton, I have to go now. Bye." She hung up.

Because of a snowstorm on Sunday night, school was canceled the next day. Nicky resolved to tell Dalton that night their relationship was over. When he called, she took a deep breath and spoke before he could say anything.

"Um, so I still like you, but I don't want to go steady anymore. I want to do more with Paizlee and Bella. Can we go back to being just friends?"

"I knew it! I knew Gage would tell you to break up with me. I knew it!"

"You'll find someone better. Lots of girls like you."

"But you talked to Gage about me, didn't you?"

"It's not his fault. I just don't want to go steady, Dalton."

"Fine. But I'm telling him to mind his own business."

Dalton hung up without saying goodbye.

Nicky started crying. This was awful. He hated her. He hated Gage. She hadn't been a good girlfriend, and she was bad at breaking up. She criticized every word she had said. She was so bad at everything. She thought about how Gage told her she shouldn't feel guilty. She wished she could take his advice, but she felt terrible. She tried to call Paizlee, but her line was busy.

The next day, the roads were clear, and school was in session. The senior high band and choir contest would be held as planned at the regional college in Sparta, where Nicky's mother had classes. Nicky found Paizlee at her locker.

"I broke up with Dalton last night," said Nicky.

"I know. He called me. Why didn't you?" said Paizlee.

"I tried, but your line was busy every time. How long did you talk to him?"

"Not long. My grandmother called, though," said Paizlee.

"I have to get on the bus, but let's talk tonight."

"OK," said Paizlee.

On the contest bus, Nicky saw Chelsea, and then she saw Gage sitting next to her by the window. Bella was on the other side of the aisle, and Nicky went to sit by her. The kids laughed and talked as the bus cruised the 20 miles to the college town.

When the band students entered the music building, they got the contest schedule. The flute ensemble had to play right away, and they rushed to find the room. They played poorly, and Nicky didn't think she was in tune. They got the second highest rating, which disappointed Nicky. She was sure it was her fault because she couldn't play the low part very well.

Bella and Nicky saw Gage in the atrium. His lips were pursed, and he was glaring. Chelsea wasn't around.

"Gage, why are you angry?" asked Nicky.

"That stupid judge gave me a second-place rating. I worked so hard on my solo and I performed it great. What was wrong with him? Now he's going to judge our percussion ensemble. I can't mess up. I won't mess up."

He paced around the atrium, went out to the bus, and came back. Chelsea was through with her solo and she told him not to be so worried, but he kept pacing and tapping his foot.

When he came back to the atrium after the ensemble played, his face was relaxed because the judge had given them the highest rating. Before he left on the bus after lunch, he wished Nicky good luck on her solo by shaking her hand five times.

Nicky didn't play as well as she could have, and she was disappointed. They didn't find out what score she got before she and Bella left the building on the last bus.

Later that week, Mr. Gillette asked Nicky and Bella to meet in his office after school.

"I have a few things to share with you. Nicky, you got a second-place rating on your solo. You did a fine job as a freshman player."

"That's better than I thought," said Nicky. She vowed to do better next time. Oh, wait…not here. She would be in a different band at a new school.

"Both of you had wonderful results for the All-State Band auditions. As you know, you were scored from the fewest mistakes, which was a 10, to the worst playing, which was a 50. Nicky, you got 20 and Bella, you got 22. I'm very proud of you."

"What should we shoot for next year?" asked Bella.

"The ones who made the cut had 14 or less. Two Eagleton students made it into the band this year. Next year, one of you could make it."

He forgot Nicky was moving away, and Nicky didn't remind him.

The next morning before band, McKenna stopped by her locker.

"Did you hear Dalton is going to the Sadie Hawkins dance with Tessa? As soon as she found out you broke up with him, she asked him to go."

"Oh, that's nice." She guessed Tessa was happy he had said yes. But she was surprised he wasn't going with Zoey.

"Grant just told me. Did you know Grant had a crush on you last year?"

"Really?" Nicky didn't want to gossip, but she liked knowing.

"He did! He also told me Gage had one on you for the longest time."

"Well, Gage and Chelsea were very 'together' at the contest."

"I saw them! But you never know."

"He probably liked me before he started dating her."

McKenna shrugged and hurried into the band room.

Nicky had no intention of getting involved with anyone else any time soon, but she felt happy knowing they liked her.

The students in all three grades assembled to watch the Air Force Stage Band play in the junior high gym. There was a guy who sang and played jazz flute and he had several solos. Nicky liked how well he played. She thought she should be allowed to play the flute in their school stage band after hearing him. She could learn how to play in a jazzier style.

On the way out, she asked Gage if they had practiced any songs for the garage band.

"Nah, we'll do it in the spring. My dad says we can't play in the house."

"I'm sorry I can't be in it now."

"If you don't move, you can still be in it."

"I wish I could."

The next night was the third dance of the year. There were more freshmen boys at the dance because girls could ask boys to it. Dalton was supposed to dance with Tessa, but he asked Nicky to dance five times, and she did. Another boy asked her once, and Josh asked her twice. Trevor asked her twice to songs she liked, and she enjoyed dancing with him. She didn't see Gage.

Paizlee was on the floor mixing with different partners, as was Zoey. Nicky tried to figure out who was having fun and who wasn't. She felt better as she paid attention to her friends. She was relaxed and happy as she talked with Paizlee, McKenna, and Kinsey.

Gage showed up, but Nicky didn't see him dancing. Nicky was by the door when Paizlee hurried up to her.

"Have you seen Chelsea? She's here with Lauren. They're in the back."

Nicky looked around and saw Chelsea dancing with Gage, and Lauren and Trevor were dancing next to them.

"They're not supposed to be here!" she said as she glared at them.

Nicky gestured with her shoulder that she didn't see a problem.

"Wait! There's Mrs. Fleming." Mrs. Fleming led the two older girls into the hall through the other east door, so Paizlee pulled Nicky out into the hall. They watched Mrs. Fleming speak sternly to Chelsea and Lauren. Other girls joined Nicky and Paizlee.

"You two know you shouldn't be here. This dance is for junior high kids, and you're crashing it. Now get your things and leave."

The girls nodded and walked down the hall, with Gage and Trevor following behind them. Nicky's friends were happy the older girls had to leave. They wanted to protect their territory.

But Nicky wasn't sure how she felt. Chelsea was only a few months older than they were, and she thought Gage should be able to dance with his girlfriend, even if it was a junior high dance. She had been a girlfriend, and she sympathized with Chelsea.

CHAPTER 28

The Shadow of "The Move"

The boys' basketball regional tournaments began in late February. The ninth-grade team won over Howell by five points. The seventh-grade team won their game, too.

A week later, Nicky sat on the pep bus alone until Paizlee came. Girls talked and passed notes, but Nicky didn't share in the activity. Why did what they say matter? She wouldn't be here next year with them. She took off her new glasses and wiped them with her shirt. She looked at Peaceful Bear Mountain with snow on the top and remembered the last time her family had climbed it.

Paizlee arrived and sat next to her. "Why aren't you talking to anyone?"

"I don't feel like it, I guess."

"Do you feel sick?"

"Paizlee! Look at this," said Lily. Lily passed a note to Paizlee, who read it.

"I thought that would happen," said Paizlee. She turned to Nicky.

"Dalton asked Zoey to go steady again, and she said yes."

"Oh." Nicky had been right to let him go.

At the tournament school, the girls visited the snack machines, then watched the teams play. They walked around the unfamiliar high school and made comments about what they saw. After the games ended, they were tired and disappointed their teams didn't win that day.

Nicky's English class studied the tragic Shakespeare play *Romeo and Juliet*, who were teenagers like the students. The teacher assigned them parts to read out loud, but Nicky and her friends didn't have the lead roles. When Romeo killed himself because he thought Juliet was dead, Nicky wondered why he acted thoughtlessly because of his passion. The teacher told the class, "No one is worth killing yourself over, even if you are crazy in love with them."

In early March, the Honors Algebra teacher chose nine students to study for the State Math Contest. Kinsey, Mia, Trevor, Grant, and Nicky were in the group. Nicky was glad the teacher chose her because algebra was her favorite subject. The test preparation classes were before school.

Paizlee's father began taking her to school about an hour early, and they stopped to pick up Nicky, which helped her get to the math prep classes on time. In the afternoon, Paizlee often asked Nicky to walk several more blocks with her because she didn't like to walk all the way home alone.

One day, Nicky was in a bad mood, and she didn't walk as far as normal, despite Paizlee's pleas. After Nicky got back to her house, she opened the wooden front door with the round glass window. Her mother's car wasn't in back and she didn't hear Ryan in the house.

"I don't want to move!" Nicky yelled as she slammed the door behind her.

The echo rang through the silent old house. Nicky stood in the hall, then leaned her right side against the stairway post. She noticed her brother's shoes in the middle of the floor, and she stepped over them with a scowl. Nicky went into the living room and stopped to look out the window. A few minutes later, she heard the door slam. Ryan was home. Basketball season was over, and he didn't have any sports until track started. But he needed to take Ginger for her walk soon.

As he went past her in a rush, he almost knocked her over. She watched him slow down to turn on some music. He sauntered into the kitchen to get something to eat. He opened the refrigerator door and stuck his head inside.

Nicky looked at her tall brother. Even though they argued sometimes, he would be the only other teen she would know after they moved. She watched as he pulled out some chicken and made a sandwich on the counter.

"What do you think we'll do after we move?" she asked him.

He turned and gave her a how-can-she-be-so-stupid look.

"Go to school."

"I mean, we won't know anyone. Doesn't that bother you?"

"We'll meet people." He shrugged and took a big bit of his sandwich.

Nicky left him, ran up to her room, and she slammed the door behind her. She took off her new glasses and flung herself on the bed. She lay on her back, her body still, her mind racing.

Nicky thought again about "The Move." It was a big, black, hot-air balloon sitting over her head, and she was in its shadow. It would crash down on her soon. She was apprehensive about her future and mad about the coming changes. Her father was almost finished with his training, and he would start soon at his new workplace in Magnus City. Then he would find a house for them all to live in. As soon as school was over, they would leave Eagleton and move into it. "The Move" was only a few months away.

She knew it would happen, but she couldn't quite believe it. Her life in Eagleton wasn't perfect, but it was the only one she knew. She had been lucky the year before when the technical school gave her father a raise and promoted him to head instructor. Then they had moved into town, which had been great for her. Why couldn't her father wait to get a new job until after she and Ryan graduated?

The phone rang and Nicky went into the other room to pick it up.

"Hi, it's Alyssa. Whatcha doing?"

"Sitting in a chair."

"Would you rather be bowling? My team in the bowling league needs another person. We had five, but Hailey's friend stopped showing up, so we need someone. You like bowling, don't you?"

Nicky thought for a few seconds. In March, options for activities in the small town were scarce, except for movies and bowling, unless someone participated in the track and field team.

"Sure. When do you meet?"

"Tuesday and Thursday afternoons at 3:30."

"OK. See you there!"

When Nicky heard Ryan go out to walk Ginger, she went downstairs to play the piano. She could see better with her new glasses, and she enjoyed playing whatever she wanted instead of an assigned lesson. As she practiced a difficult section, her thoughts wandered until she pounded the keys abruptly and stopped playing.

Later that week, the ninth graders went to a new play given by the drama and debate classes. Zoey was in the play, but Paizlee wasn't. The freshmen who were in band sat in a group together and whispered. Her friends paid little attention to the play.

But Nicky crossed her arms and watched it. She barely listened to her friends because she felt uninterested in the social situations going on around her. She did what she was supposed to do, but part of her didn't care. Se was more the observer again, like she had been in seventh grade.

After lunch, the algebra teacher stepped out into the hall while the students worked on their assignment.

"Hey, Kee. How did you do this problem?"

Trevor had been calling her 'Kee' for a week. She thought it was neat he had given her a nickname. He usually didn't ask for help in math because he was good at it. But he pointed to his paper. He was having an off day because he had gotten answers wrong on the previous assignment.

"Which one? Let me see."

Trevor had taken over the big table at the side of the room, so she had to stand up to look at his paper. Nicky opened her book and showed him the page.

"We went over that on page 209." She felt confident she was good at math when even Trevor asked her for help with problems.

Later, Nicky, Ryan, and her mother ate dinner around their octagon-shaped table.

"The driver's education class starts before school on Monday. Can I sign up?" asked Nicky.

"No, you can take it after we move," said her mother.

"But all my friends are in it."

"The state laws might be different, so you should wait."

"Couldn't I learn the basics here? Then I could read a book in Magnus City and learn more there."

"I'm sorry, but you need to wait until we get settled. That's the way it is."

Nicky frowned, and she didn't understand the logic. She would miss out on learning to drive with her friends. Why did she have to wait until after "The Move?"

The next day before band, Bella's eyes were bright, and she smiled. "My dad wants to leave Eagleton!"

"Really? Why?" asked Nicky.

"He was talking to a visiting doctor who said there were some openings in a city close to Magnus City. He said my father would be perfect for one of them."

"Wow."

"Wouldn't it be great if we lived close enough and we could visit each other? Once we get our driver's licenses, we could go back and forth whenever we wanted!" Bella laughed.

"Who knows when I'll be allowed to drive. It's so unfair!" Nicky complained. Bella was in the driver's ed class.

"But you'll get to do so many new things after you move. I dream about a fresh start somewhere else. This town is boring!"

"I wish I could be that optimistic," said Nicky.

After the talk with Bella, Nicky began imagining what might happen after "The Move." When her father talked about Magnus City, she imagined what it might be like to live there. "The Move" could be a fresh start, as Bella said. Maybe there would be a group of band kids she could get to know. Maybe there would be a cute, intelligent boy who was unattached who would flirt with her. Such thoughts kept her from crying when she felt sad about leaving.

Nicky only bowled for three weeks on Alyssa's team, but she was eligible to bowl in the tournaments on April 1st. Their mothers watched them and talked together. Nicky had some decent scores, and she was happy with them. She even got a trophy for the most improved bowler.

The algebra teacher cut three people from the prep class because only six could go to the State Math Contest. Nicky had thought she knew who would be let go, but she was surprised one boy didn't move on with the rest of them. Four boys and two girls remained.

After gymnastics, Nicky talked with Elena, who was having problems with her father.

"Sometimes my boyfriend gives me a cig and I just take it, you know? It isn't a big deal. But my father thinks I smoke all the time and says my boyfriend is a bad influence. He yells, then he grounds me."

"What will you do? Will you keep seeing him?"

"Yes! We have a blast together. But now I can't even talk about things we do because Dad growls every time I mention him."

"My father never grounds me. It's too bad your father does."

"You're lucky. My father gets angry a lot," said Elena.

Nicky's father came home for a week in early April. She felt like he was a stranger. She was angry at him, but she felt ashamed. She didn't want to argue with him like Elena did with her father. She would never convince him to let them stay in Eagleton, and the attempt would only upset both of them.

CHAPTER 29

The State Math Contest

Zoey ended it with Dalton. They had only been steadies again for about a month. Dalton called Nicky, and they chatted. He didn't mention Zoey.

A few days later, Dalton called Nicky again.

"I need to ask you something."

"What?"

"I was wondering about that night. Naw. It's stupid. Never mind." He hung up.

The same thing happened an hour later, and he hung up again after mentioning Gage had told him something.

The next morning, Nicky and Gage waited for the bell to ring after band. "Gage, what did you say to Dalton? He's upset about something you said."

"Oh, he just asked about that night we talked. I didn't tell him much."

"You must have said something."

"I just told him you thought he didn't understand you."

"I wonder why that upset him," said Nicky.

The bell rang, and they went to their next class. It was true that Nicky didn't think Dalton understood her. But the talk with Gage across the hedge was confidential, even if it occurred two months ago. Nicky was irritated.

Dalton called that night. "What were you and Gage talking about the night when he helped me get my car out of the snow?"

"We were just talking."

"Why did you tell Gage I don't understand you?"

"Because you don't. I'm a quiet person. You're a talkative person."

"You aren't always that quiet."

"I usually am. It's hard for me to talk to someone every night."

"I didn't call you every night!"

"Almost. You need someone who wants to talk more than me."

"Didn't you like talking to me?"

"Sure, mostly. But I get tired. I'm tired now. I'll see you tomorrow."

She still couldn't explain how she felt to him. But at least she tried.

At lunch the next day, Bella was unhappy.

"Bad news. My father decided not to interview for a new job. I'm stuck here."

"Well, I'm glad!" said Paizlee. "I don't want any more of my good friends to leave."

"You're lucky. Everything is going to change for me," said Nicky.

"Oh, Nicky, can you play piano at the stage band concert for me? I can't play because I have to be at a dance rehearsal. They won't let anyone out of it who wants to dance at the recital."

"Sure. I guess I'll finally get to be in the stage band. But I wish you could be there. I'll probably mess up something terrible," said Nicky. She already felt a little nervous just thinking about it.

"I'll give you the music tomorrow in band. You'll see how easy the songs are."

The senior high band needed a bus to go to the State Fair in the summer, and they needed a way to pay for it. Mr. Gillette decided the kids could fundraise by selling jewelry to earn a cash commission. A salesman came in and handed out brochures with bright photos. Nicky wouldn't be going with them to the Fair, so she didn't need to sell it.

"Do you want to buy some jewelry? Look at this shiny chain. It would look great on you," said Grant.

"It's pretty, but I don't have money." She rarely babysat anymore.

"Oh, come on. Look at how pretty this one is." He showed her the photo and tried to convince her she needed it.

Nicky just shook her head. "You'll have to sell it to someone else."

Nicky saw Grant again with the other four math students on Saturday, which was the State Math Contest. The big auditorium at the technical college in Ridgeland City was full of kids from across the state, ready to tackle different math subjects from algebra and geometry to calculus.

When Nicky looked at the first test, she couldn't believe how easy it was. She got scared then because she knew she could make stupid mistakes on easy problems. The second test was even easier for her.

After a break, the students returned to the auditorium to learn who won the top five places. The announcer started with the ninth-grade finalist who won third place. A student from another school went up to get his trophy.

"The second-place winner is Grant from Eagleton!"

The five other Eagleton students and their teacher erupted in a cheer and pumped their fists as Grant went down to the stage to get the trophy. After the other winners were announced, the group high-fived and congratulated Grant as they left the auditorium together. They felt like a true team and wanted to know how everyone below third place ranked, but the rest of the rankings would be given later.

One beautiful spring day, Paizlee and Nicky walked to school.

"What did you learn at the dance line rehearsals yesterday?" Nicky asked.

"I'll show you. Just follow me." Paizlee put down her books, and they practiced steps on the sidewalk. They counted out loud and did the routine together.

"I'll show you whatever we learn. I wish you could try out with us. They work us hard, though, and you might get tired. We barely get time to have some water."

"I'd still enjoy it. Trying out for the team is worth getting sore."

"It will be if I make it. Otherwise, I'll be sore for nothing." They picked up their books and continued walking.

Ryan had his first track meet. He competed in three events and got first in high jump, third in high hurdles, and sixth in the 440. He was happy as he talked about the meet during supper.

A few days later, Nicky asked Alyssa to go to the track and watch a practice. They met after school and walked to the football field, which had the track circling it. They watched the runners, long-jumpers, and hurdlers.

"We should have joined track, Alyssa."

"I don't know. The hurdles look hard. I'd probably knock them all down."

"Maybe they don't have to do every event." The girls watched for a while, then walked home.

At the end of April, the math class found out how the rest of the competitors placed in the State Math Contest. Twenty-five people ranked in 4th through 10th places, which meant there were many ties. Trevor and Nicky tied for ninth place, while the other three tied for tenth place. Their six-person group all ranked in the top 10 places. Nicky felt proud of them. She wondered if Magnus City students competed in a state math contest.

The senior high band went on a field trip to watch a performance of multiple Ridgeland City bands at a Ridgeland City high school. Bella and Kinsey couldn't go because of school tests, so Nicky and McKenna sat alone together on the bus. The group went to a roller skating rink before they went to the school. Gage, Grant, and Chad, a new sophomore that year, played games in the arcade for a while, then joined Nicky and McKenna on the rink.

Gage and Grant invited Nicky to "snowball." Three people held hands and skated forward until the announcer blew a whistle. The trios had to turn and skate in the other direction. Gage was the one who turned them. McKenna was with Chad and another boy. They had a blast and Nicky laughed a lot.

After roller skating, the kids got lunch at a fast-food restaurant. Gage, Grant, and Chad stood in front of McKenna and Nicky in the line to order. McKenna asked Nicky to order for her while she got a booth. Gage and Grant asked Chad to get their order, and they went to the seating area on the right. As Nicky waited, she saw Gage appear several times before disappearing.

After Chad got his order, Nicky finally got the food and went around the corner to find McKenna. She saw the other four sitting in the same booth.

"Nicky! Over here! Look, we saved you a seat!" said Grant.

Nicky set the tray on the table and slid in next to Gage. When they finished, they walked to the school to watch the bands perform. By the time they got back to Eagleton on the bus, school was already out.

As Gage, McKenna, and Nicky walked home from the school, McKenna had a problem.

"I got on the bus at the last minute. Before we left, I asked Kinsey to stop by on her way home and tell my parents. She said she didn't want to. My parents will probably kill me for going without permission!"

"They won't kill you," said Nicky.

"What would your parents do?"

"They'd probably not let me do the next thing I wanted to do."

"Gage, what should I do?"

"Just say you were so excited you forgot. Or tell them you didn't know you should tell them. Or you're really, really sorry and you'll never do it again." He came up with ideas easily.

"Maybe I'll tell them all of that."

The next week, Nicky found out McKenna was grounded for a few nights. Nicky knew she would have gone on the field trip, even if she had gotten grounded like McKenna.

Nicky's father called a few days later. He had found a house for them in Norburg, a suburb of Magnus City. It was seven times the size of Eagleton. The house was close to the school, and it didn't need fixing up, which made him happy. He sent photos, which showed a family's things all around a strange house. Nicky tried to imagine living in the house, but she couldn't.

CHAPTER 30

Award Assemblies

After Nicky's mother finished her college semester, she brought home boxes and focused on packing the family's possessions. She planned to attend the college in Norburg in the fall.

Her mother wrote an article about Peaceful Bear Mountain for the county newspaper. She described the awe-inspiring panoramic view of the Ponderosa Hills to the south and southwest, and how she felt a spiritual connection with the mountain when she hiked to the top. Nicky wondered if they would ever climb it again.

Her parents set the date for moving: June 29th. Nicky's thoughts about "The Move" became more real once they had the name of the city and an image of their next house. The house had a bedroom in the basement which Ryan wanted, and their parents agreed he could have. Nicky wanted it too, but she decided not to make a big thing about it. She was more worried about the school, which had over 2,000 students in it. That was scary big.

Who would she meet there? Would they become good friends, like her group in Eagleton? She hoped so, yet she feared she wouldn't ever have such good friends again. She often missed everyone while she was still with them. The dark hot-air balloon over her head grew bigger.

Nicky congratulated Paizlee and Bella when they made the dance team. Nicky's old neighbors, Carly, her sister, and Abby were also chosen. At least all of them knew some of what they would be doing next year. She had no clue, except she would live in a new house with her mother, father, and brother in a new city, attend a new school, and play in band.

At a junior high assembly in the second week of May, coaches gave awards to the school athletes. Their teams had two trophies, one for the ninth-grade football team for winning the conference title, and a second-place trophy for the seventh-grade basketball team. The boys in each group went up one after another to get their certificates. Some got special awards like the highest scorer in points or the most valuable player.

The week before the junior high regular band and stage band concert, Nicky practiced the stage band songs at home on the piano and at lunch with the stage band. She was nervous because she wanted to do her best, yet she kept seeing herself failing.

When concert night arrived, she made it through the piano solos. She was relieved when she dropped her hands in her lap. Before the junior high band performed, Mr. Darnell turned to the audience.

"I want to say a few words about one of our ninth-grade students who has dedicated a great deal of her time to the band these last three years. She stepped in at the last minute to play piano for the stage band, and she helped the band directors whenever they needed help. She even made a strong showing at All-State Band tryouts.

"Mr. Gillette and I would like to thank Nicky and let her know how we'll miss her after her family leaves Eagleton this summer. Please give her a round of applause!"

As she stood up, a mix of embarrassment, happiness, and sadness overwhelmed Nicky. She thanked Mr. Darnell as he shook her hand.

The spring dance the next night was the last one she would enjoy with her Eagleton friends. Gage asked her to dance four times, and two were slow. Trevor asked her twice. When she wasn't dancing, she was laughing with the group on the bleachers.

When the school newspaper came out on Monday, it included Bella's article titled "A Tribute to our Junior High." Nicky thought her friend captured the experience of being in junior high very well. She especially agreed with the words "as I look back over the last three years, I realize that every year set me more at ease with my surroundings and acquaintances."

The high school seniors, including Gage's sister, graduated on Monday night. Nicky knew some seniors' names from sports and band. As she sat with the senior high band and played "Pomp and Circumstance" for them, she thought how special it was Gage could play the song for his sister.

On Tuesday, seventh, eighth, and ninth graders talked loudly in the junior high gym as they waited for the non-sports award assembly. Gage sat next to Trevor, who sat next to Nicky, Paizlee, and Bella. Trevor took out a package of mints from his pocket and offered them to Nicky. She took one and thanked him. Then he motioned for her to pass them to the right. Dalton, Grant, and Josh sat in front of them, and soon they wanted a mint, too.

Principal Dahlke and the teachers sat on folding chairs on the stage, and they motioned everyone to be quiet. The sound system screeched once or twice, but then it stopped.

"The kids in this school are the greatest kids in our state!" said Principal Dahlke.

Everyone cheered. Gage and Trevor shook each other's hands and got up to shake other people's hands, too.

"Now, let's give out the awards. We'll start with choir and band."

The choir teacher spoke into the microphone as she called the choir students' names. Each student went up to the stage to receive a certificate. Then Mr. Darnell did the same thing. When they got to the ninth graders, the cheers from her group were very loud. Even the kids who had transferred to senior high band got certificates.

Mrs. Matthews announced the math award. "Grant, please accept the Best Math Student award. You did a great job at the math contest."

Mrs. Colsen stepped to the microphone next. "The Best English student award goes to Bella. Bella, I believe you have an exciting journalism career ahead of you." Nicky and Paizlee cheered for their friend as she walked up to the stage.

Nicky's social studies teacher introduced an award named for a social studies teacher who had retired. The teacher wanted to encourage a love of history and learning about society.

"This year, I am honored to announce Nicky will receive this award. She has shown a strong interest in this subject. Nicky, please come up!"

Nicky was surprised when her name was called. She tried not to trip over Trevor and Gage's feet as she exited the aisle to walk to the stage. Her friends gave her loud applause.

Principal Dahlke announced the last award.

"This award goes to a student who worked hard, displayed creativity, was on the honor role and helped wherever she was needed. The Outstanding Ninth-Grade Student award goes to Bella! Bella, our school appreciates your talents."

Their entire group erupted in cheers, clapped, and whistled. Paizlee and Nicky leaned over to her and said, "Bella! You deserve this! It's fantastic!"

The students got their yearbooks on Friday, the last day of school. Ryan had some good pictures on the "Remember the 7th Grade" page. The very last photo in the book was Nicky speaking at the Student Council election the previous September. What a long time ago that seemed.

The kids had study halls the rest of the day. It was a warm spring day, and Nicky's class went out to the front lawn where they sat in groups as they signed each other's yearbooks.

Nicky wrote notes to tell her friends how she would miss them. Many of them wrote notes saying they were sad she was leaving, and they wished her the best of luck. Some people told her to write. Others thought she would be a "big hit" at the new school.

Nicky wondered if she would ever see them again.

CHAPTER 31

The Going-Away Party

Ryan picked up the ringing phone, and he yelled upstairs to Nicky, "It's Dalton!"

Her mother heard. "Nicky, we're waiting for a call from the real estate agent, so don't stay on very long."

"OK, Mom." Since her mother wasn't in school, she kept a close eye on the phone calls.

"Hi, Dalton."

"Hi, Nicky. Have you heard I'm a cook at the Crossings Drive-In?"

"Oh, cool. When did you start?"

"Last week. Gage and Trevor are muggers there this summer. Why aren't you working there?"

"I didn't think my parents would let me."

Dalton was smart to make some spending money before he left. Nicky wished she could work there again like last summer, even though she didn't really enjoy it.

"I'm on the baseball team again. I can play until we move in July. When are you moving?"

"End of June. I hate people in our house looking at all our stuff. I wish it would sell so they would stop."

"Having people in the house was a drag. Luckily, our house sold already. What've you been doing?"

"Reading and writing and other stuff."

"School's out, so why are you writing anything?"

"I just want to."

The publication of her mother's article about Peaceful Bear Mountain in the newspaper motivated Nicky to write something of her own.

"Nicky! Get off the phone, please!"

"I've got to go. Hope you have fun this summer, Dalton."

"Drop me a line sometime. Paizlee will have my new address."

"Goodbye, Dalton."

"Good luck, Nicky."

At dinner, her mother discussed the arrangements about the house sale and the movers. Even though the realtors had another offer on the house, if it fell through, the realtors would buy the house. They were sure it would sell that summer.

Her father's company would pay for movers to pack up the house on June 29th. Then she, Ryan, and Nicky would start driving the same night. The next day, they would meet her father in Magnus City. They had to stay in a motel for a week until the other people left the Norburg house.

With only four more weeks until they left, Nicky repeated to herself, "My life in Eagleton is over." It didn't seem real. Sometimes, she wanted to get on with it. Most of the time, she felt like she could wait forever. She wanted to be hopeful and brave, but she was afraid of the future.

One day, Paizlee and Nicky biked up to Wicker Drive. When they passed Gage's house, he was playing drums in his garage with Trevor and Grant on the guitars. The "Wicker Drive Band" was practicing. The girls stopped and listened for a while.

"Paizlee, you should be their lead singer now," said Nicky.

"No, they won't ask me," said Paizlee.

"I wonder who they'll get."

"I'm surprised they're even practicing."

"Maybe they'll get good and make some money."

"Highly unlikely," said Paizlee.

That week, Nicky's mother's relatives came to visit. Her grandmother, aunt, and her cousin, Sophia, stayed for several days. Sophia was the same age as Nicky. The group went to the big attractions in the Ponderosa Hills for one last time.

The next day, they relaxed at home. Nicky and Sophia were in the family room when they heard the phone ring. Nicky's mother answered it. After a few minutes, it rang again. Her mother called Nicky to pick up the second phone.

"Hi, Nicky. What's happening?" asked Gage.

"My relatives are here."

"Why didn't you and Paizlee talk to us the other day?"

"You were busy practicing. The band sounded good."

"We're terrible now, but we'll get better. I hope I'll see you before you move."

"Maybe we could ride up there again," said Nicky.

After they hung up, Nicky looked at Sophia.

"Is he your boyfriend?" asked Sophia.

"No. I don't have a boyfriend now."

"It sounded to me like you like him."

Sophia put a twist on the word "like," and Nicky knew she wondered if Nicky was attracted to Gage.

"Yeah, but it doesn't matter anymore. He had a girlfriend all year, anyway."

"Why doesn't it matter? You can always write to him."

"But I won't get to see him. He'll forget me."

"You give up too easily. If I were you, I'd keep writing and calling him until I could see him again. Of course, you might meet someone new in Norburg."

"The school there is huge. No one will even notice me."

"I wish I were in a bigger school. There isn't anyone new to meet where I am!"

Nicky desperately wanted to stay in Eagleton, while her cousin desperately wanted to leave her small town, just like Bella.

"The new boys won't be as good as the boys I know here."

"You don't know that. I would be so excited if I were you."

Nicky frowned and shrugged.

"Maybe things will be different after you move," said Sophia.

After her relatives left, Alyssa came by and gave Nicky a going-away present, a book which contained sayings. Nicky read some out loud.

"The love in your heart wasn't put there to stay. Love isn't love till you give it away. Friendship doubles your joys and divides your griefs." Nicky loved the book.

Nicky thought about buying gifts for her friends to show how much they meant to her. But she had a tough time focusing. She often just stared out the window for a long time and remembered the fun that year.

Her mother was worried about how to bring Ginger with them on the trip to the new house. They couldn't have her in the motel with them. Ryan was upset their parents would even consider not taking their dog to Norburg. He often took her for walks, and it was his job to feed her, so he would miss her the most. They asked everyone they knew whether they wanted a nice dog. But they didn't find anyone who could adopt her.

Nicky went up to Paizlee's house, and they planned a bike ride to Bella's house to take pictures of each other. The next day, they met and enjoyed finding places to pose. They wanted to see a movie together in Ridgeland City as soon as they could.

A few days later, Paizlee called.

"Hi, it's me. Bella and I are going to the drive-in to get something to drink. Can we pick you up on the way? We'll be there in 10 minutes."

"I'll get out my bike."

When they arrived at the drive-in and opened the door, Trevor greeted them. He was behind the counter working as the mugger. Then they saw Gage and Grant sitting at a table. The boys waved the girls over.

After they sat down, Paizlee began. "We wanted to give you something, so you'll always remember us."

"Always," said Gage.

"And forever," said Grant as he nodded.

"We got you a present. All five of us chipped in. But Gage and I picked it out," said Paizlee. She looked shyly at Gage, and he smiled.

"Oh, that's so nice," said Nicky. She regretted she didn't have anything for them.

"Here it is," said Bella. She slid a small box with a bow around it to Nicky.

Nicky opened the box. Inside was a gold-colored ID bracelet with her first name engraved on it.

"This is great! I love it! I'll wear it every day. Thanks!"

"Put it on!" said Gage and Grant together.

She put it on her left wrist, and they all admired it.

"You have to look at your own name," said Trevor from behind the counter. "I thought we should put 'Kee' on it, then you would know it was from us."

Paizlee rolled her eyes. She often thought Trevor said silly things.

"I'll know it's from you. I won't forget. I'll never forget any of you."

"You'll make new friends so you might," said Gage. "We'll be the 'old gang in Eagleton.'"

"I won't forget." Nicky shook her head from side to side.

She carefully put the bracelet back in the box and put it in her coat pocket, so she wouldn't lose it while riding home.

In the middle of June, Nicky's father's side of the family visited. His aunt and uncle came with two of their granddaughters who were Nicky's age. She wondered why so many people were visiting them. She only wanted to be around Eagleton people. When they arrived, her mother went out and welcomed them. Nicky delayed, but she finally made herself go downstairs.

After they had eaten supper and finished the dishes, the phone rang.

"Nicky, would you get the phone please?" said her mother.

"OK. Hello?"

"Hi, Nicky. It's Gage. Mr. Gillette left some music for you with me, but I can't come down there. Can you come up to my house?"

"Really? Why did he do that?"

"Uh...I saw him at church and...he said it was a present for you, but...he didn't know how to get it to you. So...I offered to keep it until I saw you."

She was suspicious, and she wondered why he was making up a story.

"We have company, so I can't today. Can I pick it up tomorrow?"

"No, I have to go somewhere with my parents tomorrow. Just ask your mother, OK?"

"Mom, Gage says he has some music for me at his house. Can I ride my bike up there?"

"Actually, I'll give you a ride, and then the rest of us will go to the park."

"Thanks, Mom. I guess I'll be up there soon. See you later, Gage."

"See you then!"

Her mother drove Nicky, Ryan, and her two cousins up to Gage's house. Nicky thought it would only take a few minutes to pick up the music. Gage said the music was downstairs, and he led her to the basement stairway. It was dark, but he didn't turn on the light. Then the light went on, and she heard, "Surprise!!"

Almost everyone in their group was there. Trevor, Grant, Josh, Dalton, Alyssa, Kinsey, Paizlee, Bella, and Gage. After expressing her surprise and greeting everyone, she said she had to tell her mother about the going-away party.

Her mother told her Gage had talked to her about the party while Sophia visited. While her mother had greeted their company earlier that night, she told them about it.

Nicky and her friends hung out in the basement room. They played cards and other games while they listened to music. They talked and laughed a lot.

Before everyone left the party, she gave them her new address. Her friends signed a blank white poster the kids had taped to the wall.

"Hope you liked the party. Have fun and don't ever forget us. Good luck! Kinsey."

"Don't forget the super, great, terrific times we have had together!! Don't forget me either!! Luv ya. Grant."

"Remember the good times. Dalton."

"Bye Kee. Take it easy and don't forget all of us deadbeats in old Eagleton. Good luck in Norburg. Trev."

"Remember me please! You are a really nice friend. Hope to hear from you. I'd better! Love, Gage."

Paizlee and Bella just signed their names. Alyssa and Josh didn't write anything. When they were all done, Gage and Trevor took it down, rolled it up, and gave it to her.

Nicky, Paizlee, and Bella started to walk home when Gage and Trevor decided to join them. They walked down Nola Drive together until Paizlee and Bella went straight toward Paizlee's house, and Gage and Trevor walked down the hill with Nicky. They each shook her hand before they left her to go back up the hill. She watched them walk away in the fading daylight. She might never see them again.

Nicky's mother drove her, Paizlee, and Bella to a movie in Ridgeland City in late June. They talked and laughed continuously. They promised each other they would write letters every week. Nicky didn't want to part with them, and after dropping her friends at their houses, tears welled in her eyes. She blinked quickly.

The day before the movers came, Ryan and Nicky rode with their mother to take Ginger to the veterinarian, who lived outside of town. The vet said he would find a home for her. Ryan petted and reassured his dog she would be fine after they left. He got into the car, and he slouched in the back seat. As they drove away, the vet's beautiful blue and green peacock spread its feathers. Nicky thought it was a hopeful sign Ginger would be adopted by a nice family.

But Ryan was angry that night. Their dog was part of the family. How could they leave her in Eagleton? He yelled at their mother and slammed the door to his room before he turned his music up.

June 29th was a beautiful, green summer day. The movers arrived early. Nicky and Ryan had packed up their possessions, and their suitcases were ready. Boxes were everywhere. The movers took all the furniture out to the truck, and soon Nicky was sitting on the floor of her empty room. She leaned against the wall and read a book to stay out of the way. The day didn't seem real, and she couldn't think about the past or the future.

After the movers finished loading all the boxes, Nicky went outside to watch them drive off with their belongings in the moving van. Her mother had cleaned each room as the movers finished, but she went through the house once again. Ryan and Nicky carried the last things to the car, and Ryan got in the front seat while Nicky sat in the back. She watched her mother lock the front door to the old white house with the stained-glass windows and felt tears fill her eyes.

After her mother got behind the wheel, she said in a cheerful voice, "Tighten your seat belts, kids! Here we go, off on our new adventure!" She tried to put a positive spin on their departure.

As they drove south on Central Avenue, Nicky and Ryan were quiet as they looked at their small town. They looked at the white rocks on the ridge to the north, which spelled out the town's name. They looked northeast to see the top of Peaceful Bear Mountain hiding behind the ridge. They looked toward Forestview Glen where they had lived and hiked in the Ponderosa Hills, which spread out dark and mysterious to the south.

They passed the dentist's office, Devon Creek, the hospital, Crossings Drive-In, the grocery store, and Eagleton Inn. Once they were on the interstate, they passed Dalton's house, Mrs. Schmidt's house, and other landmarks Nicky knew well. She kept looking at the lovely green land and wondering how long it would be before she would see it again.

The time had come. She was leaving Eagleton and her pep band friends.

PART 2

LIFE AFTER

CHAPTER 32

The Big City

The trio arrived in Magnus City during rush hour after staying in a motel overnight. Nicky's mother drove with a tense look, and her hands clenched the wheel as she drove on the highway through the middle of the city in heavy traffic.

"Mom, there's a car on your left," said Ryan.

"I couldn't see him at all! This is crazy," said her mother.

After they crossed the Magnus River, old houses lined the hillsides above both sides of the highway. Her mother sighed with relief as she parked the car at the hotel. When they knocked on the door, her father opened it and welcomed them in.

"You're here! You made it safe and sound! I'm happy to see you."

Her parents hugged, then her father hugged his kids. But Nicky and Ryan were tired, and a little wary, so they held back. They were not as happy to be in the new city as he was.

"How did the drive go?"

"The traffic was nerve-racking. It's been a while since I drove in big city traffic," said her mother.

"I was worried about that, but you'll get used to it. I checked in here at noon. My co-worker will be happy to have his basement back." He laughed. "We'll go see them sometime this week."

"I've been sightseeing, and I can't wait to show you guys around the area. We'll ride a bus tomorrow to some places I want us to see.

There are bus routes all over the city and we can get a pass to hop on and off wherever we want."

But it rained all night and kept raining the next day until the streets were flooded. Her father decided not to tour the city until the weather cleared up. The family ate meals in restaurants, swam at the motel pool, played card games, and watched shows.

The third day was clear, and they walked across the street to the bus stop. As they rode, they saw many people on the bus and on the streets. Nicky had traveled to several large cities with her parents before, but this new city was overwhelming.

They visited downtown, the Federal Reserve building, and the tallest skyscraper. On the viewing floor, tall windows on all sides revealed a wide view of the city.

"Come over here. See the Magnus River? Follow it north as far as you can see it. Our new house is in that area," said her father.

"That looks far," said Ryan.

Nicky was stunned at how big the city was. When her father had first described the metropolis, she couldn't picture it. Even when he showed them the map, it didn't make sense. Now she could see there was no space, fields, walls, or anything dividing up the areas. Everything was one big forest of buildings and streets.

From downtown, they rode to Magnus Falls and toured the oldest house built on the west side of the Magnus River. As they waited for each bus, Nicky walked up and down the sidewalk and watched the cars whiz by. She wanted to return to the safe hotel.

On Sunday, Nicky wrote to Paizlee and Bella about some of the places she had seen and how big the city was.

Over the next few days, the family toured her father's company, then went to a big park with a zoo. They went to have dinner with her father's co-worker, his wife, and son.

The group watched the Independence Day fireworks over the State Fairgrounds from the co-worker's front yard. The loud and spectacular fireworks exploded skyward from behind the fairground's outer wall and above the houses. Nicky thought about last summer when she went with Alyssa to the dam near Eagleton. The fireworks were smaller at the dam, but they exploded in the wide-open sky. She remembered how she had enjoyed that evening.

The next day, her father drove 10 miles north along a main avenue to their new house in Norburg. He pointed out each green city limit sign. They saw three before they came upon the Norburg sign. Nicky's mind numbed as the houses went on and on.

The olive-green house was small, and it looked like all the other houses around it. The neighborhood of similar houses reminded her of a song she had heard about ticky-tacky houses all the same style on a hillside.

The detached garage had a basketball hoop, which Ryan liked. Nicky saw a garden in the back. Her father had gardened when they lived at the Forestview Glen house, and he planned to use it.

The family unpacked the moving van when it arrived. Nicky hung up clothes in the closet and taped pictures to the wall of the northwest corner bedroom. Her mother set up the kitchen and went to buy groceries. It was hot and muggy outside, and her father turned on the air conditioner. They had never lived in a house with an air conditioner, and Nicky sat near it until she got too cold.

A few mornings later, Nicky rode her bike around the flat neighborhood and out by the railroad tracks. She saw many oak, ash, and maple trees, but few pine trees. She missed the beautiful Ponderosa Hills.

The streets curved around and dead-ended in unexpected places. Some streets had the same names, but they were disconnected. She couldn't figure out where she was, but she eventually made it back to the house. She felt homesick for Eagleton's straight streets, which ran from north to south and east to west. Nicky liked the logical layout better than the Norburg maze.

The next day, Nicky and Ryan walked to the shopping center to get some comic books and treats. They walked a block until they arrived at a fenced in green space on the right with school buildings on two sides.

"These must be the practice fields," said Ryan.

"Look at the school. This one must be the high school because it's bigger. The one over there must be the junior high," said Nicky.

"They're twice the size of Eagleton," said Ryan.

"At least, maybe even three times as big."

They continued past the practice fields to Northland Avenue, a busy road. As they turned the corner and looked right across the parking lot, they saw the front entrance of the high school. The school was three stories tall and stretched two blocks long. At the end of the buildings were more sports fields. Across the road, the bleachers blocked the view of the football field. Everything seemed gigantic compared to what they had known. They reached the shopping center, got a few snacks, and walked the mile home.

Nicky wanted to talk to her friends about how she dreaded attending the big high school. She barely looked at her father when he reassured the kids they would get used to the new place. He didn't understand how she felt like a piece of luggage he had picked up and plopped down. She had no control over her life, except to withdraw.

Nicky got a letter from Paizlee, and she smiled as she reread it multiple times. Dalton wrote one on the way to his new home, which was hundreds of miles away.

The brother and sister tried to think of things to do. They played ping-pong, took their tennis rackets to the nearby tennis court, biked around the neighborhood, and watched shows. They watched the news, but the number of suburbs with unfamiliar names confused them. They were bored and tired of talking only to each other.

At the end of July, her mother went with Ryan to register at Norburg Junior High School. Then she went with Nicky to register at Norburg Senior High School. The high school guidance counselor put Nicky in the advanced sophomore math class and the German I class. But she wasn't certain which of the three bands Nicky would be in.

As Nicky and her mother left the building, Nicky walked quickly to the car as she frowned, hunched her shoulders, and barely responded to her mother's comments.

CHAPTER 33

The Quiet Neighborhood

When Ryan and Nicky were outside, they wondered how there could be so many houses and so few people around. Occasionally, a car passed by, but the neighborhood was quiet otherwise.

Nicky wished she had a job. Even carhopping like last summer would be better than the boredom she felt. However, she was clueless about potential workplaces. School began in less than a month, so she couldn't start something, anyway.

Nicky wanted to be at band camp with her Eagleton friends. She wished she could rehearse the dance line routines with Paizlee and Bella. She disliked this strange, no-friend land. She no longer had a social life, and she only talked to her family.

Nicky wrote to Gage, Trevor, and Grant. She got a letter from Elena on Monday which cheered her.

"I really miss you, and you have such a great personality everyone loves. You won't have any trouble making friends. Don't let all those kids scare you because they're just trying to make friends and getting through school, too. Let people know you care about them, and they'll come around. They're as curious about you as you are about them. Stay cool and try not to worry so much.

"Remember, everyone loves you and misses you here and we are only a letter away. That means me! Never forget me because I won't ever forget you and the fun times we had. Keep your head high and a smile on your face and you'll have so many friends you won't know what to do."

School wouldn't be the same without Elena.

Nicky got a letter from Alyssa on Tuesday. Then, on Saturday, she got a letter from Gage. Paizlee had told him Nicky felt strange about writing to boys, and he assured her he was like any other person. He went to a big music concert in Ridgeland City, and he had his wisdom teeth out.

He reminded her he knew how tough it was to move to a new neighborhood, and he offered to help with any problems. He told her to reach out whenever she wanted to.

Nicky read the letters over and over. She wanted to talk, bike, and work at the drive-in with all of them, but they were far away. She was dying of thirst for her friends in this alien place.

Her mother registered at the community college, which was over by the river. Her father worked every weekday, and when he was home, he worked on his car or watched sports. Nicky hibernated in her room and burrowed into fiction. Ryan played basketball when he wasn't helping with the car.

In early August, Paizlee called.

"My dad has to go to a specialist south of Magnus City. If we can find a place to meet, Dad says we can get together!" said Paizlee.

"That would be great! We went to this big mall in Southville. Maybe we can meet there," said Nicky.

The girls worked it out with their parents, and Nicky marked off the days until she could see her friend again.

One day Nicky was sitting on her bike in the driveway when a girl walked up and introduced herself. Her name was Kristi, and she would be a sophomore like Nicky. They timidly asked each other questions. Nicky went swimming with Kristi and her sister a week later. They met outside several times and took walks.

"Why is it so quiet around here?" asked Nicky.

"I don't know," said Kristi.

"Where do the other kids hang out?"

"At each other's houses in the basements, probably. It's so hot out here." Kristi fanned her neck with her hand.

"Do you know if people are on vacation?"

"Some are. Some work."

"Where do they work? In Eagleton, I worked at the drive-in. Is there a drive-in around here?"

"Not that I know of."

"In Eagleton, my friend Alyssa and I got this comic book and rode out to the city park. Do you like comic books?"

Kristi shrugged and looked away. Then she looked at Nicky.

"Did you watch the show about the soccer player last night?"

Nicky had, so they started talking about the show. Nicky decided not to talk about Eagleton again. Every time she brought up what she used to do, Kristi changed the subject as if she wasn't interested.

Ryan started football practice with the eighth graders. Nicky envied him because he met people and had something to do.

Nicky got more letters from her friends in Eagleton, and she wrote back quickly. She tried to be supportive and encouraging of them. She tried not to complain about her new life, but that was difficult.

When the day came to meet Paizlee, Nicky talked with her mother the whole way. She smiled when she saw Paizlee across the restaurant and hurried over to her. Nicky's mother went to a different table to talk with Paizlee's parents. Nicky asked what Paizlee had been doing.

"I've gone to a few movies and the drive-in a few times with Lily, and we saw Gage. He didn't seem very happy to me. Bella has been at a dance camp, and we've only talked a few times."

"I wish we could both work at the drive-in. Wouldn't it be fun to have shifts together?" said Nicky.

"Yes, but I wouldn't want to work in the heat outside. Have you made any new friends yet?"

"Just one, but she's hard to talk to."

"Maybe you'll have some classes together and get closer."

"Maybe. She's not in band, though."

"There might be some flutists you can become friends with."

"There are three bands. I hope I am in one with some friendly kids. But they won't be you and Bella, though."

They shared for two precious hours before Paizlee's father said he was tired, and they needed to leave. On the way home, Nicky stared out the car window, didn't respond to her mother, and almost cried.

Nicky's grandmother visited, and the family did some sightseeing. Her father planned a four-hour drive to meet his aunt, who would drive her grandmother back to the town where the sisters had grown up. Nicky wanted to watch a movie instead.

"Do I have to go? The trip will be boring, like everything here," said Nicky.

"Yes, you have to go. Why are you even asking? Stop complaining. I expect you to be nice to everyone," snapped her father. He got up from the table and went outside.

"Honey, things aren't that bad, and they will get better. You need to try harder to see that," said her grandmother. "Try to be positive."

"I don't know how. I hate it here, Grandma," said Nicky. But she went on the drive.

At the end of August, Nicky walked to the sophomore orientation at the high school. She learned three junior high freshman classes combined in the new school. After the assembly, she wandered around with her new schedule and eventually found her classrooms. The band room and her locker were at the west end of the school, but her classes were at the east end.

Nicky watched as students greeted their friends and chatted in small groups. No one talked to her. She looked down at her gold ID bracelet and wondered what her friends were doing.

Nicky remembered how she didn't want to go to school in eighth grade, then she had fun. However, she was starting from scratch in Norburg. She was a new kid, and an outsider.

CHAPTER 34

The Big High School

On the first day of school, Nicky walked the short distance with Kristi. They didn't have any classes together, so Kristi said goodbye as soon as they entered the rear school door. Nicky went to her locker and put her lunch sack in it. Her first class was Advanced Algebra. Then she had German I, Health Issues, English, and social studies. Symphonic Band was the last hour.

"This class has lunch in the middle of class," said her English teacher, Mrs. Sheplan. "We'll meet for 20 minutes, then you'll leave to eat. Please return here, as quietly as you can, at 11:35."

The cafeteria was not large enough for all the students, but Nicky swiftly calculated it must be big enough for over 700 students. She chewed her lip as she left the English class and hurried to her locker to get her lunch sack. She followed the flow of students to the basement cafeteria. As kids darted in and out of the doors, she took a deep breath and entered.

Long tables with attached benches filled the room. Students stood with trays in the winding lunch line, dashed around, or sat at the tables. Nicky looked at all the bodies and froze. She would have to squeeze between two people who she didn't know, and she didn't see anyone else with a sack lunch. Nicky turned around and left. She put her lunch back in her locker and returned to the empty classroom to read until class resumed.

As Nicky walked into the band room, she saw the chairs were arranged in a semi-circle, like Eagleton's band room. Girls with flutes sat in the first nine chairs on the right hand of the director, so she sat in the tenth chair.

"Hi, I'm Laila," said the girl in the ninth chair.

"I'm Nicky."

"You're in my English class." Nicky hadn't recognized her.

The band director told the kids the band rules. After class, Nicky walked to her locker, then met Kristi by the back door to walk home.

When the English class went down to lunch the next day, Nicky again felt overwhelmed by all the chaos in the cafeteria. But she didn't want to skip lunch again. She didn't know where to sit until she spotted Laila with a sack lunch and an empty spot next to her.

"Hi Laila. Is anyone going to sit here?"

Laila shook her head no. Laila introduced her to two friends, but the cafeteria noise was loud, and it was tough to hear what she said. The next day, Nicky brought her sack lunch to class. It would save time, so she wouldn't have to stop at her locker. When Laila saw her, she agreed it was a good idea, and she brought her own sack to English the next day.

The band kids were quiet during the breaks, which amazed Nicky because everyone talked in Eagleton. During the first week, they auditioned for chair assignments.

Nicky learned a different band, the Varsity Band, played as the pep band at games. But this band was the "Football Band," which meant they marched for halftime shows and parades. They would practice marching during band class, but sometimes, they would meet after school. The other kids had ordered their uniforms in the summer. The director asked for her size and informed her the uniform wouldn't arrive until after the band marched at a football game a week from Friday, so she wouldn't march. She didn't care.

Nicky yearned to go back to the Eagleton band. She wanted to talk to her friends as they put their instruments together. She wanted Mr.

Gillette as her band director, someone who knew her, knew how hard she practiced, and how much she cared about music.

On Labor Day, Nicky's family drove to a local lake to walk. After her father parked, Nicky kept reading a book while the others got out. Her father opened the car door.

"Nicky, let's go."

"Can I finish this chapter?"

"No. You can read your book anytime. Get out of the car."

"Why?"

"Because we're walking around the lake today…as a family. You never want to do anything with us this summer! Why are you being such a brat?"

Her father emphasized the word "brat." Nicky's eyes opened wide because her father had never said something that mean to her.

"You need an attitude adjustment, young lady. Now put your book down and come be a part of this family!" He glared at her.

Nicky was stunned and tears started rolling down her cheeks.

"You don't need to yell at her," said her mother.

Her father turned around and headed to the lake.

Nicky got out of the car, wiped her tears with her hand, and her mother locked the car. They walked in a line behind her father while her mother said the lake was pretty. No one responded.

The next week, Mrs. Sheplan told the class she was an adviser for a group called SHARE, which helped seniors by visiting them in nursing homes and assisting them if they needed something done. Nicky went to the first meeting after school that day. The girls seemed to know each other, and no one said anything to her. Nicky decided she didn't fit in with them.

The band director announced the new seating chart. He assigned Nicky to the seventh chair, and she no longer shared a folder with Laila, who was the tenth chair. Her new folder mate was a junior who didn't talk to Nicky.

Nicky kept walking to school with Kristi, but as soon as Kristi turned down the hall, Nicky felt herself shrink and disappear. She was a little fish in a vast lake. She didn't say hi to anyone, and no one greeted her. She didn't talk to people in class, except for a few words with Laila.

By the end of the week, Nicky familiarized herself with the easiest route to her classrooms. Some of her classes were two stories and a long hall apart. She found the restrooms, but they each had long lines between classes. Some teachers stood in the hall as monitors, so the kids didn't talk while they rushed to get to their next class on time.

Nicky wrote letters to all of her close friends and told them about her new school, band, and classes. She was eager to hear back from them.

Kristi invited her to walk to the varsity football game on Friday, since Nicky couldn't march in the band.

"I'll introduce you to my friends from ninth grade when we get there. I'm not sure who will be there though. Maybe Jocelyn and Morgan. If Morgan is there, her boyfriend probably will be, too."

The night was warm, and they didn't need jackets. They entered the gate and the wide green field opened up in front of them. The stadium was bigger and nicer than the one in Eagleton. The teams were on the field, about to kick off and start the game. Nicky heard the pep band music as Kristi saw her friends, and Nicky followed her over to them.

"Here's Morgan! This is Nicky. She's new here."

Kristi saw another friend a few feet away and started talking to her. She remembered to introduce Nicky, but pretty soon Kristi was talking and laughing with her old friends, and Nicky felt left out. She had lost track of their names, and she felt like a sheep as she followed Kristi, who laughed and darted from one group of her friends to another.

Nicky remembered last year when she knew almost everyone she saw. She found a seat on the bleachers, alone in the crowd, and she watched the game, saw the Football Band march at halftime, and listened to the pep band and cheerleaders. Kristi found her at the end, and they walked back together as Kristi shared news about her group.

Nicky dreaded opening the school door the next Monday and entering the crowded halls. She plodded through the following days when Laila and Kristi were the only people she knew, and she rarely saw other people twice in a day. Nicky often felt like a silent ghost, present but invisible, watching and listening to everyone else.

Nicky's Eagleton friends hadn't written since school started. She wanted to know how the first month of school went for them. Every day, she checked the mailbox, but it was empty, and she ran to her room and cried. She missed them, and she was upset they didn't seem to miss her. Nicky sat at the piano one day after playing one of the stage band songs. When her mother arrived home, Nicky's shoulders were hunched, and her head was in her hands.

"Were there any letters today?" her mother asked.

"No. No one cares," Nicky said. She wiped her eyes with a tissue, but she couldn't stop the tears.

"They'll probably write soon. The start of school is a busy time."

"Not for me this year," said Nicky.

"I'm sure things will get better. You'll start to meet people and make friends here."

"But I miss my old friends! I want to go back to Eagleton."

"Maybe we should talk to your father."

The next day after dinner, the three of them sat in the living room while Ryan watched a show downstairs.

"What's going on?" asked her father.

"I don't like this school," said Nicky.

"You just started there. You have to give it time."

"But, Dad, it's so big. Only Kristi and Laila talk to me."

"It'll take time to make new friends. When I was in the middle of my sophomore year, my parents moved out to a new farm, and I started at a different school."

His second school was fifteen miles from the first one, so he could go back sometimes to see his old friends. Both were small schools, not a mega school like Norburg. They had family in the area as well.

"I focused on my schoolwork, and I made friends and adjusted. You will, too. Since you like to read, spend more time in the library."

"How can I make friends in the library?"

"Well, think of something else then."

Nicky was frustrated, and she felt hot tears swell. Her father must not have had close friends like Nicky had in her old school. Otherwise, he would understand what it was like to leave and miss them.

"I want to go home," said Nicky.

"Where your mother and I are is your home."

"This is not my home! I want to go back to Eagleton."

"We all live here now, and you WILL be happy here." He emphasized "will," as if he could force her to be happy. "You need to accept the way things are."

"But I hate it here," she sobbed.

He turned his head and looked out the living room window.

"If only my friends would write more, that would help."

"Funny thing about friends." He looked at her. "They tend to forget you until you come into their lives again."

His remarks made her cry harder. She knew her friends wouldn't forget her. She wanted to see them intensely, and she was in pain.

"You need to pull yourself up by your own bootstraps. You'll have to make the best of this place." He went downstairs to watch television with Ryan as she dashed to her room and shut her door.

Nicky sat on the edge of her bed, doubled over, and tensed her abdominal muscles as she screamed silently. Norburg was a horrid, huge school, and she would never have close friends there. Her father had sentenced her to prison, and he didn't even care. Her anger ran through her body. He made her feel like she made a big deal out of nothing. She thought he loved her, but she had been happy, and he destroyed that happiness. She wanted to be back in Eagleton.

The next morning, she awoke with tired eyes. She grudgingly told herself that she would have to deal with the problems alone. Her parents wouldn't help her.

Her father was so wrong. Her friends hadn't forgotten her because they were great friends.

CHAPTER 35

Incredible Thirst

Nicky began reading some poetry, and she wrote a few poems to help her express her feelings.

A Lonely Beginning

Out of breath
Trying to outrun all the emotions
Pushing against my chest.
Now the dam breaks:
The flood begins all over again:
The mailbox was empty,
No letters today,
No word or thought sent by a friend.

Our residence is no longer
Where I wish it to be:
My father has moved our family.
With the severing of ties
Came the wretched feeling
That lingers in my heart.
I had just begun to know
The persons I called friends.

Leaving Pep Band Friends

Now the good times are over.
Why must all strings be broken
Between friends so young
Who have no choice
But to go along?
The road lies ahead
Though I would like to return
To those times in the past.

I write, no response.
I am alone
Without friends
In a world much bigger
So much more impersonal.
The people who love me
Try to protect and comfort me
In this sea of tears.

Though they try
My feelings
Do not change.
Why can't they see
All that's going on
Inside of me?
No way to go back
Without hurting the people I love.

I must go forward.
New experiences await
If only I choose.
Shall I accept
Or reject
The change in my life?
Confusion inside.
Loneliness.

Nicky was separated from her Eagleton friends, and the car of time drove her farther away from them each day. Every morning, she took out her gold ID bracelet and looked at it. She thought about the friends who gave it to her. At least, she would finally get to take the driver's education class the last week of September. She dreamed about driving back to Eagleton.

Nicky caught a cold virus. Over the weekend, she grew thirsty, and hunger gnawed at her even as she blew her nose. On Monday at school, she stopped at water fountains to guzzle water multiple times, and at home, she drank glass after glass of water. Her mouth was still dry. Her thirst was incredible, and it grew on Tuesday.

On Wednesday, Nicky rushed to the bathroom immediately after every class. She was in agony as she awaited her turn. She didn't sleep well that night, and she was exhausted on Thursday morning. She found her mother at the kitchen sink.

"Mom, something is wrong with me. I can't stop drinking water, and I barely slept last night."

"I heard you. I've noticed you're eating a lot."

"I can't go to school because I can't sit through a class."

"I have tests this morning, but I'll try to get a clinic appointment this afternoon."

Nicky stayed at home until the appointment. At the clinic, the medical assistant asked her to step on the weight scale. She had lost five pounds that week, which was odd.

The doctor came into the room, asked questions, then did a physical exam. He asked for a urine sample, and Nicky had no trouble providing it. When he returned to the room after a long delay, the doctor sat across from Nicky on his rolling stool, but he didn't look at her. He opened a manilla folder, and he spoke slowly.

"Nicky has juvenile Type 1 diabetes," he said. Then he stopped.

Nicky saw her mother's jaw drop. Her mother looked at her and tears welled in her eyes. What was it? What was diabetes? It must be bad because her mother was upset.

"Nicky, your pancreas has stopped making insulin for your body. Your blood sugar is 520 when it should be below 100. You could die if you don't get some insulin soon, so you must go to the hospital right away. You'll have to give yourself insulin shots and learn how to eat according to the diabetic diet. It will be difficult, but if you follow the guidelines, you'll learn to live with it."

"When will it go away?" asked Nicky.

"It will never go away." The doctor looked at her with sad eyes.

Nicky looked down at her hands, and her mind went blank.

"What do we need to bring to the hospital?" asked her mother.

"May I go to the car now?" asked Nicky before the doctor answered.

"Yes. I'll be there as soon as we make the arrangements." Her mother gave her the car keys.

Nicky rushed out of the exam room, and as soon as she was out the clinic door, she ran to the car. She wanted to keep running past it, to run away. But she knew she couldn't escape her body. Her tears rolled down her cheeks as she got into the car. She gulped for air as if a landslide was crushing her. She used her hands to wipe the tears, and she leaned her head back to breathe better. The doctor said she could die without medication.

When her mother got in the car, she was crying, too. Somehow, she drove home to get some things for the hospital stay. She called Nicky's father to let him know what they had learned, and he would meet them at the hospital.

The first insulin shot wasn't painful because she had allergy shots, but soon Nicky wanted the nurses to stop. After a few days at the hospital, her mother joined her for the diabetes education classes. When Nicky gave herself an insulin injection the first time, she had trouble because her brain didn't want her arm to pierce her skin. But after several days, she learned to count to five and insert the needle.

Nicky learned until her head was ready to explode, but the educator said it was all important. If Nicky wasn't careful, she would develop complications, such as kidney disease, heart disease, limb loss, or blindness. The ultimate complication was death from too much or too little insulin, and that was a daily risk.

While Nicky was in the hospital, she missed the start of Driver's Ed class, and her parents said she should wait to take it the next spring. She wondered what other horrific events would happen in the meantime. Incredibly, the big, dark, hot-air balloon of despair had reached a gigantic size. She was trapped in its shadow.

After Nicky was home, she watched the Homecoming Parade on Northland Avenue on Friday afternoon, and she saw Laila and the other flutes pass by. She was supposed to be marching in it, but she was still absent from school, and she didn't have her uniform yet.

Laila called, and Nicky told her she had diabetes. She was sympathetic, and she invited Nicky and Gwen from their lunch group to her house. Nicky ate nothing because the snacks weren't on her meal plan, and she looked with envy at the other girls as they ate without thinking. They didn't need insulin to help them digest what they ate.

Nicky got a letter from Paizlee and one from Bella. They told her all about their first month of school. They were overwhelmed with homework and higher expectations. The dance line required hours of their time every day. Paizlee had stopped playing flute in band, but Bella still played, and she was on Student Council.

Nicky wrote back to them, and also to Alyssa and her cousin Sophia. She let all of them know she had diabetes. What would they think of the new disaster that happened to her?

In the first week of October, she marched in the band at halftime of the varsity football game. Her uniform was uncomfortable, and she had to wear a huge furry hat, which didn't stay on well.

As she watched the second half of the game, Nicky was reflective as she sat in the midst of the cheering crowd of fans. Since moving to Norburg, her life had turned upside down. Her social life wasn't what she wanted, and she had gotten a terrible disease. Once upon a time, she had felt content. She hadn't realized how lucky she had been.

Nicky regretted some of her actions and words in eighth and ninth grade. She wished she had been more active in Student Council. She wished she had not stopped piano lessons. She wished she had been nicer to Dalton. She wished she had been a better friend. She wished she could take back some of the times when she had been irritated at people. She wished she hadn't ever gossiped.

Dalton and Gage had been successful and well-liked after they moved to Eagleton. She guessed Dalton was doing great because he could talk and joke easily with people. He would make friends in sports, like her brother. But she was a failure because she couldn't even make more than one friend in band.

Over the next several weeks, Nicky began criticizing herself if she made any error. If she forgot a book at home, bumped into someone, or made a mistake on homework, she told herself she was an idiot. She didn't know how to do anything right.

*Nicky thought about ways to end her misery. Maybe she could ride her bike out to the swampy area near the creek not too far from the railroad tracks. She could hide and freeze to death overnight. Or, after she learned to drive, she could drive far into the country where no one would find her body. They would all just think she ran away. Her anguish would be over if she died.

She could never do any of those things. She didn't know why she was thinking about them.

*This passage may trigger those who have considered suicide. Please see Appendix A "Suicide and Crisis Prevention Lifeline" for help.

CHAPTER 36

Her Refusal

When she wasn't catching up on her homework, Nicky watched and read a lot of news. She rarely saw good news, only a terrible world of politics, the dying planet, endangered species, disease, and violence. If she grew up, everything would still be awful, so what was the point of growing up? Why even go to school?

Even thinking about her Eagleton friends didn't help sometimes. They were lucky. They were at football games, dance line practices, band practices, and enjoying life together without her.

When Nicky awoke one morning, she thought about how tired she was of her life. The doctors had told her she would die if she didn't have any insulin. She had been thinking about that fact for a while. She didn't know how fast she would die, but she would die. After she got dressed, she went to lie on the couch.

"Nicky, hurry up and get your coat on. You'll be late for school," said her mother.

"I'm not going," said Nicky.

"You have to go. Now get off the couch and get ready."

"I hate school. I won't go to a place that I hate. I'm quitting."

"I've never heard you talk like that! What's wrong with you? I have to get to my class, and you can't stay home."

"I didn't give my insulin shot." Nicky said the words softly.

"Nicky! What do you mean? You've been doing so well taking care of your diabetes. Why won't you give your shot today?" Her mother knew the danger if she didn't give it.

"Because...I...don't...want...to...live."

Nicky was serious, and she wouldn't budge. Her mother pleaded with her to give it, but Nicky faced the back of the couch and refused to speak or look at her. Her mother called her father, and he drove home to deal with her.

"Nicky, get off that couch now! We'll talk at the table" said her father when he arrived.

She huddled for a few more seconds, then stood and followed him to the kitchen table. Her mother sat with a tissue and wiped away tears. Her father tried to reason with Nicky, but she kept her chin in her crossed arms on the table and wouldn't respond. She was done trying to adjust to the friendless school and diabetes, and she didn't care about her life anymore. She wasn't even crying.

They convinced her to listen to a doctor tell her about what would happen without insulin, so they drove her to the emergency department of the hospital. She sat on a hospital bed while the staff and her parents discussed what to do in the hall. The doctor who told her she had diabetes came into the room to talk to her alone.

"What's wrong, Nicky?"

"I hate my life." She didn't look at him.

"Your parents said you won't give yourself insulin. What's going on?"

"I want to die."

"I have a hard time believing that. Did something happen?"

She shrugged and avoided his eyes as she stared at the curtain.

"What do you believe happens to you after you die?"

"It doesn't matter."

"Do you believe in heaven?"

"No."

"Well, I do, and most Christians do. Doesn't your family go to church?"

"No."

"Do you know who Jesus is?"

She turned her head and squinted at him. "Not really."

"Jesus can save you from sin and suffering. Because He died for our sins, those who believe in Him will go to heaven. But if you don't, you won't. You'll go to hell."

Nicky stared at him, then looked away. Her parents never talked about sin. She was sure that they didn't believe anyone needed to be saved from it. Why was he talking about it?

"I know a group of young people who could help you. They go to my church, and they have a Bible study group. Would you let me talk to your parents to see if they would allow you to meet with them?"

Nicky's astonishment grew. She wanted all her unhappiness to go away, yet her doctor wanted her to study the Bible. She had read enough about teens who were depressed and threatened suicide to know that she needed psychological help, not a religious conversion.

"May I see my parents, please?" She looked at the curtain again.

"Sure." He left, and soon her father and mother came into the room.

"I want to go home now."

"Will you take your insulin shot? Will you go to school?" asked her mother.

She took a deep breath. She wanted to get away from that doctor.

"Yes. I'll go to school tomorrow," agreed Nicky.

The nurse came in with a syringe of insulin and injected it into her arm. The family left the hospital, and when they arrived home, her mother wanted to talk. Nicky sat at the kitchen table with her chin in her hand and gazed outside. Her parents sat across from her.

"Your father and I are very concerned. We want to understand why you want to die," said her mother as her voice trembled.

"Mom, I keep telling you. My friends aren't here. I never smile. I feel like a robot every day. Go to this class, sit alone, listen to the teacher, work, hear the bell, go to the next class, sit alone, hear the bell. I can't live like this."

"Most people are unhappy. Try harder to make friends if that's what's important to you," said her father.

Nicky made some circles on the table with her finger. He blamed her for not being able to make new friends in that huge school. Besides, she wanted her old friends. Why didn't he understand new friends wouldn't replace the old ones?

"I don't like my job, but I go there every day. I try to be friendly with people. But it isn't what I want to be doing," said her father.

Nicky crossed her arms and pursed her lips as she listened to him. Twelve jobs in the past twenty years hadn't satisfied him, yet he moved them to Norburg for a new one, as if this job would. He now admitted that it didn't, so why had he ruined their lives? She was angry at him, even if she couldn't say that directly to him. Then she felt guilty because he was her father. He loved her and took care of her.

But what was the point of living if she didn't have her good friends around her? She needed to talk to them, do things with them, and laugh with them, otherwise her life didn't have any purpose.

"The doctor wanted me to study the Bible, as if that would help me. He said I'd go to hell if I died. Why did he talk like that?" asked Nicky.

"He believes in the God of the Bible and Jesus Christ as His son. Many people in our country have those beliefs. But your mother and I don't share them," said her father.

"I was raised Methodist, but I stopped going to church as a teen. Now I believe in an essence or spirit everywhere, which people call God, but I don't think it belongs just to Christians. It's a loving presence, but it's mysterious, so we can't know it personally," said her father.

"My parents were Baptist, but I didn't want to go to church. I'm agnostic, which means I don't know which spiritual beliefs are true," said her mother. After some discussion about religion, her father put on his coat.

"I need to get back to the office. You seem to be fine now." He left the house.

"Mom, I'm going to the park. I need a walk," said Nicky.

"Are you going to hurt yourself?" asked her mother.

"No, I just want to be outside. Can I go for an hour? I promise I'll come home."

Nicky's mother sat back in her chair with a worried look.

"Please come back, Nicky. We love you."

"I love you, too, Mom. I just wish we still lived in Eagleton."

"I know. It hasn't been an easy time for you."

Nicky put on her coat, took her notebook and a pen, then walked to a little park nearby. As she sat under an aspen tree with bright yellow leaves under a cloudless sky, she opened her notebook.

She wrote about what the doctor, her mother, and her father had said. They didn't understand how exhausted she was, and how she wanted to stop being angry, sad, and lonely. Nothing had worked out the way her parents had assured her it would. Nicky had hoped for a while that she would find some happiness, but she was sure now it wouldn't return.

She wrote about Norburg and the high school. People weren't friendly, and teachers didn't even put kids in small groups to work together when they might get to know each other. No one in band ever talked to her, besides Laila. The neighbors never talked to each other. People existed in their own little worlds in this big city.

Yet her father blamed her for becoming isolated and unhappy, not the fact that he dragged them to an awful place where they didn't know anyone. She was sentenced to a life without her friends, but she wouldn't threaten to kill herself again, at least not to her parents or doctor.

She closed the notebook, put the pen in her pocket and walked back to the olive-green house. As she walked, she wondered whether her life had any meaning at all.

CHAPTER 37

The Weekend Trip

Nicky's father decided the family needed to spend more time together. Over the teacher conference days off, they drove east to the Cross River, where they stopped at a wayside park and walked along the trails up a ridge. The scenery was beautiful even though the peak of fall color was past. Many oak trees around the area had dark or bright red leaves. When the sun shone on the orange and yellow ones, the leaves were bright and beautiful. The Ponderosa Hills had little red, only a lot of yellow nestled in the dark green pines.

The stillness of the forest felt timeless and peaceful. As the four hiked, they came upon some stone steps carved out of an enormous boulder next to a dry creek bed. They followed it until they looked down a high cliff. If the stream had been running, the waterfall would have been breathtaking. They went to the lookout point and viewed the surrounding valley. The view of the Cross River was awesome.

After the hike, they checked into a motel, ate at a restaurant, and went to a movie that night. The next morning, they drove to a different state park with many flat hiking paths. They all started out together, but at the first fork in the path, Nicky took the right path, while her parents and brother took the left. The scenery was beautiful, and she felt calm and content in the natural setting. She walked for a while and returned to the trail center.

When everyone was back at the car, her mother broached an idea.

"Your father, Ryan, and I talked about moving to a new town. None of us are fond of Norburg. We could find a better place with a smaller school."

"It still needs to be close to my work," said her father. "But maybe we could look at towns as we drive around this weekend and see if one of them appeals to everyone."

"It would be nice to leave Norburg," said Nicky.

"Maybe we could find a neighborhood with kids in it," said Ryan.

As her father drove away from the park, he slowed down and explored some nearby small towns. But her father dismissed them as too far away from his work. They returned to Norburg.

The next day, Nicky and her mother went horseback riding. Then the family went bowling in the afternoon. All of that was pleasant, and Nicky enjoyed the activities.

Nicky turned in the last of her catch-up homework before the end of the month. She was still lonely, yet she was starting to adjust to her new life. Her mother had classes and spent a lot of time with a book open on the desk. When Nicky's father got home, he usually went out to the garage as he finished work on his car.

One day, after she got home from school, she went downstairs to say hi to her mother.

"Your father and I were talking about moving. It would be tough on all of us to move again, and it would cost a lot. We just bought this house and got settled."

Nicky stood by the desk and waited.

"It's a lot of work to find a new house and move. Selling this one could be a challenge. Even though your father makes more money here, it isn't that much more because our mortgage is higher in the city."

Nicky sat down.

"There's no guarantee that a new house and school would be any better. You still might not make the kind of friends you want. It might be better to keep trying to find friends here."

"Maybe we could move back to Eagleton. I bet the school would give Dad his job back."

"I know you care for your friends, but even if we went back, they might not act the same around you. We've been gone for four months."

"I guess we're not moving, then?"

"No, I don't think so."

Nicky stood up and went up to her bedroom. Even though she wanted to leave Norburg, she didn't want another place to get used to. She only wanted to go back to Eagleton. She had changed since they moved because she smiled less, and she had more negative thoughts. Perhaps her mother was right, and her friends had changed, too. Maybe they had new friends, or maybe some new kids had moved to Eagleton who they liked more than her.

Nicky knew being around her family wasn't enough to make her happy, and she needed more people to interact with. She wasn't 10 anymore; she was almost 16. Although she was still financially dependent on her parents, she needed to find a way to change that. Her parents didn't always have satisfying answers when she needed help emotionally, either. In fact, they were in her way now. But she didn't want to hurt them.

Nicky asked if she could have the downstairs bedroom. Ryan was younger than she was, and she hadn't made a fuss in the spring about him getting the room. But now, she wanted to be near the extra bathroom and away from her parents. She needed some independence.

Nicky had to get through high school somehow. Later, when she was on her own, she could do what she wanted, even end her life if she still wanted to. But how was she going to get through the next two and a half years?

CHAPTER 38

Intense Heartache

The band director was all business, and he never smiled or told any jokes during band practice. Nicky was still in seventh chair, and she wasn't sure if she could even challenge the sixth chair flutist to move up. She practiced hard music, just in case.

The band marched in a parade on a rainy, cold Halloween in a town northwest of Norburg. It had a Main Street, and Nicky liked it. She wished her father had chosen a house there.

The concert for all three Norburg high school bands was on the first weekend in November. The boys had to wear suits, and the girls had to wear long dresses. Nicky didn't have a long dress, so her mother took her shopping. She chose a lovely pale blue dress with a tie in the back. At the concert, Nicky was embarrassed when she saw another girl in her band wearing the same dress.

After the concert, the band director moved people around within the instrument sections. He moved Nicky to third chair, and it boosted her confidence.

Nicky's social studies teacher could be entertaining. He made sarcastic comments on the meaning of some historical events, like a comic would. Nicky would get the meaning or twist, but she suppressed her smile so no one else would see her. She didn't want the other kids to know that she liked the class, because when she sneaked a look at them, they weren't even paying attention.

Nicky went to talk to the school counselor one afternoon. While she waited in the office, she glanced around to see if he had any pamphlets to help kids who were unhappy, but she didn't see any.

"What do you need, Nicky?"

"I just moved here, and I'm down all the time," she said.

He paused a minute, then turned to look at her school record.

"I'm not sure what I can do. Your grades look fine. Maybe you should join an activity."

"Oh. Thanks." Nicky got up and left his office. She could see he would not give her real advice about how to become happier. She felt like she was wasting his time.

It snowed in mid-November and Nicky felt boxed in, so she went out for a walk in the snow. She thought about her friends in Eagleton and how being with them made the day go faster. They always laughed and had such a good time. Nicky missed their joking around.

She missed how Paizlee gently teased her and helped her overcome her seriousness. She missed all of Paizlee's notes and how she came up with clever things for them to do. She missed how she and Paizlee supported each other through all their ups and downs. She even missed peeling Paizlee's oranges at lunch.

She missed talking to Bella in band and her observations about what was going on with people at school. She missed practicing flute with her for duets. They had commiserated about teachers and weird things that happened around them. Bella was a true friend.

She missed Alyssa, how they talked at lunch and enjoyed doing things together. She missed Elena's smiles when they shared gymnastics and science activities. She missed Zoey's self-confidence, McKenna's energy, and Kinsey's quiet strength. She missed seeing them and supporting them with homework and their troubles.

She missed talking to Gage, his friendship, and his poking fun at her. He was so handsome, motivated, and smart. Trevor was quiet and kind of awkward sometimes, but he was gentle, and he made her smile. She missed seeing Gage and Trevor laughing until they almost fell out of their chairs. She missed Dalton's cheerfulness and grin. She missed being around Grant, Josh, and Preston. She would never forget any of them. Her heart ached to see them again.

She missed talking at football games, basketball games, and wrestling matches. She missed playing in the pep band. She missed gymnastics and piano lessons. She missed Ginger. She missed the town where she knew where everything was, and how long it took to walk there. She missed the Forestview Glen house. She missed the old white house with the stained-glass windows and the street where many of her friends walked every day.

She missed the teachers and neighbors who knew her parents. Both Ryan and Nicky had status in Eagleton because of their parents. They had identities. In Norburg, they were lonely strangers who no one knew. They were not a part of the community.

She missed seeing the picturesque Ponderosa Hills around her. She missed taking hikes among the pines. She missed seeing Peaceful Bear Mountain looming in the northeast like a guard protecting the town.

She missed her old body, before diabetes. Now every day was difficult. She hated giving insulin shots and, especially, having insulin reactions when her heartbeat was rapid, and she couldn't think. She hated how thirsty she was most of the time. She hated feeling different from other kids who didn't have to think about their blood sugar.

Nicky returned to the house and went down to her bedroom. She cried for a while. Then she twisted her ID bracelet around her wrist a few times. She loved her friends, and she needed them terribly. She could never replace them, even if she made new friends.

She wanted to have good times again. Maybe next semester, she would meet some friendly kids, and she would spend time with them. Maybe she was hoping for a miracle.

She turned up her music.

CHAPTER 39

Another New Job

One evening, Nicky made dinner with her mother, who had talked with one of her professors earlier in the day.

"She has a daughter who's a senior at Norburg and is on the gymnastics team. After I told her you like gymnastics, she suggested her daughter talk to you about it. Would you like that?"

"I guess. But they're probably lots better than I am," said Nicky.

"After you have information, you can figure out if you'd like to try."

Two nights later, Sandy, the woman's daughter, visited Nicky.

"We have a great group of girls on our team. I've been on it since seventh grade."

"How many sophomores are on it?"

"I would guess at least 10."

"Do you have meets here?"

"Oh, yeah! We have invitationals and sometimes we've had four teams in our gym. It's so much fun. I hope you'll come to the first meeting."

"When is it?"

Sandy gave Nicky the details and left. Nicky felt excited as she thought about joining the team. But on the morning of the meeting, she convinced herself she was worthless, and they wouldn't want her. It would be a disaster, especially because she had diabetes. She didn't go to the after-school meeting.

Nicky didn't know how to make her negative thoughts stop. She pretended to be pleasant around her family, but inside, she wasn't pleasant to herself. When Nicky was absorbed in watching, listening, or reading something, she wasn't as miserable. She barely controlled herself from watching the screen from the time she got home from school until she went to bed.

Nicky continued to write letters to Eagleton friends, and sometimes, she got one back. She wanted to call Paizlee, but she was afraid to ask her father if she could. When he saw her writing a letter one time, he commented.

"Why aren't you making new friends instead of writing old friends?" He said it with a fierceness.

"Because they're my friends, and I miss them!" She retreated to her room and tried to ignore his criticism. She knew he was disappointed in her because she hadn't made many new friends.

But she was becoming better friends with Laila, who invited her to see the junior high play of "Peter Pan."

"Wasn't the play good? Some of my friends were in the play last year. My sister was in the light booth tonight. Let's go up and see her."

They walked up the aisle and Laila knocked on the tech room door until her sister let them in. Her sister explained the equipment, then turned out the lights and shut the door.

"Over here was my locker last year. Come on, I'll show you the band room." Laila said goodbye to her sister.

Laila and Nicky walked through the hall until they reached the band room and looked through the classroom door window. Then they left the school. Nicky tried to imagine what it had been like to be a student there. It was Ryan's school, but he didn't talk about it with her.

Just before Thanksgiving, Nicky and her family sat at the dinner table, and her father's eyes lit up as he gave them some news.

"I'm accepting a new job! I answered an ad several weeks ago."

"How did the meeting with the hiring manager go today?" asked her mother.

"Great, and he thinks I can advance to become a manager in the department. He's mailing the offer tonight, and the salary is a bump up from what I make now. I think this job will be more challenging, too."

"How long is the drive?" asked her mother.

"About 30 miles," said her father.

"Are we going to move?" asked Nicky.

"We're not sure yet," said her mother. "But it's possible."

"Rush hour will be worse, so I'm thinking about it," said her father.

At Thanksgiving dinner, their father made a toast to new beginnings, just like last year. This time, Nicky felt a ray of hope.

The job offer came on Saturday, and her father's start date was the first of December. The next day, the family drove around the southwestern suburbs near the company and found a nicer area than Norburg. Her parents decided the family would move in March or April after they found a house.

After Thanksgiving weekend, Nicky received a letter from Gage. Although he had played on both junior varsity and varsity football in the fall, he felt out of place in both. He decided not to join the basketball team, but he was preparing for track in the spring. Gage was having problems with Chelsea, plus he was depressed because his sister was at college, which left him home alone with his parents.

Included in the envelope was his school picture, which Nicky taped to her wall. She smiled as she reread his letter. But she also sympathized with his mention of depression. Depression wasn't a word she had used before, but it fit her, too. She was still in the shadow of the hot-air balloon.

When she answered the letter, she asked Gage if he ever thought about hurting himself in some way. She admitted she had because she thought she wasn't doing anything right anymore, and she missed having friends she could talk to. Nicky told him she wanted to study psychology to understand herself, other people, and their emotions.

She hoped he would write back quickly.

CHAPTER 40

Déjà Vu with a Twist

As soon as Nicky's father started his new job, he flew to another state to get information on a new computer to buy. After the family dropped him off at the airport, they drove around a town called Westville, which was near her father's new job. It had a downtown area, and the streets had number names like First, Second, Third, and so on. Westville had started as a small town, but the city grew around it until it became a suburb. They found the rolling hills attractive and prettier than Norburg's flat land.

Nicky felt déjà vu. Like last year, her father had a new job, he was gone for a while, and the family talked about a new place to live. The new high school might be smaller, and talking to people might be easier. She would have a new chance to find people she could fit in with. But she still wanted the old Eagleton world, not another new one.

Nicky opened her locker one morning to discover her Health Issues and German notebooks were missing. The German notebook was the new one with few notes in it, but the Health Issues one had all of her notes, and she wasn't doing well in the class. Laila had to change lockers because someone took five new notebooks. The school suddenly seemed unsafe.

Mrs. Sheplan talked Nicky into shopping with the SHARE group on Thursday. The SHARE group had been meeting since September, but she hadn't gone to another meeting. Nicky rode with three other girls and her teacher to the mall. The snow and outside lights were festive as they drove into the parking lot. Several mothers drove more girls, and they met in front of a department store. When they went inside, Nicky admired the many holiday decorations.

The other girls talked and laughed together, but no one reached out to Nicky. When everyone broke into small groups to shop, she found herself alone. She shopped for an hour, then she returned to the meeting area and watched the rest of the group arrive in pairs or trios. Once again, Nicky felt like an outsider.

After everyone returned, the group drove over to an ice cream parlor. Nicky couldn't order one of the yummy treats, so she had a small bowl of ice cream. She watched and listened, but she didn't talk, except for a few words with her teacher. Nicky was the last one in her teacher's car after she dropped off the others.

"Are you getting used to Norburg, Nicky?" asked Mrs. Sheplan.

"I guess."

"Are you making some friends?"

"A few."

"Moving to a big school like this must be tough. It's hard for most sophomores to feel comfortable, even if they didn't just move here. You'll get to know more people by the end of the year."

"I won't be here then. We're moving again at spring break."

"I'm sorry to hear that." The tone of her teacher's voice was sad. "Where are you moving?"

"We're not sure. Somewhere near Westville."

"That's a nice area. There are two high schools and neither of them are as big as ours. I hope it works out for you. I've enjoyed having you in class."

"Thanks," said Nicky. "I like your class."

Nicky would miss Mrs. Sheplan, but she told herself it didn't matter. After semester break, she might already be with a new teacher. She couldn't allow herself to get attached to anything at Norburg.

The next day, Nicky walked home alone, which she had done since October because Kristi had volleyball practice. After a week of cloudy days, the sun shone brightly in the clear blue sky. The powdery snow on the practice field, where the kids had made a path as a shortcut, was about a foot deep. The field was an open space, and she breathed deeply as her mind quieted. When she was alone outside, she was aware of the natural world, and she was content as she observed the area.

She got home and wrote letters to Bella, Paizlee, and Alyssa. She tried to be positive about the upcoming changes as she wrote about moving to a different new place.

Ryan played basketball whenever he could. He was on two teams: the school team and a community traveling team. Nicky and her mother went to one of his Friday school basketball games. His school team had only lost one game so far, and they won that day. The junior high gym bleachers were half empty. Nicky was surprised because the junior high had so many students. In Eagleton, many fans attended the junior high games.

Nicky made Ryan a birthday cake. His birthday was the same week as Gage's. She wondered if Gage was having a big 16th birthday party. If she were there, she would wish him a happy birthday, and give him another card. She daydreamed about giving him a kiss and wished they could dance together again.

During band, Laila invited Nicky to watch the senior high dance line rehearse. After the bell rang, they went to each other's lockers.

"My sister said the dance team is in the B gym," said Laila.

When they opened the gym door, they saw a group of girls sitting on the polished wood floor watching the group of dancers, who were dressed in shorts or sweats.

"She's over there." Laila motioned to her sister, and they sat next to her. Laila whispered to Nicky, "There's Winnie. Isn't she good?"

Nicky thought Winnie was beautiful as she twirled and kicked her way through the dance. The team leads directed the girls by clapping and counting as the dancers rehearsed the routine.

Nicky had a sudden urge to try out to see if she could belong to the group. It took her a minute to remember she wouldn't be in Norburg in the spring. She scolded herself as she dismissed the idea.

She wouldn't be good enough anyway. Besides, Nicky was already checking her rearview mirror as she mentally drove toward a new school.

That weekend, Nicky babysat for a woman who usually had Kristi, but Kristi was busy that night. She enjoyed the kids, and having a little money for presents was helpful. She thought about looking for an after-school job.

Oh, wait. Once again, she couldn't apply for a job yet. She was stuck waiting to see what would happen after the next move.

Nicky and the lunch group exchanged gifts before the winter break. They had continued to eat together, but they might not all have the same lunchtime after the semester ended. Who would Nicky eat with then? She couldn't count on anything staying the same.

Paizlee sent a package to her with a little photo album, which had pictures of Gage, Grant, Josh, Bella, and Mr. Gillette. Paizlee had new glasses, which were cute and made her look older. She also sent some photos taken at the band contest last spring. Nicky loved the pictures. It was wonderful to know what was happening in Paizlee's life.

Then she received letters from Alyssa and Bella. Bella finally wrote! She didn't write often, but she wrote many pages when she did. Nicky relished the letter and reread it multiple times.

Nicky received a holiday card and a letter from Gage. He thought about hurting himself sometimes when he felt like he wasn't good enough to meet his father's expectations. He said if Nicky ever felt so depressed again, she should call him. He gave her his phone number, and he reassured her if she ever felt no one cared, she should remember he was someone who did.

CHAPTER 41

The Conflict Over Two Houses

When Nicky's father returned from his trip, the family sat around the dining room table after dinner. Her father crossed his arms.

"We want you guys involved in choosing our next house. Last year, you were back in Eagleton, so I looked around, but we're all here now. Of course, I could live in an apartment and be happy not doing any more yard work or house maintenance. But we've had houses since you can remember, so that might be too big of a change for you."

"I think we need a house," said her mother.

"Well, we'll probably sell it after the kids graduate. That's less than five years from now. Since we know it's temporary, your opinion isn't as important." He frowned at her mother.

Nicky thought his comments were odd. Her mother should have a say in the decision. Her mother dropped her eyes, then looked back at her father with her lips pursed and her brows close together.

"I can live anywhere," said Ryan.

Nicky raised her eyebrows as she wondered why he didn't care.

"Nicky, we know you didn't like this house from the moment you stepped into it. What should we look for in a new one?" asked her father.

"Well, I don't want an apartment," began Nicky.

"We know. What do you want?" asked her father.

"Could we get a place where all the bedrooms are upstairs and have windows?" asked Nicky. She didn't like being in the basement.

"That means three bedrooms on the main floor, or an upper level. What else?"

"A garage with a basketball hoop for Ryan. A few trees. Sidewalks. Could it have a wide, pretty view from the living room window? Like our Forestview Glen house?"

"We can try to find something, but we'll never have a spectacular view like that again," said her mother.

"It would be nice if it was unique. The houses here all look the same," said Nicky.

Her father snorted. He didn't see that as a problem.

"I guess the biggest thing is smaller schools we can walk to."

"Well, we'll look around and see what's out there. We might be limited," said her father. He took his plate to the sink.

The family went to five open houses in the Westville area that Saturday and debated pros and cons of each place. A week later, her parents went to look at houses without the kids. When they returned, the choice was down to two houses. They would decide between an old house right in Westville or a new twin home in the suburb to the south called Elk Prairie.

The old house had two stories with a basement, and it had an old garage in the back. The high school and downtown area, with a movie theater, were a short walk away.

The new house was in a growing suburb without a downtown. The twin home was brand new, one of a group of newer twin homes several miles away from the large new schools. A wall divided one building into two homes. Behind the houses was a big, shared area, like a field, without fences. The homeowners all paid a contractor to mow the grass and shovel the snow. Her father liked the idea he wouldn't have to do those things.

As her father raved about the twin home, he made clear that was his preference. Her mother liked it, and Ryan said it sounded good.

"What do you think, Nicky?" asked her mother.

"When we drove around Elk Prairie, it didn't have any big trees. It was an ugly prairie." She stopped when she saw her father's piercing stare. Nicky dropped her head and clammed up.

Why did her father want to take them to a new suburb with large schools like Norburg? She hated the idea of living with just a wall between their neighbors. She wouldn't be comfortable playing piano or flute because she didn't want anyone to hear her practice. What if she or Ryan wanted to play music loud when no one was home? It might bother the neighbors. Or what if the neighbors were loud, and the noise bothered her?

Nicky could tell her parents were going to buy the twin home. She thought the idea was to choose a town with a school which was smaller, where they could feel more like they did in Eagleton. She felt betrayed.

As the others kept talking about the twin home, Nicky left the table and went downstairs to her room. Her mother knocked and opened the door a crack.

"Nicky, we need to talk to you more about houses. Please come upstairs."

Nicky's father stomped down the stairs. He swung open the door, and he was angry.

"You left the table before we finished talking."

Nicky got up from the bed and stood.

"Look, we know you want the older house because you can walk to school. But the twin home is what we need. I'm the one who has to take care of it. It's been years since we lived in a new house, and it would be a beautiful place to live. There are a lot of benefits."

"Fine." Nicky shrugged.

"We want you to be on board. This would make us all happy."

Nicky shrugged again. "I wouldn't be happy in that house."

He practically growled. Then his anger rose and burst out.

"Why don't you ever like anything? Everything I try to do for you isn't good enough. We've been here six months! Six months! I chose this nice house near the school, but you don't like it because the school is too big!" He threw his arms around as he talked.

"You're getting too angry at her. Please stop yelling," said her mother.

"You're just as stuck as you were in September. You're always grouchy and complaining! You criticize everything!" He jabbed his finger at her as he talked, and she was afraid he was going to hit her. She backed up.

"Every house we've looked at is wrong! Wrong! Wrong! 'Westville is OK, but I don't want to live right downtown. We can't move into the Lund school area because the school has modular scheduling. Elk Prairie doesn't have any big trees.'" He used a voice to imitate her.

"Why can't you be agreeable? Why can't you act like a normal human being? You're going to have to get a whole lot nicer so you can marry some rich man who will support you. Otherwise, you'll have to become a doctor or a lawyer so you can buy everything you want!"

Tears rolled down her face. He was very loud and very scary. He kept yelling and criticizing her. He pointed at her and glowered.

"You better shape up soon!"

He slammed the door and went upstairs and out to the garage. Her mother went upstairs after him.

Nicky flung herself on her bed as tears streamed from her eyes. She couldn't stop sobbing. She had never feared her father before they moved. But that night, he seemed to hate her. He said she could have a vote in choosing a house, though. Why did he get so angry?

Why did he say no man would ever marry her? They were talking about a house, not whether she was nice enough to get married someday. But maybe he was right. Maybe she wasn't good enough for a boy to love her. Maybe no one would ever want such an unhappy girl.

Finally, she sat up and thought, "Sorry, Dad, but I don't like everything you do. I can't be happy because you tell me to be. It's your fault I'm like this. You took me away from my friends. I was happy with them! You wrecked my life! I'll never tell you how I feel again!" She would close up now she knew he could verbally attack her.

When she went upstairs the next morning, her father didn't mention the previous night. He said they were driving down to see the twin home. Nicky tried to keep her face still and not betray any emotions, so he wouldn't get mad at her. She got ready to go.

Upon arriving at the twin home, she saw it was one of 12 houses surrounding a large field. As a child, it would be fun to play out in the field with other children. As a self-conscious teenager, Nicky needed privacy and friends her own age who wouldn't even use the field.

If they moved there, Nicky and Ryan would both have to ride a bus to their schools. Their parents would have to drive them to every activity until they got their drivers' licenses. Once she had her license, she would most likely have to chauffeur Ryan.

When the four went inside, Nicky liked how new everything was, but she could hear people next door through the wall. Didn't the shared walls bother her parents? Couldn't they find a different new house which wasn't a twin home?

A few days after the holiday, the family had another discussion. Her parents didn't mention the twin home. Instead, they talked about the older house near the high school in Westville. They had decided it would be better for Nicky and Ryan to be in a small town again. After Nicky graduated, the others would decide if they wanted something else. Everyone was calm. They asked if she was OK with the choice. Nicky nodded.

Her parents were trying to understand. Nicky didn't want any more conflict.

CHAPTER 42

Friendly Voices

At Laila's holiday party, Ryan played games with Laila's younger brother. Laila invited the lunch group as well as Phil, the boy Laila had a crush on. He played some songs on the guitar for them.

Nicky got a letter from Mrs. Schmidt, her former piano teacher. As she remembered her lessons, Nicky wanted to find a new piano teacher. She reminded herself she couldn't start anything new in Norburg.

The family got a card from their realtor and friend in Eagleton. She said the bank painted their old house gray, and it looked good, but it hadn't sold yet. Nicky wished again they could move back into it.

After the New Year, Laila talked about Phil at lunch until Nicky grew bored and tuned out. Even when Nicky had told her she was moving again, Laila only asked where to, then she resumed talking about Phil. Nicky tried to pay attention, but sometimes she didn't care. She couldn't support her new friends the way she had her old friends. She remembered her philosophy of life conversation with Gage and Trevor, and felt she wasn't following her own. Her Norburg friends would fade into her past soon.

When Nicky heard about sports games, dances, plays, and other high school events, she dismissed them as meaningless. For the first time, she realized there was more to life than those activities. She had to find other ones which would help her get through school. She spent most evenings and weekends alone in her room, reading and writing.

With her birthday soon to arrive, Nicky asked for a guitar. Her mother had learned to play folk songs on a guitar when Nicky was eight, and Nicky learned some chords and simple songs on a small second guitar. But they had given away the instruments before one of the moves. She wanted to play again.

Nicky spoke little to her father after he yelled at her. She refrained from doing anything that might irritate him, and she felt like she was walking on eggshells. Six months earlier, he had pushed her over a cliff when he took her away from Eagleton. Although she wasn't recovered yet, they were moving again. She had no one to talk to about how she felt. Her close friends weren't nearby, and her new friends weren't close.

Gage sent her another letter, and he enclosed a key chain. He said he recalled she had once said she wanted a car. He couldn't get her a car, but he could give her a key chain to use when she got it. She put her house key on it. When she had a car key, she would slide it on, too.

Nicky wanted to drive back to Eagleton, but she had no license and no car. In the fall, when she asked when her family could go back to visit their old town, Nicky's parents had replied they would visit in the summer on the way to her grandparents' house. Nicky counted on the trip.

She longed to be in the Ponderosa Hills on a hike again when she would savor every moment. She yearned for clean air and few houses. Most of all, she wanted to be with her friends again. Nicky daydreamed constantly about ninth grade events and joining her friends in new activities. Activities weren't meaningless when shared with her friends.

After Nicky got a letter from Paizlee, she asked her mother if she could call her friend, and her mother approved.

"Hi, Paizlee! Your letter was so nice, I had to talk to you."

"I can't believe you called! I've missed you so much."

"Me, too! How's dance line?"

"Awful, truly awful. The seniors criticize me and Bella all the time. I wish they would lighten up. We try really hard."

"That's rotten," said Nicky.

"Bella's father is talking about moving again. She can't move! I'm not even used to you and Dalton being gone. Did I tell you he called me? He asked about you. Didn't you ever write to him?"

"No. I don't know what to say. He's probably happy, but I'm such a mess now."

"He's having some troubles, too. I wish I could see both of you again. If Bella leaves, I won't have close friends here."

"What about Zoey, Lily, and Kinsey?" asked Nicky.

"We hardly do anything together anymore. They've changed. They hang around more with the popular kids. Are you coming to visit this summer?" Paizlee asked.

"Definitely, even if I have to run away to do it!"

She was determined to go, no matter what. After they hung up, Nicky found her mother cleaning.

"Mom, when will we have our vacation in Eagleton?"

"I'm sorry, dear. We probably won't go. We have so much to do this spring, buying the house and selling this one. Your father doesn't have time off because of the new job."

"Couldn't just you and I go?"

"I don't think so. I'm quitting school when the semester is over, and I'll get a job to help pay for the new house mortgage."

"Could I just go? I mean, after I get my driver's license?"

"We'll see. It might work out if you rode the bus."

The answers reduced the certainty of a trip to a slim possibility.

Laila invited Nicky and Ryan to her 16th birthday party. The group went ice skating, and Laila mainly focused on Phil. Nicky spent half her time in the warming house, where she met Tina, a seven-year-old who was there with her older sister. Tina chatted effortlessly with Nicky. Why didn't kids in high school reach out like Tina?

Back at Laila's house, Nicky talked with Gwen until Gwen's mother drove them both home. Nicky found a note on her bed. "Gage called. He'll call back tomorrow a.m." Nicky's heart jumped! Why did she stay at that party? If she had been home, she would have talked to Gage.

She walked around the living room for a few minutes, then she picked up the phone and called him back.

"Hi Gage. It's Nicky. Mom told me you called."

"Hey. Paizlee said you called her. I was jealous. How are things?"

"Weird. I feel like I'm in limbo. I can't get into things here."

"It was tough to care after I knew we were leaving our old town. Your birthday is in a few weeks. What do you want?"

"I liked the keychain, so you don't have to get me anything else."

"But I want to, so think of something."

They talked about school and their families. Gage talked about a misunderstanding he had with Chelsea and asked for her advice. She asked him some questions and offered her thoughts.

"Thanks, I'll try that. You'll be a good psychologist because you listen so well."

"Maybe after I get myself figured out, I can help other people."

"Paizlee said you're going to visit. We should get together then."

"I'd like that."

Gage called the next day. He was lonely at home because both his brother and sister were gone. He said he often sat in the dark to think. They shared their sadness, and it helped to know that someone else was struggling. She understood his depression in a way his other friends didn't.

If she hadn't been forced to move away, maybe the whole group would be having more fun. If she were there, she would try to get them together and support them in as many ways as she could.

Laila continued to talk about Phil, although she had no classes with him after the semester ended. Phil gave her a late birthday present: a gold necklace with her initials in a gold circle.

Nicky thought of the birthstone necklace Dalton had given her. She wore it the next day along with her gold ID bracelet, and each time she looked at them, she smiled. Boys used to like her, too.

CHAPTER 43

The Gym Teacher

When the new semester began, Nicky was relieved to find four of the five girls still shared a lunch period with her. The Health Issues class was over, and gym class took its place. Nicky recognized many of the girls from her health class in it. She looked forward to gym class all morning.

The boys' class joined them for the dance unit, where the first one they learned was square dance. On Tuesday and Wednesday, the number of girls and boys counted off into couples, and Nicky had partners. But on Thursday, the guys picked partners, and the girls outnumbered them by one. Nicky was the girl who didn't have a partner. She stood by herself until the teacher made a boy dance with her for a while. She was grouchy after that because she thought that never would have happened in Eagleton.

On Friday, one guy who had been in her square on Tuesday asked her to be his partner. He made her laugh by making funny faces at her. Gym was enjoyable because someone paid attention to her.

"Dance with you next time," he said.

"OK." Maybe she wasn't so bad after all. They danced together for the last weeks of the unit, but they didn't see each other elsewhere.

Nicky's other classes were all work. English would be a pain. The male teacher had a voice that grated on Nicky's nerves, so she wanted to yell at him to shut up. She had never thought that before about a teacher. But many things irritated her now.

Algebra was a fast-paced class because the teacher had a definite schedule. Correct papers in the first couple minutes, then go through complicated problems on the board. He explained the homework assignment thoroughly, then he let them work alone. He allowed no discussion.

Nicky's mother made it onto the college Dean's list for her good grades. She brought home a booklet for Nicky to read about careers in psychology. Nicky read it cover to cover. It described the profession, but it didn't help her figure out her own problems.

Nicky didn't go to any Norburg varsity basketball games or wrestling matches because she wasn't in pep band, and none of her new friends went to them. She wanted to go to movies, but she couldn't drive yet, which was another irritation.

"Mom, since we're moving, I can't take Driver's Ed in Norburg in the spring. I'll need to drive to a job this summer. Can I take it somewhere as soon as we move? Could I go to a private driving school?"

"I don't think your father wants to pay more for the course when it's usually offered free at school. Let's see if you can get it in your schedule at Westville," said her mother.

"I found out the state requires a person with diabetes to fill out an extra form before they can get their driver's license. They have to renew it every year."

"Why?"

"The state wants to make sure they won't cause an accident if their blood sugar is out of control."

The information about the form gave Nicky one more reason to hate her disease. She clenched her jaw as she thought about how the state treated people with diabetes like potential criminals. It didn't seem fair to her.

At the end of January, she went to a roller skating event with Kristi. The rink wasn't as big as the one in Ridgeland City. The event was a benefit for Mary, a sophomore who was in a terrible car accident in September. Mary was well enough to be at the roller skating rink for a while and watch. Nicky thought how awful it must be to have to use a wheelchair for the rest of your life. Her diabetes was frustrating, but she could walk.

Kristi skated a lot with a boy she knew. Nicky was alone, and she felt like an unwanted third party. Many little kids skated across in front of her and she was afraid of running into them. She wanted to snowball again, as she had last year with Gage and Grant. But they didn't snowball at this skating rink, and even if they had, Gage and Grant weren't there to do it with.

Nicky got a few birthday wishes in the mail from her Eagleton friends. She made Valentine's Day cards and sent them off.

For her birthday, her mother gave her a folk guitar and a book of folk songs with a chord chart in it. Nicky's other gift was a trip to the hair salon. The stylist cut her long hair into a shorter style with curls, but Nicky struggled to replicate it. She got angry when her hair looked ugly and felt relieved when it looked good.

The dance unit was over in gym and the girls learned cheerleading stunts. As they learned a new stunt, another girl fell on Nicky and Nicky felt pain in her left arm.

She told the gym teacher, who sent her down to the nurse. The nurse called her mother and suggested Nicky needed an x-ray at the clinic. The x-ray showed her arm wasn't broken, only bruised.

As her mother drove them home, Nicky started complaining.

"That girl was talking to her other friends, and they were so loud. The teacher was talking to another teacher by the gym door, and she wasn't even watching us. She does that all the time. It's dangerous. Mrs. Tanner was always near us and telling us what to do. I don't like this teacher, Mom."

"It doesn't sound like a good situation. How old is the teacher?"

"I don't know. Maybe your age."

"I wondered if she was young. Well, we won't be here much longer and maybe your next gym teacher will be more attentive."

Two days later, the gym teacher called her into her office.

"Nicky, your mother came to see me. Did you know that?" said the teacher.

Nicky shook her head no.

"Did you tell your mother I don't supervise this class?"

Nicky's mind went blank. "Maybe."

"What do you know about supervising a gym class? Have you ever done it before?"

Nicky shook her head no.

"Then why would you talk to your mother? I've been teaching for over 20 years and no student has ever had their mother come to me to tell me I wasn't watching out for the kids. I know how to do my job. Do you think you could do a better job? Do you?"

Nicky shook her head no, and her nose started tingling as she held back tears.

"This had better not happen again."

"OK." Nicky said softly.

"Get back to class now."

As Nicky left, she held her arms in front of her stomach and almost tripped as she stumbled into the gym. No teacher had ever confronted her that way. The teacher was mad at her.

On her way home, she blamed herself, and she decided she couldn't complain to her mother. Her mother couldn't fix problems for her anymore, even if she wanted to. The rest of that week, she didn't want to go to the gym class because she was uncomfortable around the teacher.

Nicky couldn't wait to leave Norburg. She wanted the move to be done so they could settle into the new house. She wanted to get into activities at the new school without worrying about getting pulled out of them again. She counted down the days until the move.

CHAPTER 44

Two Homesick Sisters

The phone rang on a Sunday afternoon in late February. Nicky jumped when it rang because the family got few phone calls.

"Happy Birthday, Nicky!" She heard Paizlee, Bella, and Gage.

"We're late, but it's still your birthday month," said Paizlee.

"That's OK. What's been happening?" asked Nicky.

"We had our best performance at the Sparta game last night," said Bella. "We have the regional contest next week."

"Is it fun now? How is the boys' basketball team doing?"

Gage had joined the basketball team, and he talked about the season. Sometimes he wanted to play in the pep band instead.

"I went to the winter dance, but it wasn't very fun. It wasn't like our junior high dances," said Paizlee.

"We used to have such good times at the dances," said Nicky.

"Yeah, well, I had a worse night. Chelsea broke up with me," said Gage. "I guess we were together too long."

"When are you moving to Westville?" asked Bella.

"The middle of March," said Nicky.

The sellers of the Westville house accepted her parents' offer, and the Norburg house was on the market. They would move during Norburg school district's week-long spring break.

The four friends continued to talk and laugh easily. Nicky felt like her old self, like she belonged with them, and she didn't want it to end.

In Paizlee's next letter, Nicky learned Gage, Paizlee, and Bella had spent time together after her calls with Paizlee and Gage in January. Gage gave them rides home from basketball games, and the three went ice skating. Then only Gage and Paizlee went ice skating. She had fun and thought he had matured since the summer.

Bella wrote next. Gage had given them a "peace offering" of peanut butter and chocolate chip cookies. He invited Paizlee and Bella to eat popcorn and listen to music in his basement.

When Gage's letter arrived, Nicky read about how he enjoyed spending time with Paizlee and Bella. He sent photos of himself.

Nicky's heart ached to be in Eagleton with her wonderful friends. Yet perhaps she would spoil their growing friendship. She didn't have the same confidence as before. She doubted more each day whether she could make friends after she moved to Westville.

When her mother drove Nicky down to Westville Senior High, they saw the school was older than the Norburg school. It had three stories, but the campus was more compact. The school counselor talked with them about the classes Nicky needed. The school only had one band, and she was relieved. She wanted to be in pep band again.

On the way back, Nicky said, "I have to write a short story for English. I don't know what to write about."

"Maybe you could set the story in the Ponderosa Hills."

"I wish I'd hiked in the Hills more often. I wish I'd appreciated the town and the people more when we lived there," said Nicky.

After a few moments of silence, her mother said, "You can never go home again."

"What does that mean?"

"It means that when someone leaves a place, that person naturally changes. Even if they return, the situation won't be the same. I tried to go back once. But I wasn't as happy as I'd been, and I became very homesick." Nicky's mother, Nancy, started reminiscing.

When Nancy mother was little, her folks moved around because work was scarce. The only stable place was her grandparents' house. because her family returned there when they needed a place to live.

Her family settled in a new town on the West Coast for a brief time until her father joined the military. Nancy's mother took her and her older sister back to her parents' house to live while he was gone.

Nancy had happy memories of her grandparents and their land, despite her grandfather's illness. They had a few acres on the side of a hill, which were covered with trees, weeds, and no lawn. The roads leading to it were dirt, not paved. The house lacked running water, with only a hand pump and an outhouse.

Her grandparents had a mule as old as Nancy's mother. The house had a wood-burning stove, so they had to fetch wood for it, and they hauled the wood in a wagon attached to the mule. Nancy's mother would guide the animal up the hill while Nancy rode in the wagon behind it. Then Nancy sat on the mule's back to ride down the hill with the loaded wagon.

The sisters found places to play as they pretended wide, flat stones were floors of a make-believe house, and used small rocks to mark the walls of the rooms. They played in a clear stream nearby and challenged each other to cross the log over it without falling off.

They climbed trees with low branches and grabbed onto strong vines to swing back and forth. Two black walnut trees grew in the front yard, and they dropped green fruit. Nancy's older sister showed her how to peel a round green walnut husk to get to the hard shell in the middle. They had to wash their hands right away in the creek because of the green stains from the husk. Then they would crack the shell and dig the nutmeat out with a hair pin. Their reward was to eat the nutmeat. Nancy still loved walnuts and thought about her sister whenever she ate them.

After her father got out of the military, the family joined him back on the West Coast. Nancy became homesick for her grandparents. She asked her mother, who was busy with her little sister, over and over if she could go back. When her aunt and her uncle decided to return to where they grew up, they offered to take Nancy with them. Her parents agreed to let her visit her grandparents for a while.

During the long drive back in the old car, which took several days, Nancy stretched out in the backseat. She put her feet up on the window, sang with the radio, and played with her nine-month-old cousin.

Nancy stayed with her grandparents, and her uncle and aunt rented a place nearby. She attended part of third grade at the little school and she babysat sometimes. She spent most of her time playing alone because other kids weren't nearby. Nancy's mother and sister had been there with her before, and she was unhappy without them. Nancy decided to return to live with her parents in their small town, where she eventually graduated from high school.

But once Nancy was back, her sister, who was in high school then, wanted to go back to live with her grandparents. She had left close friends, and she missed them. She hadn't adjusted to her new school. After months of yelling and door slamming, her sister took the bus to her grandparents' town. She lived in a boarding school with her friends until she graduated from high school. Nancy's family didn't seem the same without her sister, and Nancy missed her.

Nicky thought about her mother's experience. She envied her aunt who got to finish high school with her old friends. Her mother and aunt were lucky because they were able to stay with their grandparents. Their family was apart, but the sisters got to be where they wanted to be.

Nicky realized her yearning to return to a place she missed wasn't so unusual. But she didn't have grandparents or relatives in Eagleton where she could stay, and she didn't know how she could return for more than a brief visit.

Nicky wanted her family and Eagleton friends to be in the same place. It was becoming clear they never would be again.

CHAPTER 45

Another New House

The week before the move to Westville, the gym teacher called Nicky aside.

"You left gym early one day. You'll have to show up for detention this afternoon. I gave the monitor your name."

"When? I only left early the time I hurt my arm."

"I show an unexcused absence. Stop arguing and just show up."

Nicky frowned because she was certain she hadn't left early otherwise. It was unfair when the teacher refused to verify the date. She had never had detention before. As she found the room after school, she was angry. She sat at the desk, hunched over as she scribbled on a piece of blank paper.

She questioned whether the adults in her life knew what they were doing. When she got the Optimist Club award, she trusted adults to help her live a good life, and she wanted to be a vital part of the community. But no one knew her here, and adults were not helping her like they used to do.

When she got home, she ate some candy and cookies to relax. She wasn't supposed to eat sweets, but she had started eating more after the holiday. Her blood sugar was always high, so she stopped testing it. She didn't care if snacking hurt her body. Eating was one of the few ways she could shift her mind away from her feelings of powerlessness, confusion, anger, and fear.

Her math teacher talked her into taking the national math test. Nicky was tired when she arrived at her regular math classroom early on the day of the test. She wasn't invested in the score, and when she found out that she got a lower one than she expected, she didn't care. Taking the national math test didn't compare to her ninth-grade experience of being part of a team and having a field trip to the technical school auditorium in Ridgeland City.

The day before spring break, Nicky said goodbye to Laila and the lunch group. She walked home with Kristi and said goodbye to her, too. Leaving Norburg was far less heart-wrenching than leaving Eagleton. Only a few people had known her in Norburg, and she didn't believe that they would miss her. She was relieved she was leaving a place where she had felt so lost and alone.

Brown boxes sat everywhere in the Norburg house. Her mother had listed their contents on the side of each box with a black permanent marker. They were moving themselves this time because they didn't know anyone who could help them, plus her father didn't want to hire a company, except some piano movers.

Moving day was chilly and overcast, but it didn't rain or snow. Nicky blew her nose because of a cold virus, and Ryan was getting one. Ryan helped his father move the big furniture into the moving van, while Nicky helped her mother pack up the food in the kitchen.

After three days of many trips between the houses, the furniture and most of the boxes were at the new place. They returned to the Norburg house one last time to finish loading and cleaning up. Nicky felt no sadness when they locked the door to the empty house, which was just a house they lived in for a while.

At the Westville house, they unpacked and tried to find things. Her father and mother attempted to keep a light tone. Nicky set up her room, which was upstairs and had two wonderful windows. She went downstairs and saw her brother watching basketball.

"What game is that?"

"Girls state basketball tournament Class A quarterfinals."

"Who's playing?"

He named two schools she didn't know.

"Norburg made it to the Class AA quarterfinal game," he said.

She raised her eyebrows in surprise. When the girls' team made it into the tournament, the Norburg students at the pep rally the prior week expressed energy as they supported their team. The pep rally was one of the few times she had witnessed school spirit. The band director said any band member could show up and play with the pep band. Nicky might have enjoyed playing and watching the team win in the big sports center, but she had already left the school.

As Nicky watched the game with her brother, they learned Norburg had won their quarterfinal game. On Friday evening, she watched their Class AA semifinal game with her father and her brother.

"There's the pep band!" Nicky said. "There's Laila!"

She recognized a few other members of her old band. In another part of the arena, she saw Phil. She wondered if Laila knew he was there.

The Norburg team lost the game by seven points. Nicky felt a little disappointed since it was the only school she knew anything about. She didn't pay attention to whether the Westville team played.

The first day of class at the new school was Tuesday, after a teacher's workshop day to start the last quarter of the year. Westville's spring break wasn't until mid-April.

Nicky's stomach felt unsettled Monday night. She would know soon whether the new school would be better than Norburg, yet she was afraid of how the first day would unfold. She wanted to enjoy attending the new school, yet she doubted she would. Her parents encouraged her to be optimistic.

She wanted a fresh start and some good luck to shine on her. She tried to believe that it would.

CHAPTER 46

Another New School

On Tuesday, Nicky's hair turned out well, and she put on her ID bracelet for good luck. Her father drove her to school.

The guidance counselor greeted her warmly and asked her to wait. Another new girl, Lynn, needed her new schedule. Twenty minutes later, the counselor took Nicky to the band room. Nicky still had her coat on, and she carried her notebooks and her lunch sack. The band practiced in second hour. The director's youth surprised Nicky.

"Good morning, Mr. Alvarez, Nicky is a new student who plays the flute."

"Hi, Nicky. Welcome to the Westville band. You can play for me later and we'll figure out where you'll sit."

"Nicky moved from Norburg. Our band and school may seem small compared to theirs."

"The teacher's workshop speaker said we're getting even smaller. Do you know when the school merger will happen?"

The two adults ignored her as they discussed their shrinking school system. Its two high schools would become one school soon.

After they left the room, the counselor took Nicky upstairs to her first-hour class, Driver's Ed, where she asked a girl to come out into the hall.

"Arielle, would you help Nicky find her classes today? She just moved to Westville. Here's her schedule."

"Sure, Mrs. B." Arielle looked at it and gave it back.

The counselor left the schedule with Nicky as the two girls went into the classroom. Nicky was excited to learn about driving at last. After the bell rang, Arielle and Nicky left the classroom together.

"Did they give you a locker yet?"

"No."

"We better go to the office and make sure you get one. You have band second hour?"

"Yeah."

"What do you play?"

"Flute."

"I have friends in band, but I don't play an instrument."

After they got Nicky's locker assignment, Arielle found it, and Nicky stored her coat, hat, and lunch. Because there were so few students, she had her own locker. Arielle walked with her through dark halls back to the band room.

"Why aren't the lights on in the halls?" asked Nicky.

"I don't know, but they never are. I can't walk with you to the next class after this one. What is it?"

"German."

"It's straight down this hall and to the right. I'll meet you in the office before lunch."

"Thanks."

After band rehearsal, Nicky found the German room, and the teacher greeted her in German. She asked whether Nicky was in third or fourth year. Nicky said she was in "erstes Jahr," first year. The teacher said she didn't have a first-year class. Nicky returned to the office where the counselor told her she might have to be in a German class all by herself. Nicky bit her lip as she considered the idea.

Nicky asked where the nearest bathroom was, and the counselor gave Nicky directions to one on the way to her next class. As she opened the restroom door, Nicky smelled cigarettes and saw butts and ashes littering the floor. She looked up to see three girls smoking under the window. They glared at her, so she turned around and left.

Algebra II was in the new addition of the school. A small group of kids talked with each other, while the teacher wrote equations on the board. During the class, he seemed somewhat absent-minded, and he didn't tell them to be quiet.

Nicky met Arielle in the office and walked to the lunchroom, which was filled with round tables, each with eight chairs. Nicky unpacked her lunch bag while Arielle stood in the hot lunch line. Kids talked and joked around, while Nicky sat alone. Arielle came back with her tray, but instead of eating, she went over to talk to some friends at one table, then another. Arielle seemed popular, which meant she already had many friends. She didn't seem interested in talking to Nicky.

When she finished eating, Arielle walked with her to the English classroom on the second floor and left. The teacher met with all the students on Monday, but she met with half of the class on Tuesday and Thursday to discuss one book, then with the other half on Wednesday and Friday to discuss a different book. The teacher assigned Nicky to the Tuesday book group. On the days they didn't meet with the teacher, the students had free time when they were supposed to read the book in the library or the cafeteria. Nicky wondered if they actually read it.

After English, Nicky found another bathroom, but it was dirty, just like the first one. She went into the gym for her next class. The gym teacher waved her off while she talked to another student, so Nicky and the other new girl sat on the gym floor and watched the boys and girls play basketball. Half the class time passed before the gym teacher talked to them and assigned them gym lockers.

American history was the last class, and the other students were juniors. At Norburg, sophomores took it. When the bell rang, she found her locker, put on her coat, and hurried out of the building.

Nicky felt disillusioned by all the problems. Her main worry was the band director's comment about the school merger. This school might close before she graduated, and she would be back in a different and bigger school as a senior. Her luck had definitely not changed.

CHAPTER 47

A Crushing Wave of Despair

When Nicky entered the house, her mother wanted to know all about Nicky's day. Nicky felt miserable, and she considered not talking about it. But she needed to unload. As she complained, she made the day and the school sound awful.

Tears rolled down Nicky's cheeks as a crushing wave of despair swept over her. Her intense desire to go back to Eagleton flared up, and she resented how she had been taken away from her hometown.

"I don't want to go back there. They're all strangers. Everything here is bad like Norburg!"

"Nicky, it couldn't be that bad," said her mother.

When her father got home, she didn't feel like talking to him.

"How was your day, Nicky?" He sounded upbeat. He hoped to hear that she liked everything.

She said, "Don't ask."

After supper, her father said they should talk about what was bothering her. They sat around the old gray table on green chairs in their new green and gray kitchen.

"Your mother says you had a difficult day, and you don't like the new school. Let's try to find some positive things about it. How was band?"

"Fine. There are ten flutists, but only a few brass players. The director graduated from college last year."

"Did you like the director?"
"Yes."
"That's a start. What else?"
"I have to take German all by myself. They don't have a German I class. Everyone is way ahead of me."
"You'll catch up."
"The algebra teacher doesn't have control of the class."
Her father snorted as if her observation wasn't important.
"The gym teacher barely noticed that he had two new students."
He snorted again.
"The school is practically dark. The halls don't have lights on."
"Maybe they're trying to conserve energy. School building maintenance is expensive."
"Kids smoke in the bathrooms, and they stink."
"There must be other bathrooms. How many did you try?"
"Two."
"You'll find another one."
"No one talked to me, except the counselor and the girl they assigned to me. But she ignored me at lunch, and she probably won't talk to me again."
"You don't know that. You're being very negative and critical."
Nicky dropped her eyes. He had taught her to be critical, but he didn't want her to criticize a new opportunity.
"The counselor said the school would close in a few years."
"I haven't read about it, and it doesn't seem likely."
He didn't believe what she said, and she was tired of trying to convince him the school was a mess.
"I'm not going back to the school tomorrow."
Her father exploded. "You're a smart girl who gets good grades. You know that you have to be in school. It'll be good if you want it to be good!

"I'm disappointed in your negative attitude. Nothing makes you happy. Why is that? We expect you to figure out how to be happier and soon. We're not moving again, and you're not going to bring us all down with your attitude." He crossed his arms and glowered at her.

Nicky was despondent as she listened. She wasn't a grown-up in a 16-year-old's body. She was a teen girl trying to get through her life. Since she was unhappy, she wasn't doing a decent job of it. Since she wasn't handling it well, she must not be smart or sensible. She felt stupid for thinking anything would change in another new place.

Nicky felt no hope anyone would ever want to be her friend, and she felt worthless. She believed then nothing would ever get better, and going to high school was pointless. If she kept living, she might always be miserable. She didn't want to live in Westville, so she begged for the only thing she thought would make her happy again.

"Please, can we go home? To Eagleton? Please?"

"No! You can't manipulate us. I won't let you ruin this family with your begging! Now you behave!" he said vehemently.

"Eagleton is not your home. Eagleton is not your home. Eagleton is NOT your home!"

He repeated the phrase as if he could brainwash her into believing it.

She yelled at him. "Eagleton IS my home! THIS is not my home!"

Her father scoffed angrily. She suddenly had to get away, to stop listening to him. Nicky pushed back her chair, and she dashed from the kitchen. She went up to her room, got her coat, then flew out of the house, and rushed down the street in the dark.

Before she got halfway down the block, her mother came running after her.

"Nicky! What are you doing? Please don't run away! We love you!"

"Mom, where would I go? You know I don't have anywhere to go! I don't know anybody here! I just have to get away from him! I'll come back later."

She walked away and her mother didn't follow, but Nicky heard her mother's sobs. Nicky didn't want to hurt her mother, but she wanted to hurt her father, which was confusing because she loved him, and he knew way more than she did. She must be the problem because she couldn't do what he wanted her to do, which was be happy. He had said she was a disappointment to him, and she saw herself as a failure.

Nicky went to the little park just a few blocks from the house, then she walked to Bright Street, the town's "Main Street." They had only lived there one week, and she had not been downtown yet. As she walked along the street, Nicky thought about various methods of suicide. She dismissed all of them, except using insulin, because it would be easy. She wanted candy, although she knew it was bad for her body. What did that matter now?

She looked at the store windows along Bright Street while she tried to find some place to buy the candy. She noticed a couple of junior-high-aged boys across the street near a bus stop.

Without warning, one boy darted out to the street, picked up a stone, and threw it at her. It hit her on the chest. He ran back to the shelter of the bus stop and laughed while he waited with his friends to see her reaction. Nicky hurried away, and she was afraid the boys might run across the street and attack her. This was a new, strange place, and she knew nothing about it.

Nicky found a store and went inside, where she bought a bag of candy bars. She was cold, so she ran all the way back to the house. She couldn't let her mother see the bag. She planned to eat the sweets until she got sick.

When Nicky entered the new house, she hurried up the stairs, and hid the candy in her room. Then she went back down to get some water. Her mother got up from her chair.

"Are you OK? Where did you go?"

"I walked downtown, then a boy threw a rock at me and hit me in the chest!"

"That's awful! Are you hurt?"

"No, he threw it from across the street, like I was a target."

"I'm sorry that happened, but I'm glad you aren't hurt. You should go tell your father you're back. He's in the kitchen."

Nicky grimaced and hesitated, but she slowly went into the kitchen. Her father was reading the paper, and he looked up.

"So, you came back."

He said it as if he knew she wouldn't run away. She gritted her teeth. She wished she had run away, just to show him she could. Instead, she knew she had to apologize. He paid for the roof over her head.

"Dad, I'm sorry that I cause you so much trouble. My ideals are different from yours. Eagleton is my home, and that's the way it is."

"We know you miss it," said her mother. She had followed Nicky into the kitchen. Her father just stared at her without speaking.

"I'll go back to the school."

Her father nodded.

"Maybe I need to talk to someone that isn't you or Mom, you know, a counselor or someone like that."

"We'll find someone," said her mother.

Nicky turned around and ran upstairs, where she started eating the candy. She didn't think she could wait until they found a counselor for her. She was miserable now and she needed to do something. The black hot-air balloon of despair and depression had crashed down, and it was smothering her.

CHAPTER 48

Hope

Nicky sat in her room and ate her third candy bar. She hated her life, and how she was handling it. She wanted to talk to a friend who would support her. She called Paizlee. Paizlee's mother said she was at a play rehearsal and would be sorry she missed Nicky's call.

Nicky desperately needed to talk to someone. She decided to call Gage because he understood the experience of switching schools. He was the only one who knew that she had felt like ending her life in October. He said to call her if she ever felt like that again.

"Hi Gage. It's Nicky."

"Hey! This is a surprise."

"Can you talk with me? I'm having a bad time."

"Sure."

"I found out today that this new school is as awful and as strange as the old one. I can't take it anymore, so I ran off tonight."

"Where are you now?"

"I'm back home, but it's only because I don't have anywhere to go."

"If you were in Eagleton, you could come here."

"I wish I could. I don't even feel like I have a home now."

"Eagleton didn't feel like home to me at first, either. It took me a long time to meet people."

"At least Eagleton is a small town and friendlier than this place. People don't care in this city."

"Wow. That sucks."

"Yeah. I mean, what's the point of living if you can't make friends?"

"You've got friends back here. So, you gotta keep living. You can't give up, so keep trying."

"I guess."

They talked for a while more, then hung up. Nicky felt better as she went downstairs to watch TV with Ryan.

"Did some kid actually hit you with a rock?"

"Yeah."

"What a jerk. Kids shouldn't throw rocks at people. What if he had hit your eye? You would have had to go to the hospital like I did. What a jerk!"

"At least no one threw rocks at us in Norburg."

Ryan nodded. Then he said, "But this is obviously another dumb place."

Nicky knew her brother was also facing a new school and strange people. His empathy comforted her.

"What was your first day like?"

"No big deal." They went back to watching the show.

Nicky was tired the next day, and she begged to stay home. Her mother let her. She wrote about everything which had happened at the new school and the discussion with her father. She ate some of the candy, but she was calm. Gage was right. She had to keep trying, somehow.

Her mother entered her room.

"Your father had an idea about letting you visit Eagleton. Would you like to do that?"

Nicky's face lit up as she nodded. "When?"

"Westville has spring break in a few weeks. What if you flew out to Ridgeland City on Saturday, stayed a week, and flew back? You need to find somewhere to stay, and someone who could pick you up."

"That would be terrific, Mom."

"You could ask Paizlee if you could stay with her, or Bella."

Paizlee called Nicky back that night. Nicky didn't want to get upset again, so she didn't tell Paizlee about the previous day.

"Guess what? I get to visit Eagleton! Do you want to see me?"

"That would be so great! When?"

"How about the week after next?"

"Wow! Can you really come?"

"My parents said I could. Can my mom talk to yours to arrange it?"

"Sure, hold on."

The mothers discussed the details of the stay. They talked more than Paizlee and Nicky did. But the friends would get time to talk face-to-face soon. At last, Nicky had hope to keep her going for the next week. She could scarcely wait to see her friends and be back in Eagleton. She made a list of what to take, and she thought about who she should write.

Nicky walked to school the following day. The school counselor had worked out her schedule. She had English third hour, and German fourth hour. The same teacher welcomed her, but she only stayed half of the hour before she left Nicky alone in the room.

The lunchroom with windows was better than the basement one in Norburg. Four boys sat across from her at a round table, but they ignored her, and she felt like a pariah. How many times would she be alone here?

After lunch, she went to a different math class, and she liked the new teacher better than the first one. She tried the nearby bathroom, and it was clean. It would be the only one she would use.

For the rest of the week, she adjusted to the schedule and the school building. Some problems were solved, and she began to like the smaller, more relaxed school. But she still didn't want to be there. No one reached out to her, and she was a ghost again. Somehow, she had to make it through the days until spring break.

At dinner, her father brought up the trip.

"I'm not comfortable with you flying out to Ridgeland City alone," he said.

"And I want to visit my parents, so I'll drive you and Ryan to Eagleton. After we drop you off, Ryan and I will keep going," said her mother.

"I like that idea," said Nicky.

"I've decided to rent a car for you, so I don't have to worry about car trouble," said her father.

A few days before the trip, Nicky called Paizlee to give her an update on driving instead of flying, and to figure out activities for the week. The girls chatted like they had only been apart for a brief time. She also called Bella and made plans to see her.

As Nicky perked up, her father noticed. When he got home on Thursday, he asked Nicky and her mother to join him in the kitchen.

"Your mother reminded me she left home when she had just turned 17. I was 18 when I went to college, and 20 when I went into the Air Force. You're almost that old. If you want to finish school in Eagleton, we could figure out how to make it work."

"Really? That would be great. Thanks, Dad." She smiled.

"Well, wait a minute. It won't be easy. You'd need to find a place to live, a job, and a car, so when you're back there next week, you'll need to ask people for help with all of that." Her father paused a minute to let that sink in.

"I'd have to drive back and forth in the beginning to help her get set up," said her mother. Her father's eyebrows inched close together.

"Maybe at first, but once she's settled, she needs to take care of herself."

Nicky felt a stab of guilt as she realized her mother wouldn't be taking care of her father and brother if she were in Eagleton with Nicky. But the elation of any possibility of going to school again with friends felt wonderful. She hoped her friends still wanted her around. If they didn't, she wasn't sure what she would do. She thought about not being around her family and felt sadness mixing with her joy.

On Friday night, Nicky finished packing her suitcase. The next night, she would be back in Eagleton, where the streets were familiar. She was eager to see Paizlee, Bella, Alyssa, and Elena. She longed to see

Gage and the other boys. She wanted to talk to everyone. It had been so long since she had enjoyed talking with her friends in person.

Her mother drove Nicky and Ryan through Westville and Elk Prairie early in the morning in the rental car. Traffic was light as they merged onto the interstate highway. They were leaving the big city and its suburbs behind them. Nicky felt tremendous relief, as if someone had lifted a weight off her.

After they ate lunch, Nicky and Ryan slept, read, listened to the radio, and played the car license plate game. Nicky's eyes sparkled with happiness as they reversed the trip taken last June.

She held her breath as they got closer to their destination. At long last, she saw the dark shadow of the Ponderosa Hills on the horizon. The old mountains grew bigger as the car crept along. Dark green pine trees, granite, and limestone rocks filled her vision. She drank in the view that she had missed so much. They passed Ridgeland City as dusk descended, and she noticed how the houses spread out in the green foothills with an expanse of land around them. She opened the window for a moment to breathe the fresh, piney air. She relaxed and smiled.

The car sped over the remaining miles as they drove through the familiar land. They reached the Eagleton exit and got off the highway. They drove north on Central Avenue, past the Eagleton Inn and the Crossings Drive-In. They saw Peaceful Bear Mountain in the distance. Soon they turned at the stoplight and passed their old house, which was still empty. Then they drove up the hill to Paizlee's house.

As they pulled into Paizlee's driveway, Nicky saw a sign with pink and white balloons tied on it. "Welcome Back, Nicky!" She smiled widely, opened the car door, and walked to Paizlee's door. She was home at last, with her stellar friends.

SUPPORT

FOR TEENS

WHO HAVE BEEN

MOVED

MESSAGES OF SUPPORT

A Teen and Her Grandmother

Imagine a teen who was moved from a small town to a big city, similar to Nicky, but in a decade when people exchange text messages. She experiences a rough time adjusting to her new house, city, school, lack of friends, and her changing sense of herself. She feels lost and overwhelmed as she tries to handle the challenges on her own.

What if that teen has an adult close to her and she text messages with them? She feels she can honestly express her emotions to that person. She knows she is loved and supported no matter what she texts or how she feels.

What if that person was her grandmother? If her grandmother was knowledgeable about psychology, she could help her grandchild identify some of the issues she faces and provide some strategies to adjust to the move and to assist her in figuring out how to feel some contentment. The communication could be a way for the teen to explore her emotions and not feel so alone.

TEXT MESSAGES OF SUPPORT

Topic 1. Feeling Lost..246

Topic 2. Missing Friends..248

Topic 3. Learning Mindfulness Meditation......................250

Topic 4. Feeling As If No One Cares.............................254

Topic 5. Feeling Lonely...257

Topic 6. Having Doubts about Joining a Team...............260

Topic 7. Having Conflict with a Parent.........................263

Topic 8. Hating School..267

Topic 9. Asking for Help..271

Topic 10. Feeling Some Hope......................................275

1. Feeling Lost

> **Hi Honey. How do you like your new home?**
>
> Hi Gram. I don't like it.
>
> **Being moved to a new place can be difficult, especially at your age. You didn't have a choice. What don't you like?**
>
> Everything! I don't know where anything is. I don't know where to hang out anymore. It's awful. 😨
>
> **You haven't been there long, so it's natural to feel lost, as if you're in a maze. It takes time to adjust to a change. Remember when you didn't like your summer camp? By the end, you knew where everything was and you didn't want to leave!**
>
> But I feel stupid here. I knew our old place so well. I miss it SOOO much. 😔

Feeling Lost

> It's OK to miss your old home. You liked your life back there. It's tough to let it go.

> I'll never let it go! It will always be my home.

> Are you thinking about it a lot?

> What else do I have to think about here in no man's land? This place is so alien. 👽 🪐

> Could you take a bike ride or walk around your new neighborhood? It might distract you. There's lots to learn about your new world.

> I have, but I don't want to be here.

> I get that. But when I come to visit next month, will you show me around?

> Sure. I'll find a few places to show you.

> I'm sorry this move is so hard. Remember that I love you. 🌚

2. Missing Friends

> Hi Honey. How are you doing?

> I'm SO lonely. I miss my friends!

> That must feel awful. You were close to them. You knew them a long time.

> Yeah, like years. We went to elementary school together! They were my peeps, my fam. Now I don't have anyone.

> You have your parents and brother, even though you're getting more independent from them. Of course, you're at the age when you need people who understand you and who talk about things you want to know about.

> My friends are so far away! Texting isn't enough. I need to see what they're doing, and chill with them. I'm tired of being by myself. I cry a lot. 😭

> It's definitely OK to feel sad. You might be sad for awhile.

Missing Friends

> People grieve when change forces them to leave people or places, not just when someone dies.

Leaving them really hurt. 😨 Every time I think of them, I fall into this dark hole. I'm miserable.

> Oh my! How do you get out of that hole?

Watch TV or listen to music until I stop thinking. I wish I could visit back home. 'Course then I'd have to say goodbye again.

> Saying goodbye isn't easy. But if you went, you would at least have fun for a while. That would lift your spirits. Why not ask your parents if they will take you?

I'll ask! I hope they say yes! 👍

> Me, too!

3. Learning Mindfulness Meditation

> Good morning! Since I got back, I have been thinking about the nice visit with you. 😊

> I wish you didn't have to leave.

> Every goodbye now must feel like a bigger loss than it usually would.

> Uh huh.

> Have you tried the mindfulness practice that I taught you?

> No...Why?

> Wanting things to be different is part of why you're suffering. Mindfulness meditation can help you feel more grounded in the present. It might help you deal with these tough feelings. If you practice it, you may relax a little and feel less unhappy.

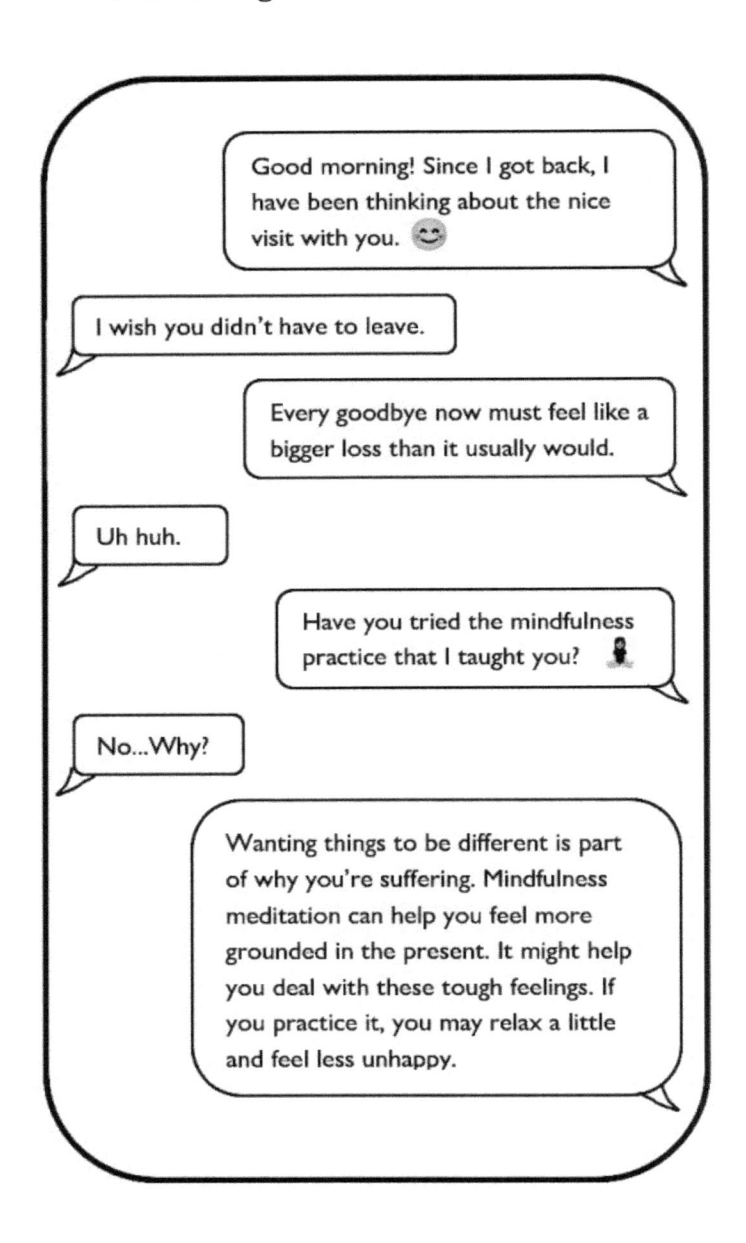

Learning Mindfulness Meditation

> Oh. How do I do it again?

> First, get out the cushion I gave you.

> Just a sec

> Ok. I'm sitting on it.

> Cross your legs and gently place your palms on your thighs. Keep your eyes open and look about 5-6 feet in front of you.

> Then pay attention to your breath. One thing you always have with you is your breath. Just breathe in and out naturally. Don't force it. Just focus on it. If you have a thought, just say to yourself, "Thinking."

> For how long?

> Set your phone timer for 2 min then gently raise your head. Text me again after that.

> Done.

Learning Mindfulness Meditation

> How did that go?

I couldn't focus because I kept thinking.

> Yes, our minds seem full of thoughts, but that isn't a problem. Your mind is like a wild horse right now. You need to train it. Just focus on your breath again whenever you become aware that you're thinking. But do so gently.

I have so many stupid thoughts, Gram. I must be stupid for thinking stupid thoughts. 😿

> Try not to criticize yourself or your thoughts. Thoughts are just brain activity. Your thoughts aren't actually solid. Part of doing this is to learn how to accept yourself as you are. Just return to focusing on your breath.

OK. I can't to do it very long.

> You'll learn how. Your thoughts will start to settle down if you practice this way. You'll build the mental muscle so you can sit longer.

Learning Mindfulness Meditation

> Learning to be present will help you as you adjust to your new reality. It will help you be kind to yourself and others.

> Would you please sit for 5 min each day this week? If you keep at it, you'll want to do it every day because you'll feel calmer.

> Do YOU want to do it every day?

> There are days that I don't. But when I make the effort to practice working with my mind, I feel more capable of dealing with the crazy world inside my head and outside my door. There's a lot of stress everywhere. Taking care of yourself is important.

> 'K. This is doing nothing but I have nothing to do anyway. So bored. 😔

> That's not quite the attitude I was hoping for, but it's a start. Let's talk about it in a few days on the phone. Hope your day goes well!

4. Feeling As If No One Cares

> Gram, my new school sucks. 😟

> I'm sorry to hear you think that. It's a new place to get used to. It's bigger, isn't it?

> It's huge! I get lost and it takes forever to get to my next class so I'm always late.

> That must be embarrassing. Once you know the hallways, you'll figure out a faster way. You could let the teachers know that you need more time for now.

> No way! I don't want them to think I'm a slow poke who can't walk fast enough. 😜

> How could you solve your problem then? Could you ask for a map of the school to see if there's a quicker path?

> I'd have to go to the office. I don't want to.

Feeling as if No One Cares

> You might have to ask someone for help. What else bothers you?

> The halls smell weird.

> Smells can seem strange at first but they often fade from our attention. Once you start talking to people, you'll think more about them than the weird smells.

> But no one talks to me! No one cares about me! I'm nobody here.

> There will be some people who will care. You just don't know them yet.

> I want my OLD friends who care now!

> You made good friends before, so you can make good friends again. Finding new friends takes effort and time. But it will happen. Try to be patient for awhile longer.

> How?

Feeling as if No One Cares

> Have you done the mindfulness exercise? That will help you accept how things are.

> A few times...

> I'm happy to hear that!

> I went outside once. All I noticed were some ants crawling up my leg. Well, I thought the leaves were pretty. But I couldn't follow my breath.

> Those were good observations. When you're at school, try to notice something you don't hate. That's a first step to learning to like it.

> I will...if I remember.

> Please try it. And hang in there.

5. Feeling Lonely

> Hi Honey! How are you?

> IDK. I wish someone would talk to me at school. I feel like I'm a ghost. 👻

> It sounds like you haven't made any new friends yet. Most people want a group to belong to, where we feel that people see us.

> Yeah. Nobody sees ME here. People I sit next to in class don't say hi. I even eat lunch alone.

> Have you asked someone to eat lunch with you?

> No. I'm new, they should talk to me first!

> I know you're more introverted so it's harder for you to speak first. But if you want friends, you'll need to make that desire clear to them. Other kids can't read your mind. If you're friendly, others will be friendly back. 😊

Feeling Lonely

> I can't do it, Gram. I start shaking and my mouth doesn't work whenever I even THINK about talking to someone I don't know.

> It helps to practice something to say before you speak. Try practicing with your mother or in front of the mirror.

> But I know I'll say dumb things. People will think I'm a loser. 👆

> You're thoughtful and sensitive, not a loser. Just smile at someone and ask them a question. Chances are good, they'll talk to you.

> What kind of question?

> Well, since you like to bike, ask them if they know of a good bike path nearby. Or if they're drawing something, ask what they're drawing. Think about what you would say to someone at your old school.

Feeling Lonely

> But I knew everyone there! It's too scary when I don't know anyone.

> Have you seen anyone who doesn't talk to anyone else before class? They might be new to the school, too. They might be happy if you talk to them. They may feel just as afraid to reach out as you are.

> I never thought about that.

> You aren't the only one who feels shy and lonely at that school. Many kids do. You could help each other.

> But I don't know if I'll like them.

> You won't know until you talk to them.

> What if they don't like me?

> What if they do like you? You could find a new best friend. Let me know how it goes!

6. Having Doubts about Joining a Team

> Your Mom says you are joining the gymnastics team. That's great to hear!

> I said I MIGHT go to a meeting…

> Is something holding you back?

> They're probably all better than me.

> It sounds like you're not feeling confident. But you were a good gymnast in the other school. You can be just as good at this school.

> Maybe I'm not any good any more.

> A sports coach will help any child who wants to learn. So if you show up, the coach will show you what you need to do.

> It's not the coach I'm afraid of. Maybe I don't want to. Maybe that's not who I am anymore.

Having Doubts about Joining a Team

> Well, what about meeting new friends by joining the team?

IDK. Maybe people will laugh at me and won't want to be my friends.

> Let's do a visualization. See yourself laughing and having fun on the team. You're strong and you help the team win.

I can't even imagine that. Maybe I can't have fun any more. 😟

> That sounds like your defeatist voice.

What's that?

> It's the inner voice that often tells you that you aren't good enough to do things or you do them wrong. But that voice is often unkind. Don't let it keep you away from trying a new opportunity.

How?

Having Doubts about Joining a Team

> First, find a mirror. Then take a deep breath and let it out. Then say, "You are a gymnast. You belong on the gymnastics team. You ARE good enough! You're confident!" Then smile. Every time you feel doubtful, say that to yourself. You could even write it down.

> That sounds like that Sound of Music song you always sing.

> "I have confidence in sunshine, I have confidence in rain, I have confidence that spring will come again! Besides which you see, I have confidence in me!" It's a great song. It helps me when I'm anxious. So are you going to go to the team meeting?

> Yeah, I'll go, but just to see who my competition would be.

> And who your new friends might be! That's the spirit! Hugs! XXOO

7. Having Conflict with a Parent

> Gram, why does Dad hate me? 👩

> I know that he doesn't but what happened?

> He keeps planning dumb family stuff and I don't want to go. Then he says I'm not participating and he's so mean when he says it, like I'm bad. Why do I have to go?

> Parents often want to enjoy spending time with their children. I wonder if he was looking forward to a place but because you were unhappy, he couldn't enjoy it. He may have felt frustrated. I know he's been worried about you.

> Wish he'd been worried before he moved us.

> Do you feel angry at him?

> Yes 😠

> Have you yelled at him?

Having Conflict with a Parent

> Maybe once or twice…

> When I was there, we talked about the difference between your emotions, thoughts and behaviors. It's OK to feel angry, but it's not OK to yell at other people.

> But he's the one who ruined my life!

> Why do you think that?

> Because he took me away from my friends! People I loved! My old school, the teachers, our house, our dog!

> Have you talked to him calmly about how you feel?

> Yes. But he didn't care. I asked him if we could go back home and he said that where he and Mom are is my home. But it's not my home! I don't want to live here. I wish we'd never moved.

Having Conflict with a Parent

> It seems that you are fighting against accepting that you can't go back to your old life. Fighting doesn't make your life any better. It only causes you more pain.

> So I just have to be depressed for the rest of my life??? 😣

> Of course not, dear. You have some control over your feelings and how you move forward. You have the power to make a choice to do something different — and that may change how you feel.

> But I want Dad to know that he was wrong to move us!

> Accepting that your life has changed isn't the same as showing approval. Acceptance is nonjudgemental. It's simply acknowledging what is now.

> I guess I'm an awful person because I don't want to accept it. I'm so mad.

Having Conflict with a Parent

> You're not an awful person. Feeling angry is something you can work through. Your father loves you and he didn't know how unhappy you'd be after this move.

> He should have.

> You can get through this. What things have you been doing to help yourself feel better?

> I watch videos mostly. Sometimes I take a walk.

> How about asking your dad to play a board game that you both like? Having some good times together may help you get back to a better relationship.

> OK. I hope he doesn't get upset at me when I win.

> Maybe you could set some ground rules so that you'll both be respectful and just have fun. It's worth a try. ☺

8. Hating School

> How did you do on the French test today?

Think I failed it. I don't like that class. I'm too dumb. 😟

> I know you aren't dumb. French can be tough. Why don't you like the class?

The teacher doesn't let us work together.

> Maybe that will change. Have you been doing your homework?

Mostly. I think I'm failing all of my classes actually.

> What's going on?

I hate that school. I really hate it! I don't want to go any more. It's too much. I can't handle it. I am tired all the time. Too tired to care about dumb homework. 😣

Hating School

> That sounds like more serious depression. Are you still crying a lot?

> Pretty much ALL THE TIME. Before school, after school, after dinner etc. etc. 😟

> Have you made any friends yet?

> I met some people, but they aren't friends. I still miss my old friends. They're having fun and I'm NOT.

> It's taking you awhile to adjust to leaving them. That's OK. But you do have to get good grades. It's important for your future.

> I don't care about my future.

> That's a new way of thinking for you. What about your dream of becoming a professional musician?

> I hardly ever think about it now.

Hating School

> I probably couldn't any way. The band teacher doesn't like me. No one does. I don't even like me.

> That attitude concerns me. Why don't you like yourself?

> Because I'm a mess. I can't get my act together. That's what Dad says – Why don't you get your act together? He's right. I should be doing better by now.

> What do you think you should be doing?

> Have lots of friends, go to the games, with them, get invited to parties, have a boyfriend, be on the honor roll, get a solo for the concert…

> That's quite a bit. I know you're impatient, but please understand that good things take some time. Step by step, you'll get there.

Hating School

> I used to be smart, Gram. I used to talk to people all the time. I was first chair flutist. Now, nothing. Worthless. I'm just worthless. 😵

> I understand that you feel that way, that you're telling yourself that. But remember that critical, defeatist voice we talked about? You don't have to listen to it.

> What else do I listen to? I'm alone all the time.

> Listen to your wise self instead. Make a list of activities that you like to do and start small. You don't have to be perfect, just make one attempt. Once you feel more confident, you may stop feeling so down.

> Well, there's an essay contest I was thinking of entering…

> Well, what are you waiting for? Just entering it gives you a chance to win!

9. Asking for Help

> Gram, I need help.

> Certainly. What do you need?

> That's just it. I don't know, but there's something really wrong with me. I just got mad at Mom. I never do that. I'm a terrible person. I don't deserve to live!

> I'm sure your mother will forgive you once you apologize. But I agree that it may be time to get some help. Remember the quicksand scene in The Princess Bride? You may need a hand to get out of the quicksand of your depression.

> I doubt I will ever get out. I keep waiting but things are worse, not better. The move broke me, didn't it?

> I don't think you're "broken." Struggling with issues and adjustments is pretty much what life is about You have basic goodness and you can bounce back.

Asking for Help

> **What does that mean?**

> It means that underneath your impatience, frustration and unhappiness is a shining sun just waiting to come out. It's tough for you to believe that right now, but it's true.

> **But I can't do anything right.**

> Says your critical, unkind inner voice. What you're facing is challenging, but you CAN feel whole again. It's time to find a mental health counselor, someone who can help you understand your feelings and learn some skills to deal with them.

> **Who? How do I do that?**

> There are many psychologists who are trained to work with teens just like you. We just have to find someone to teach you some strategies to build your confidence and help you feel joy again.

Asking for Help

> I'll support you in any way I can. First, let's meet with your parents. I'll set up a Zoom call.

> OK. But don't tell anyone else! I don't want them to know I can't handle this by myself.

> This info will be private. But you're dealing with big issues. It's mature of you to ask for assistance.

> What will a counselor do?

> They'll ask you questions and listen to your answers. They'll evaluate the level of your depression and help you deal with it. You need to respond to them and not just expect them to fix you, though.

> How long will it take?

> Your grief over losing everything except your parents is very deep so it may take awhile.

Asking for Help

> **Will I have to take pills?**

> I am not qualified to answer that. Everyone is different. A pill may sound like an easy treatment, but inner work needs to go along with medication, if you need it.

> **And what if they can't help me?**

> A good counselor can help just about anyone feel better about themselves. In my experience, just talking to someone and taking what they say seriously helps change your perspective.

> **All I really want is to find friends.**

> Once you like yourself again, that will be easier. Your counselor may teach you some communication and assertiveness skills that you can practice.

> **OK, I'll try it.**

10. Feeling Some Hope

> Hi my most excellent Granddaughter! How are things?

> Good. Guess what?

> What?

> I started volunteering at the food bank and I met this cool girl who's in my history class. She lives right down the block!

> Great news! Did you use some of the communication skills you learned with your counselor?

> Yeah, I guess. We both reached for the same bowl and apologized then we started laughing. We laughed the rest of the time! 😊

> I'm so happy to hear that you were laughing. Are you going to do anything together? 👧 👩

Feeling Some Hope

> Yep! Skating on Saturday. We're going to work on the history paper together, too.

> It sounds like you have some similar interests. Have you been feeling better?

> Yeah, a lot.

> Last time I called, you said you liked your counselor. Are the sessions still going well?

> Mostly. Sometimes I don't know what to say. I don't always get the homework done.

> Well, I'm proud of you for trying and learning more about yourself. If you can make one friend, you can make more. Volunteering is a good way to feel like you can help others, too.

> I like helping! It makes me feel good about myself.

Feeling Some Hope

> And that means you're respecting yourself more. Is your critical voice easier to quiet?

> It's still pretty mean. But I'm not letting it get its way so often.

> Have you had any more fights with your dad?

> A few but I don't feel like yelling as much. We take a breath when we start to ramp up.

> Excellent approach. I hope you'll keep going to counseling so you can keep growing, keep finding your strengths and keep dealing with your emotions.

> Mom made 6 more sessions so I have to keep going.

> Good. Well, enjoy skating and getting to know your new friend. I'm glad you're happier. 💕

> Me Too!!!! 😊

Author's Thoughts on Being Moved as a Teen

Being moved as a teen is a traumatic life event. I use the phrase "being moved" because, as a teen, you are not in the driver's seat. Your parents or caregivers decided to move you even if they consulted with you. It can be especially tough to accept the way your situation changes when you have no choice.

Growing up is difficult enough without such a major life change. If you were moved and have trouble afterward, know you are not alone. Many teens do not adjust well after a move. They feel lost and far outside of their comfort zone.

Negative feelings about the move do not make you a bad or weak person. You are a basically good person who is encountering some temporarily difficult lessons. Your conscious and subconscious mind must work through many emotions.

Dug Up

After a move, you may feel like your caretakers dug you up like a flowering plant, then carried you away, and transplanted you to a new location. Your roots experience stress after being pulled out of that safe old ground, and it may take time to settle into the new ground. The new soil might not ever feel as good as the old.

You are forced to face unfamiliar people, places, and routines. You may have to attend a new school. You learned certain ways of being in your old location, but after the move, you cannot do normal activities the same way. You must learn an activity which used to be automatic, such as how to get from your house to school or the store. You may feel overwhelmed, and like a plant, lose your blooms or even your leaves for a while.

Your Brain Is Changing

As a teen, you may have more difficulty with a move because your body, including your brain, is in a specific phase of growing. You are in the middle of learning new ways to respond to what happens around you. Although you are more mature than when you were younger, your brain is not in its adult form yet. Your brain is quite impressionable, which makes both good and bad experiences seem more intense. You are in an extremely sensitive period of your life.

Social Interaction

You are in the middle of learning more about how to interact with people around you. Every school year, you make new friends, and your acquaintance group grows. You learn how to communicate with them and with adults who are not your parents or caregivers.

Communication with other people is complex. It includes talking, writing, body language, facial expressions, eye contact, emailing, texting, commenting on posts, using emojis, etc. Friends are incredibly important when learning how to interact well with others. Certain communication skills, like those learned in assertiveness training, help you communicate better.

But even if you have not had specific instructions, when you spend time with friends, family, and other adults like teachers and neighbors, you usually figure out how to take part in a conversation in a way so you and your partner both feel good. If someone does not respond like you think they will, then you adapt your approach. You want to feel seen, and so do the people you are with.

If you belong to a group of friends, you likely enjoy the feeling that you contribute to that group. They may be your primary focus outside of your family, schoolwork, or employment. You spend much of your time thinking about them as you build meaning with them.

As you become independent from your family and move into the bigger world, learning how to communicate, and especially talk, to others appropriately is important. Trainers can help you learn the skills needed, and if you keep practicing them, you will feel confident when interacting with new people.

A Move Interrupts Social Development

After a move to a new location, your forward social growth may be interrupted, at least for a while. You will not have the same amount or quality of interactions with new people as you did with your old group. It makes sense you still want to belong to your old group, and you may think about them frequently. You miss seeing them, and you do not feel like yourself without them.

Grief

Grief is a mental and emotional state of sadness and distress when you experience change and loss. It can sometimes result in physical responses, including tears and even health problems. Many people do not sleep well after loss, which makes it more difficult to get through the time after the loss. Your brain needs time to heal from separation.

You can experience deep grief after a big change, or a small change, not related to the death of someone close. You need time to learn how to live without all that was familiar to you. Caregivers may not understand the pain you feel, and they may get impatient that you are not "moving on" more quickly. Your caregivers often want and expect you to act as if nothing happened. They may not understand what you need, and you may need to figure out how to take care of yourself. Follow your own path at your own pace despite their demands.

You may experience a great deal of sadness about the loss of your old friends. You trusted them and now they are no longer around to talk to and see every day. It is natural to miss them.

Personality Differences

Your temperament and personality may help or hinder your adjustment and the time it takes you to feel comfortable again. Some researchers have found that moves during later school years can be difficult for introverted teens but not as bad for extroverted teens.

Extroverts. If you adapt quickly to a new middle or high school and start making friends, you may be an extrovert. Extroverts are more likely to reach out to new people and have curiosity about new surroundings. They tend to be talkative and sociable because they enjoy getting to know new people. Extroverts may not be inhibited or afraid of rejection or they have learned how to move past that fear. They may see the move to a new place as a wonderful experience and appreciate the new opportunities ahead.

Introverts. If you need time adjusting to a move, and you have trouble meeting new people, you may be an introvert. Introverts feel more comfortable focusing on their inner thoughts and ideas. They enjoy spending time with one or two people and exploring those relationships, rather than hanging out in large groups. Introverts may compare the new place unfavorably to the old place, and a negative opinion may interfere with their comfort level in the new place.

Identity

With new people, you may feel that you have lost your identity, and you do not know who you are anymore. You may long to be seen in the same way that your old friends saw you, the ones who knew you and accepted you. You think of yourself differently without them. You may not feel as confident or have as high self-esteem after the move.

Relative Deprivation

You may feel as if your new surroundings are not helping you thrive. You may feel that you are missing certain elements you needed to feel good about yourself in your old place. You may feel what is called "relative deprivation," which means even if you have a positive situation with no abuse or neglect in your new place, you may still feel as if you have less compared to what you had. You may feel you were robbed.

You may resent your parents or caregivers who moved you and feel anger toward them. With that anger, your relationship with them shifts, and they may be angry at your words and behavior in return. Suddenly, it seems like you lost another good part of your old life, your positive relationships with your close family members.

High School and Fun

Getting through high school takes three or four years of your life. Most teens want to have as much fun as possible during those years. Your culture, via movies and other media, drives expectations that everyone else is having more fun than you are. After a move, you may be angry with the changes in your life which seem to deny you that fun.

You may think you deserve a great school experience, and you lost it because you moved. The reality is many people who stay in one place are unhappy in high school. Many are not having a positive experience because most teens encounter the pain of growing up, which often does not meet their expectations and desires. If you had stayed in your old place, you might be having struggles with school, friends, or other situations. There is no way to know what might have gone wrong there.

In fiction stories, many writers put a new character in a high school story and that character somehow overcomes all obstacles to become the star of the team or part of the popular group. In real life, most kids do not end up conquering their new school. More often, teens who move in real life feel lonely for an extended period. It is nice to dream about succeeding when you are not coping well, so go ahead, read those books, and enjoy those movies. But do not compare your own real experience to fictional characters, or those who make their lives seem better than yours.

By knowing that not everyone has fun throughout high school, you may feel more comfortable reaching out to find other people and sharing your experience with them. Gather your courage, practice some opening conversation, and take a risk.

Life is Stressful

Difficulty making new friends can be a frightening and confusing experience when you are in school. It may feel that you will never get through the loneliness, and time may seem to drag while you figure out how to function after the move.

Throughout life, there will be times when you feel alone, upset, or disappointed. One task of growing up involves learning how to navigate through, around, or over hurdles like those feelings. With your growing independence from your family, you may think you should be able to figure it out on your own. Do not be ashamed if you cannot.

If you cannot handle the stress alone, you may need a helping hand for a while. Smart people ask for help when they need to learn something. The desire to figure out how to get back to feeling good after a move is an excellent reason to ask for some guidance.

Suicide is NOT the Answer

If you are seriously depressed (see Appendix C), if you are thinking about killing yourself, and especially if you have made plans to do so (see Appendix B), call a crisis helpline in your area. See Appendix A for numbers. Call now and do not delay.

What Can You Do to Cope?

As you struggle to cope with change, you may want to consider some of the following:

1. **Accept Your Disappointment**. Understand that other people have experienced similar difficulties adjusting after a move to a new place. You are normal if you feel stressed out by all the changes.
2. **Make Friends with Yourself**. Your inner voice may bully you into thinking you do not deserve to be happy again. That inner critic can be toxic. Just let yourself feel what you feel (without hurting yourself or others). Tell that critic that you need some

time. You could learn and practice some mindfulness meditation to be with your true good nature.

3. **Find New Hobbies.** Explore healthy hobbies that you can do, like playing games with your siblings, drawing, building something, or riding your bike in a local bike race.

4. **Exercise.** Exercise has been proven to help people feel better about themselves. Walk around, bike, skateboard, play tennis, or whatever else you like to do.

5. **Take a Social Skills Class.** Find a local class which teaches social skills to teens, join a teen Toastmasters group, or take an assertiveness training class. The instructors will give you exercises and allow you to practice in a safe environment.

6. **Be a Friend.** Ask someone next to you a question. If they do not respond positively, it may have nothing to do with you. They may have something else on their minds and their lack of positive response may not be related to you at all. Try again with another person, but be gentle and watch for cues that the new person is open to a talk. You might find someone who needs your friendship.

7. **Join an Activity.** Find an activity that you like which is offered in person at a school, a community center, or spiritual center, and show up even if you are nervous. You might have a great time and find friends who share that interest.

8. **Find Employment.** Sometimes teens who work together become friends. If you can find a job where there are other teens, it may help you get to know people.

9. **Volunteer.** Find a way to volunteer to help other people who need it. Many people struggle with life or need help with events and your helping hand will mean a lot to them.

10. **Use Your Phone Wisely.** Turn off notifications from social apps if they make you feel like you are the only person in the world experiencing pain. Better yet, turn off your phone and practice a sport, a song, a game, or work on a project.

11. **Talk to a Counselor**. If you still feel overwhelmed, find an adult who can listen and give you feedback. Ask your parents or your school counselor if you feel comfortable. Search online for help lines for teens. Once you have a number, gather your courage and call. You do not have to keep feeling so bad.

Back to the plant analogy: With time, your roots stretch out, and you learn how to be in your new soil. You cannot go back to your old home again and have things be the same as before you left. You have changed and your old friends have changed, too. But you can keep in touch to continue your relationships to some extent.

At the same time, you can look around and get to know new people in your new place and not be disloyal to your old friends. You may have to be the one to reach out and talk to new people. Unless you approach, other teens may not reach out to you. They may be afraid to do so. Yet if you make a connection, a new person may be someone you will care about deeply someday, as deeply as you did for your old friends.

Making friends with yourself is especially important in life. You may find some peace inside yourself if you search. Sometimes you have no choice but to adapt to unfriendly soil and figure out how to keep growing toward the sun despite new challenges. It may be hard, but you are often stronger than you think you are.

It took me some time, but I found the strength to be my own friend. Caring for myself helped me feel more content in my life, and able to care for others, too. Give it a try because you may surprise yourself and find some happiness in life again.

APPENDICES

APPENDIX A

Suicide and Crisis Lifelines

If you are triggered by the subject of suicide or are in crisis now, I strongly encourage you to talk to someone who is trained to help you deal with your distress. It is far better to reach out for help than to feel so overwhelmed that you take action that can never be undone.

You matter! Even if you don't believe that right now, others can help you understand and explore the wonderful gifts you have to offer the world.

USA: Suicide and Crisis Lifeline call or text **988**

- It's Confidential.
- It's Free.
- A trained counselor will listen and help you.
- It's available 24 hours a day, 7 days a week, 365 days a year.
- Visit 988lifeline.org for more information.

Additional Numbers*:

Argentina:	Suicide Hotline call +5402234930430
Australia:	Lifeline Australia call 13 11 14
Canada:	Crisis Text Line: text "DESERVE" to 686868
China:	Lifeline Shanghai www.lifeline-shanghai.com/
Finland:	Crisis Line call 010 195 202

Germany: Hotline call 800 111 0111
India: Sneha India call 91 44 24640050
New Zealand: Lifeline call 0800 543 35
South Africa: Helpline call 0800 12 13 14
Spain: De La Esperanza Telefono 717-003-717
UK / Ireland: Samaritans UK call 116 123

Other countries:
suicide.org/international-suicide-hotlines.html

*Author is not responsible for changes in this information. It is provided with the hope it may help in a time of crisis.

APPENDIX B

Warning Signs of Suicidal Intention

Many books, magazines, websites, blogs, and video resources can give you information to help you recognize if you, or anyone you know, is at risk of suicide. The following information is found on HelpGuide.org, a nonprofit mental health group, website page *Depression Symptoms and Warning Signs*.*

Warning Signs

Depression is a major risk factor for suicide. Deep despair and hopelessness can make suicide feel like the only way to escape the pain. If you have a loved one with depression, take any suicidal talk or behavior seriously and watch for the warning signs:

1. Talking about killing or harming oneself.
2. Expressing strong feelings of hopelessness or being trapped.
3. An unusual preoccupation with death or dying.
4. Acting recklessly, as if they have a death wish (e.g., speeding through red lights).
5. Calling or visiting people to say goodbye.

6. Getting affairs in order (giving away prized possessions, tying up loose ends).
7. Saying things like "Everyone would be better off without me," or "I want out."
8. A sudden switch from being extremely down to acting calm and happy.

If You Notice Warning Signs in Someone

Call a suicide and crisis prevention lifeline without delay!

Be aware that, sometimes, a person may not show any suicide warning signs, especially if they have tried suicide before. Some people shut down and do not want others to know how they are feeling. If a person changes and you are worried about them, try to be aware of what is going on and ask respectfully if you can help.

If You Feel Suicidal

When you're feeling suicidal, your problems don't seem temporary. They seem overwhelming and permanent. But with time, you will feel better, especially if you get help.

There are many people who will support you during this difficult time, so please reach out to someone you trust or call or text the suicide lifeline (See Appendix A).

---

*Smith, Melinda, Robinson, Lawrence, Segal, Jeanne. Depression Symptoms and Warning Signs of Suicide, HelpGuide.org, 08/14/2023, https://www.helpguide.org/articles/depression/depression-symptoms-and-warning-signs.htm, last accessed 08/24/2024.

APPENDIX C

Depression

Feeling down sometimes is a natural feeling for most people. However, if you experience serious mood changes that affect how you think, feel, behave, and handle daily activities, such as sleeping, eating, or working, you may be depressed.

Major or Clinical Depression can affect all ages, races, ethnicities, and genders. Some people with it may cry frequently and feel helpless while others may feel like they don't care about anything anymore, feel empty and remote. Some may express anger and irritability because expressing anger is more acceptable to them. People with depression may suppress or hide their symptoms from others, it may be a surprise to learn that the person deals with depression. No matter how they express it, someone who is depressed is more than just unhappy.

"My forest is dark,

the trees are sad,

and all the butterflies

have broken wings."

- Raine Cooper

A depressed teen may experience a wide variety of symptoms. If you frequently have more than five of the symptoms listed below, you may have a depression.

Common Symptoms of Depression (Teen)

Based on the PHQ-9 and PHQ-A (© Pfizer)

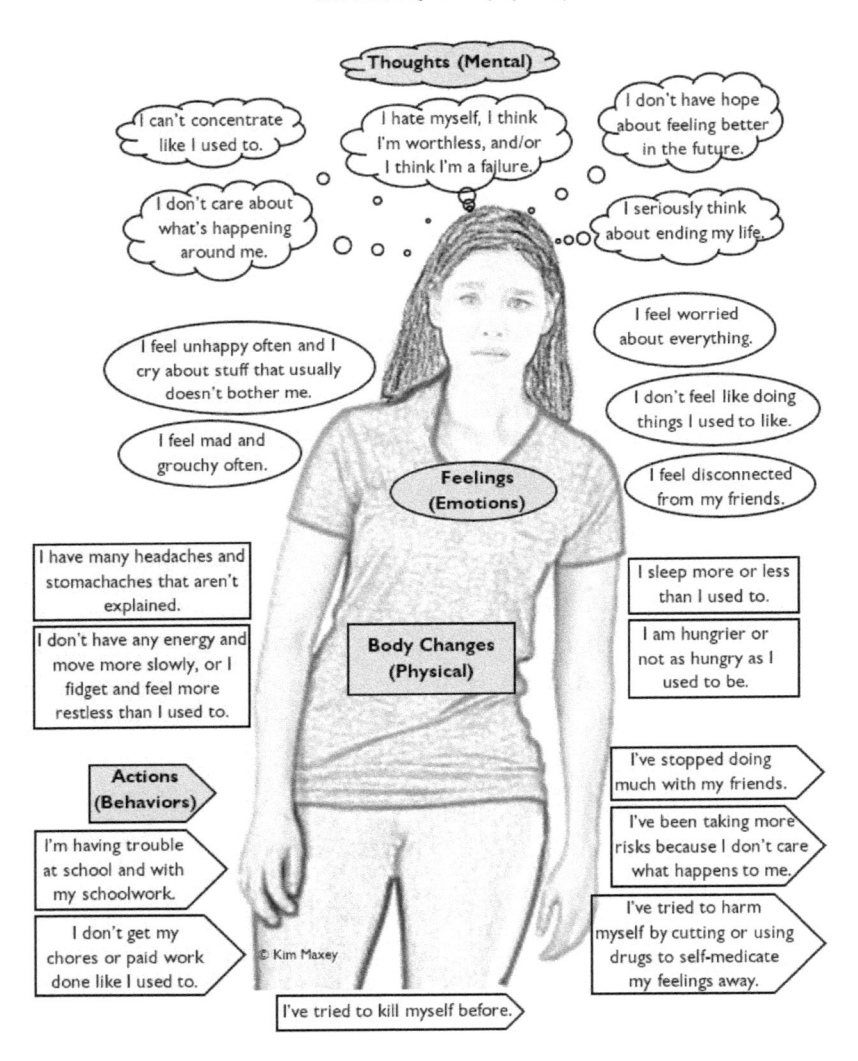

Thoughts (Mental)

- I can't concentrate like I used to.
- I hate myself, I think I'm worthless, and/or I think I'm a failure.
- I don't have hope about feeling better in the future.
- I don't care about what's happening around me.
- I seriously think about ending my life.

Feelings (Emotions)

- I feel unhappy often and I cry about stuff that usually doesn't bother me.
- I feel mad and grouchy often.
- I feel worried about everything.
- I don't feel like doing things I used to like.
- I feel disconnected from my friends.

Body Changes (Physical)

- I have many headaches and stomachaches that aren't explained.
- I don't have any energy and move more slowly, or I fidget and feel more restless than I used to.
- I sleep more or less than I used to.
- I am hungrier or not as hungry as I used to be.

Actions (Behaviors)

- I'm having trouble at school and with my schoolwork.
- I don't get my chores or paid work done like I used to.
- I've stopped doing much with my friends.
- I've been taking more risks because I don't care what happens to me.
- I've tried to harm myself by cutting or using drugs to self-medicate my feelings away.
- I've tried to kill myself before.

© Kim Maxey

Teens with Type 1 Diabetes (T1D) have an especially heavy self-care burden and may have additional symptoms of depression and distress.

Symptoms of Diabetes Distress (Teen)

Based on the Type 1 Diabetes Distress Scale, (T1--DDS) and Type 1 Diabetes Distress Assessment System (T1DDAS), Behavioral Diabetes Institute, William Polonsky et al.

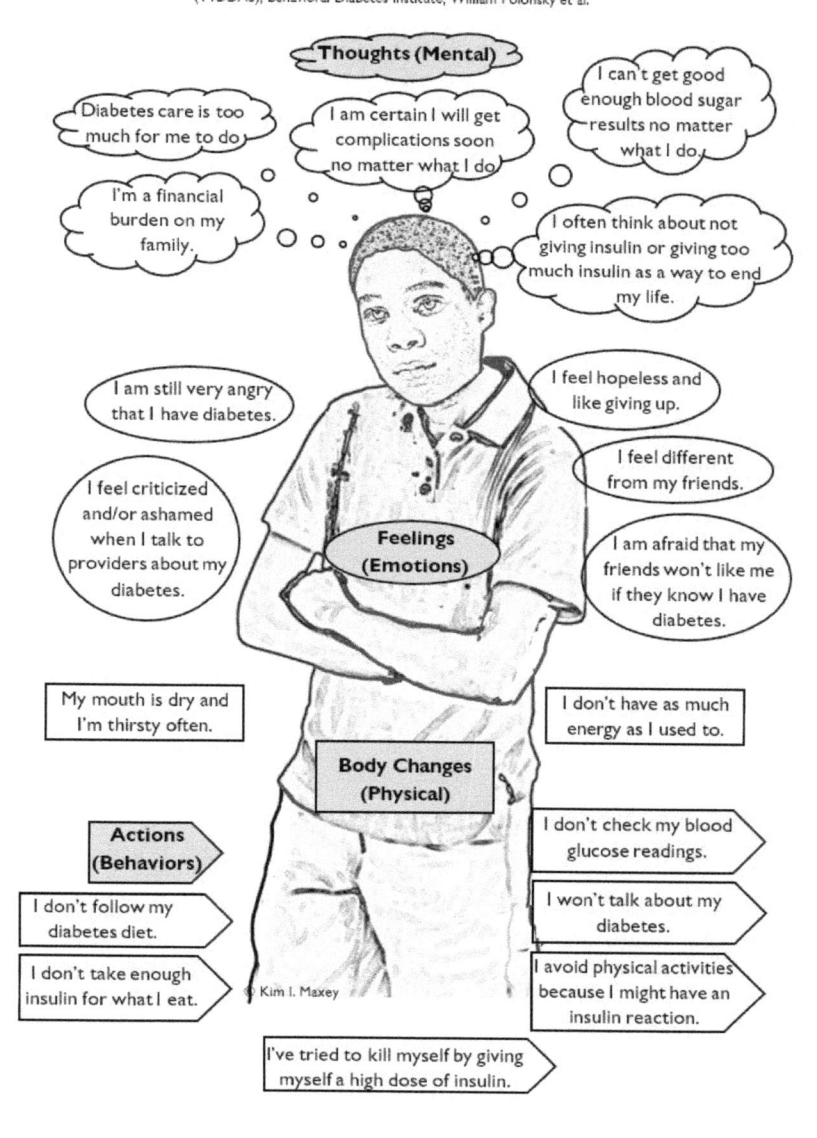

Thoughts (Mental)

- Diabetes care is too much for me to do.
- I am certain I will get complications soon no matter what I do.
- I can't get good enough blood sugar results no matter what I do.
- I'm a financial burden on my family.
- I often think about not giving insulin or giving too much insulin as a way to end my life.

Feelings (Emotions)

- I am still very angry that I have diabetes.
- I feel hopeless and like giving up.
- I feel criticized and/or ashamed when I talk to providers about my diabetes.
- I feel different from my friends.
- I am afraid that my friends won't like me if they know I have diabetes.

Body Changes (Physical)

- My mouth is dry and I'm thirsty often.
- I don't have as much energy as I used to.

Actions (Behaviors)

- I don't follow my diabetes diet.
- I don't take enough insulin for what I eat.
- I don't check my blood glucose readings.
- I won't talk about my diabetes.
- I avoid physical activities because I might have an insulin reaction.
- I've tried to kill myself by giving myself a high dose of insulin.

© Kim I. Maxey

What Can You Do?

If you have multiple strong, long-lasting symptoms of depression or distress, you don't have to struggle alone. Many other people understand what it's like to deal with depression. But they can't read your mind. You need to speak to a trusted adult such as your parent, guardian, teacher, school counselor, or health care provider.

It's normal to have trouble reaching out. You may think your situation is unique, or people will judge you in a way you can't handle. You may have to talk to yourself as a best friend would, someone who cares about you and wants you to get better.

If you seek answers, you'll find some, and your life will get easier. Professionals and teens have written numerous articles on how to feel better.

Once you take the risk, you may find yourself at your clinic where a health care provider may ask you to answer questions which are part of the Patient Health Questionnaire or PHQ. Some forms have two while others have nine questions. Below is an image of the PHQ-2:

Over the last *2 weeks*, how often have you been bothered by any of the following problems?	Not at all	Several days	More than half the days	Nearly every day
1. Little interest or pleasure in doing things	0	1	2	3
2. Feeling down, depressed, or hopeless	0	1	2	3

If you have depression, finding a qualified counselor is a wise next step. If you have diabetes distress, ask about counselors who have worked with teens who have diabetes.

A mental health counselor will talk with you and teach you how to use tools which will assist you in coping with and recovering from depression.

While you wait for an appointment, think of ways you can help yourself.

1. Search on the internet for "teen depression." There are <u>multiple articles on teen mental health</u> that will give you information.

2. Look for a <u>mental health workbook</u> to learn to handle your thoughts and feelings better. *Don't Let Your Emotions Run Your Life for Teens: Dialectical Behavior Therapy Skills for Helping You Manage Mood Swings, Control Angry Outbursts, and Get Along with Others* by Sheri Van Dijk is a good starting place.

3. Repeat <u>positive affirmations</u> to retrain your brain, so you begin to view yourself and your capabilities in a healthy way. Multiple websites provide instructions and statements.

4. Try a <u>meditation app</u> like Calm, Headspace, Insight Timer, Ten Percent Happier, Mindfulness.com, or Healthy Minds Program. Smiling Mind is specifically for youth. Some have a free option.

Many types of depression will lighten after some therapy and with some time. You have it within you to feel contentment and joy, even when life is tough.

Locks That Seemed Real

Like layers of a heavy chain,
Mean, dark thoughts still remain,
Creaking as I move around,
I can't escape their awful sound.

Locks on my mouth, no speech,
Locks on my hands, can't reach,
Locks on my heart, can't feel,
These horrid locks seem so real.

In front of me I see
A kind friend turn to me,
"May I help? I'll go slow."
I shrug to say, "I don't know."

"Take a breath, close your eyes,
See the sun, visualize,
Gravity you can defy,
You are a bird about to fly."

I close my eyes, warily,
One link dissolves, quietly,
More disappear, quickly,
As I guide myself, gently.

With open eyes, widely,
I thank my friend, kindly,
"Your words lifted me so high,
Now I see the bright, blue sky."

© Kim I. Maxey

Love Swims Below the Surface

With an app spewing meanness,
My phone is not on my side,
It's wacky with its coldness,
It forces me down a slide.

But then I get my hammer,
I breathe in and then I moan,
I swing the hammer down,
Three times against my phone.

The quiet is inviting,
I hear the babbling brook,
My friend sits on the boulder,
I go to take a look.

We sit in yellow sunshine,
We have so much to say,
Love swims below the surface,
My thoughts are kind today.

© Kim I. Maxey

BOOK RECOMMENDATIONS

Especially for Teens

Boehm, Sara. *The Essential Moving Guided Journal for Teens: My Life and My Thoughts Before and After Moving.* N.p., CreateSpace Independent Publishing Platform, 2014.

Crist, James J. *What to Do When You're Scared & Worried: A Guide for Kids.* United States, Free Spirit Publishing, 2004.

Galbraith, Judy, and Delisle, James R. *The Gifted Teen Survival Guide: Smart, Sharp, and Ready for (almost) Anything.* United States, Free Spirit Publishing, 2011.

Fig. 1 by the University of California (Berkley). *Why the Teenage Brain has an Evolutionary Advantage.* https://youtu.be/P629TojpvDU?si=g4mV2P_ylid-F5PA, 4 minutes 15 seconds. December 6, 2017, Last accessed February 5, 2024.

Skeen, Michelle, et al. *Communication Skills for Teens: How to Listen, Express, and Connect for Success.* United States, New Harbinger Publications, 2016.

Thelen, Tom, Neeley, Kirleen, Hooge, Kimberly, Kagan, Elliot. *Mental Health 101 for Teens*. United States, Independently Published, 2020.

Van Dijk, Sheri. *Don't Let Your Emotions Run Your Life for Teens: Dialectical Behavior Therapy Skills for Helping You Manage Mood Swings, Control Angry Outbursts, and Get Along with Others*. United States, New Harbinger Publications, 2011.

Vigil-Otero, Ashley, and Willard, Christopher. *The Self-Confidence Workbook for Teens: Mindfulness Skills to Help You Overcome Social Anxiety, Be Assertive, and Believe in Yourself*. United Kingdom, New Harbinger Publications, 2023.

ACKNOWLEDGMENTS

Many wonderful people contributed to my life so I could write this story. Without them, this book would not have been written and published.

I am forever grateful to my mother, Kay Mouchet, who died while I was writing the first drafts of this book. Her love was a lifeline during rough times. While I was writing, I felt as if she was in the next room, which gave me solace.

I am forever grateful to my father, Jim Maxey, who died before I finished this book. He gave me a solid foundation of love, curiosity, and strength. He challenged me to never stop questioning the nature of the world.

Thank you to my brother, Jay Maxey. Moving multiple times and changing schools was a very challenging experience for both of us. You saved my life when you donated one of your kidneys to me after Type 1 diabetes took both of mine. I can never repay you for your generosity and support.

Thank you to my stepparents, Jim Mouchet, and Jill Walter Maxey. I'm glad you came into my life after my parents divorced. I love you both.

Thank you to my daughter, Lienna Libersher Soderling, for the wonderful times and the life lessons we have shared. Becoming a mother brought a new dimension to my life, filling it with much more joy than I could have predicted. As I watch you parent your own daughter, I am impressed with your insightful and kind nature.

Thank you to J. Hilt, D. O'Loughlin, L. Bellew, J. McGough, and L. Popowitz. We shared a time of life that shaped us in ways we hardly understood. I will always treasure our friendships.

Thank you to the many friends and family who I wrote about in this memoir. I think fondly of our past together, and I tried to recreate it as best I could.

Thank you to the family and friends who were part of my journey by proofing or otherwise supporting me as I wrote: Jody Grande, PhD, LICSW, BCD, Patrick Dallas, MSE, Anita Howe, Gloria Zampedri, Sheila Martin, Bonnie Anderson Maxey, and Eva Maxey.

I especially thank Karen Sonday, M.A. Special Education, B.A. Child Psychology, for providing significant feedback.

Thank you to the many wonderful teachers who guided my efforts to write and think critically. You cared greatly for your students, as most teachers today do.

Thank you, Lisa Whalen, author of *Stable Weight: A Memoir of Hunger, Horses, and Hope*, for allaying my fears about publishing a memoir, which is a rather scary prospect.

Thank you to The Minneapolis Writer's Workshop members who provided writing assistance and other helpful information. Thank you to the many writers who have walked the self-publishing path guided me in numerous ways. They include: The Self-Publishing School (https://self-publishingschool.com), The Nonfiction Authors Association (https://nonfictionauthors association.com/), Book Launchers (https://book launchers.com), and the Alliance of Independent Authors (https://selfpublishingadvice.org).

Thank you to the Bees pep band. https://youtu.be/LD6RljlVtIs "Baldwinsville (New York) Bees Marching Band at varsity girls' basketball game - 1/28/20 | 4K." You gave a great performance which brought back many memories.

Thank you to the readers of all ages for giving this story a chance. I hope it helps you sort through any difficult isolations which may have occurred in your own life.

ABOUT THE AUTHOR

Kim I. Maxey lives in the Minneapolis, Minnesota area. *Leaving Pep Band Friends* is her first book.

She comes from a long line of restless families who moved from one end of the United States to the other, and she experienced a traumatic move before her sophomore year of high school.

Kim wants teens who have been moved to know it is natural to feel grief over what they have lost.

ENCOURAGEMENT

If you are a teenager:

I encourage you to take the high road as you struggle with and master the hurdles appearing in your life. The older generation needs your voice and participation because you can impact the future culture around you in beneficial ways.

May you be worthy of an Optimist Club certificate as you uphold the dignity of youth, show a sincere devotion to the welfare of others, and offer generous and unselfish contributions to our society.

Milton Keynes UK
Ingram Content Group UK Ltd.
UKHW040819121024
449514UK00022B/56